Palestinian Refugees after 1948

Palestinian Refugees after 1948

The Failure of International Diplomacy

Marte Heian-Engdal

I.B.TAURIS

LONDON • NEW YORK • OXFORD • NEW DELHI • SYDNEY

I.B. TAURIS
Bloomsbury Publishing Plc
50 Bedford Square, London, WC1B 3DP, UK
1385 Broadway, New York, NY 10018, USA
29 Earlsfort Terrace, Dublin 2, Ireland

BLOOMSBURY, I.B. TAURIS and the I.B. Tauris logo are trademarks of
Bloomsbury Publishing Plc

First published in Great Britain 2020
Paperback edition published 2021

Cover design by Adriana Brioso
Cover image: A Palestine refugee family leaves behind their makeshift dwelling
to hopes of a better life, Amman New camp, Jordan. (© Undated UNRWA Archive)

A catalogue record for this book is available from the British Library.

A catalog record for this book is available from the Library of Congress

ISBN: HB: 978-1-7883-1226-4
PB: 978-0-7556-4558-9
eISBN: 978-0-7556-0183-7
ePDF: 978-0-7556-0182-0

Typeset by Deanta Global Publishing Services, Chennai, India

To find out more about our authors and books visit www.bloomsbury.com
and sign up for our newsletters.

To all those still displaced

Contents

Acknowledgements

While researching and writing this book, I have been fortunate to have had my home in three very different cities – Jerusalem, Washington, D.C., and Oslo. I am convinced that both the book and I have benefited greatly from all that this has entailed. Over these years, in all these locations, there are many people who have contributed to this project and to whom I want to extend my heartfelt gratitude.

First, I want to thank the Department of Archaeology, Conservation and History at the University of Oslo for providing me with the funds for this research and clever and supporting colleagues with which to discuss it. The department also houses Professor Hilde Henriksen Waage without whom this study never would have seen the light of day. Hilde has been there during ups and downs, constantly cheering me on, pushing me to dig deeper and to answer my own questions clearer. To have her as an academic mentor has been very important to me. Many thanks also to Professor William B. Quandt, for his incredibly insightful comments and suggestions on ways to improve earlier versions of the text, for his continued interest in the work and for his heartfelt encouragement – it has meant a lot!

I have also benefited greatly from many stimulating conversations with colleagues at the Department of History, who have offered valuable insights, comments and, not least, excellent company and support. Moreover, I am thankful for all input from the many brilliant scholars connected to the Oslo Contemporary International History Network. Financial support has kindly been awarded to me by *Thorleif Dahls legat for historisk forskning* and *Ella og Robert Wenzins legat ved universitetet i Oslo*, for which I am grateful.

I also want to thank the Peace Research Institute in Oslo (PRIO), for being an exceptionally warm, supportive and intellectually stimulating workplace. For running groups, discussions, seminars and panels – thank you!

Heading down the homestretch, the book and I moved to NOREF Norwegian Centre for Conflict Resolution. This was a match made in heaven.

The work at NOREF has brought many of my academic observations, ideas and insights into the rather stark light of the realities of the conflict resolution industry. It has been a humbling experience and one that I am very grateful for. The practitioner's angle has caused me to rethink and rewrite my scholarly work, and hopefully, I will also be able to bring some of the scholarly learned lessons back to the practical work, in the years to come. NOREF's wonderful, hard-working and dedicated staff inspire me every day, as do the people we meet in our work: Often harmed and traumatized by conflict, but despite all their losses, willing to look up and ahead for solutions to past and current conflicts, they are a constant source of motivation and inspiration to me.

I want to extend my sincere thanks to all the staff that have helped me find my way in the various archives I have visited – at the *Israeli State Archives* in Jerusalem; at the *United States National Archives*' different branches at College Park, Maryland, the Herbert Hoover Library in Iowa and the JFK Library in Boston, Massachusetts; at the *United Nations archives* in New York City; and at the *Public Records Office* at Kew Gardens in London – I have met nothing but friendly faces and helpful assistance.

A heartfelt thanks also to I.B. Tauris for publishing the book and to all those that have been involved in the process. My editor Sophie Rudland has been smart, patient and always supportive, and I am thankful for her inspired comments and work on the manuscript. I also want to thank the two anonymous reviewers for their time, effort and constructive comments on an earlier draft.

I am also fortunate to have many close to me – friends, family and framily – who have always been interested and supportive of my work, who have asked me to explain it again, only better, and who have helped with the logistical hurdles of combining book writing with family life.

Finally, Jesper, Sofia and Olav. You are the last ones mentioned here but let there be no doubt that the three of you are always first on my list. J&S – rays of sunshine and source of never-ending love, and Olav – my greatest sparring partner and most devoted fan and friend – there are no words to describe my gratitude and love to you.

Despite all this help and more, I am sure there are remaining flaws, omissions and inaccuracies. They are naturally my sole responsibility.

1

Introduction

A U.N. Commission of three
Sat for long on the poor refugee
They talked for some years
Then with crocodile tears
Decided they could not agree.[1]

Considering the limerick's inherent brevity, the author of the one above must be commended not only for his wittiness but also for his prescient analytical accuracy. In this book I argue that years and years of crocodile tears is an apt summary not just of the efforts of the UN Palestine Conciliation Commission (PCC) but also of the international diplomatic community's effort to deal with the Palestinian refugee problem in general.

Despite the attractiveness of such a glib conclusion, the questions raised in this book – regarding how the international community treated the Palestinian refugee problem in the first twenty years of the Arab–Israeli conflict – call for a somewhat more complex set of explanations. Drawing on a wide range of primary sources from multiple archives, this book provides a systematic analysis of this key issue, largely missing from the otherwise rich existing literature on the history of the modern Middle East. By doing so, it aims to investigate who the key actors were and, moreover, to chart the tendencies and developments of the international diplomatic community's perceptions and thinking about the refugee problem in this crucial first phase of the Arab–Israeli conflict.

Throughout these two decades of the conflict, a set of dominating tensions can be identified. They arise, in brief, from questions about whether the refugees' solution laid in repatriation or resettlement (and compensation), whether a peace process should follow a piecemeal or a package approach, and whether the Palestinian predicament should be understood as political or humanitarian. Was the solution to the problem to be found in repatriation of the refugees or in their resettlement in other nations? Was the refugee issue best tackled in isolation, or did its solution rather belong in a larger framework of a regional peace agreement? And finally, the most defining tension, should the international diplomatic approach to the Palestinian refugee be to seek a solution along political lines or did this problem belong within the humanitarian realm?

In brief, four factors stand out as the main obstacles to finding a solution to the refugee problem throughout these two decades: Israel's tactical skills in the international diplomatic game; the clear domination of domestic political gain over international strategy and policy in consecutive US administrations; the problem of timing in international relations; and, last, the minimal cost of no agreement for Israel and the Arab states and the inability and/or unwillingness of any of the relevant actors to alter or to redeem this situation.

Detailed knowledge and understanding of the international treatment of refugee question in this period is important in its own right. The Palestinian refugee issue was – and remains – at the very core of the conflict between Israel and the Palestinians. By looking at it within the framework that is applied here, however, it is a topic that feeds important insights into other, more overarching themes such as the conduct of international diplomacy; the role of the UN in the Middle East; the development and execution of US Middle East policy; the establishment and development of US–Israel relations and the roots of the pattern and dynamic that dominates that relationship today, as well as the intertwined worlds and dynamics of foreign and domestic policy.

The Palestinian refugee issue: At the core of the conflict

Up until the 1980s, there were two distinctly opposed narratives about the origin of the Palestinian refugee problem: the traditional Zionist and the Arab narratives. According to the former, the creation of the refugee problem was largely the responsibility of the Arab regimes, who ordered hundreds of thousands of Palestinians to flee their homes so that the Arab armies could invade and strangle the Jewish state at its birth.[2] In this narrative, the Zionist movement is relieved of any responsibility for the creation of the problem.

The Arab narrative, meanwhile, maintains that the Palestinians were forcibly expelled. In the early 1980s, however, the conflict of narratives took a new turn, when a group of 'new' or 'revisionist' Israeli historians emerged onto the world stage. With newly declassified material from British, American and Israeli archives, these historians challenged and refuted many of the 'old', revisionist Zionist myths about what had or had not happened at the time of the establishment of the state of Israel.[3]

The new historian who has done most to debunk the Zionist narrative on the origin question is Benny Morris.[4] In what has now become the standard reference work on the topic, *The Birth of the Palestinian Refugee Problem*, Morris gives a meticulously detailed account of the four different waves of the Palestinian exodus.[5]

Despite the later controversy surrounding Morris's views, his account of the Palestinian exodus remains the most systematic and detailed study of the reasons behind it. Morris distinguishes among four different waves of flights: December 1947 through March 1948; April through June 1948; early July to mid-October 1948 (this wave was interrupted by two truces); and from October through November 1948.[6] Morris shows that there was a complex set of reasons behind the Palestinian flight and refutes the traditional Zionist claim that the Palestinians fled on orders from the Arab regimes.[7]

The first (and smallest) wave of refugees began immediately after the UN decided to partition the British Mandate of Palestine in November 1947, though the roots of this decision reach back to the late 1800s in Europe. As the situation for European Jewry grew increasingly grim, Theodore Herzl and the Zionist nationalist movement began to formulate a solution to the Jews' problems in diaspora – one involving the establishment of a Jewish state in Palestine.

The Palestinians, unlike the Jews, had done next to nothing to prepare themselves for statehood. Part of the Arab Higher Committee (AHC), the Palestinians had rejected the UN partition plan out of hand.[8] The Palestinians who fled during this first period were first and foremost residents of the areas slated by the UN to comprise the Jewish state. They represented the wealthy urban families with the highest levels of literacy, skills and education; they were, in short, the Palestinian leadership.[9] This first wave of refugees left largely because of ensuing Jewish militia attacks or the fear of such attacks.

The second wave, from April 1948 through June 1948, was the largest wave, numbering between 250,000 and 300,000 refugees in total. It followed an intensification of the military offensive led by the Jewish leadership and the forces under their command, notably the *Haganah*. In early March 1948, the *Haganah* chiefs developed and prepared the implementation of the infamous Plan D (*tochnit Dalet*). Plan D called for the securing of all areas allotted to the Jewish state and to the border areas surrounding that state. In these territories, all Arab villages and cities were to be emptied.[10] As Ilan Pappé notes, the Arab regimes played an 'important, albeit negative role in the dynamics of the exodus'.[11] Not only did the local Palestinian elite leave its constituency in the most crucial hour, but it also failed to give those who remained any kind of guidance as to what to do or how to behave in the context of both overt and covert battle against Jewish forces.[12]

After the formal establishment of the state of Israel in May 1948, the deteriorating situation on the ground turned into a formal war, as the Arab states declared war on the newborn Jewish state. What this transfer meant in relation to the Palestinian question was that the mass flight, which had commenced during the days of the *Yishuv*, now had become an urgent matter on the Israeli *Cabinet's* table. The Jewish state had come into being, that is, while the independent Arab state that was intended to persist alongside it remained amorphous, demonstrating the ultimate success of the Zionist movement and the failure of the Arabs. This was also the starting point of an imbalance and asymmetry that, to this day, is one of the principle primary trademarks of the conflict between Israel and the Palestinians.

In essence, Morris's conclusion is that 'war, and not design, Jewish or Arab, gave birth to the Palestinian refugee problem'.[13] With the flights of the third and fourth waves of Palestinian refugees, the total number to an estimated 700,000 to 750,000 people had fled their homes since December 1947.[14]

The new historians, and in particular Morris, were attacked by those who upheld the Zionist narrative for attributing to Israel the 'original sin'.[15] The criticism was twofold: (a) the new historians were professionally flawed, and (b) they sought to delegitimize Zionism and the state of Israel. One of Morris's main antagonists was Shabtai Teveth, the author of a biography of one of Israel's founding fathers, David Ben-Gurion.[16] But this was not the only position from which Morris's work was attacked. From the other end of the spectrum, representing the Palestinian narrative, historians Nur Masalha and Norman Finkelstein took issue with Morris's ultimate conclusion – that the refugee problem was a product of war – rather than Zionist design.[17] They commended Morris for his meticulous research but faulted him for what they perceived to be a failure and/or unwillingness to see that his own findings implied a much greater degree of Israeli responsibility for the exodus than Morris was prepared to endorse.[18]

In Masalha's view, Morris and the other new historians had plainly settled for a 'happy medium' characterized by a sense of 'shared responsibility'.[19] The association of the Palestinians with their own expulsion is, to Masalha, but a further indication of Israel's 'politics of denial' and continued 'hegemonic discourses'.[20] Likewise, it proves to him that the new historians remain 'firmly attached' to their 'Zionist roots'.[21] Masalha has remained convinced throughout his career that there was, from the very beginning, a conscious Zionist plan to evict the native Palestinian population and this was the meaning of Israel's Plan D – *tochnit Dalet*. Morris, on the other hand, maintained that the plan was nothing more than a military program, and, furthermore, that it was not relevant in any case, since it was never really implemented.[22] Masalha (and others with him) maintained that Morris failed to see Plan D in its wider historical context as a 'master plan' for the expulsion of the Palestinian population.[23] Furthermore, they argue that a consistent thread runs through the Zionist movement, from Theodor Herzl to David Ben-Gurion, in relation to the 'desire to empty' the future Jewish state.[24]

Historian Avi Shlaim's more nuanced approach argues that Plan D was never a 'political blueprint' for the expulsion of the Palestinians, but as a military plan it had military and territorial objectives and consequences.[25] By implementing it, Shlaim writes, the *Haganah* 'directly and decisively contributed to the birth of the Palestinian refugee problem'.[26] Shlaim elsewhere points out that Masalha undermines a good case 'by over-stating it' and focusing too narrowly on one aspect of the thinking within a multifaceted and complex Zionist movement.[27]

There is little added value in a detailed blow-by-blow account of every article and op-ed published in relation to this debate.[28] Suffice it to say that at some point the debate was no longer strictkly about what had happened, it was highly charged, accusatory and political dispute.[29] However, despite the disagreement over the degree of responsibility and the interpretation of the meaning of Plan D, Morris's version and the Palestinian narrative had much in common. Or, put differently, Morris's findings more or less confirmed what the Palestinian narrative had maintained all along – that the Palestinian population had not fled voluntarily.[30]

Simultaneously, throughout the autumn of 1948 and the spring of 1949, abandoned Palestinian villages were destroyed and new Jewish settlements were established on abandoned lands and sites and in abandoned houses throughout the country. The *New York Times* journalist Anne O'Hare McCormick, who covered the events as they unfolded, described the flight as 'a phenomenon only less extraordinary than the precipitancy with which the vacuum is being filled'.[31] Where the Palestinians fled from, Jewish immigrants moved in and settled down.

Most of these processes of exits and entries occurred under the 'protective carapace' of the Israeli army. As Jewish immigrants cultivated and settled the conquered land, Israeli Defence Forces (IDF) soldiers made sure that no refugee 'infiltrated' the country by making his or her way across the borders.[32] While Israeli leaders were quick to reject the claim that the flight of the Palestinians was a result of a deliberate policy on their part, McCormick noted that they 'cheerfully' admitted that they certainly had 'lost no time in taking advantage of it'.[33] In the summer of 1948, the Israeli cabinet decided that no refugees would be allowed to return. This stands out as one of the most important decisions taken by the new state. The decision, and the upholding of the policy, has remained Israeli policy to this day. Israel employed its military power to enforce the decision. Today, due to natural population growth, the Palestinian refugees and their decedents total almost 5 million people and constitute the world's most protracted refugee problem.[34]

The refugee issue is a core issue in more ways than one. It is a core question in the Israeli–Arab conflict and notably in the Israeli–Palestinian conflict. It is also at the core of the conflicting parties' collective memories and collective identities.

In any society, the sense of a shared history or set of societal beliefs – defining issues for that society – is an important social construct. In times of conflict, and in particular for societies living in protracted conflict, that conflict itself becomes a major driving force for the development of the society's collective narrative.[35] The refugee issue resonates formidably throughout Palestinian society – among those who are determined to return to their homes and those who are not as well as those who never lost their homes in the first place. It cuts across social, political and geographical barriers in a society that is otherwise both physically and psychologically divided. Spread across the increasingly volatile region, and split between the West Bank, the Gaza Strip and within

Israel, there are today many different layers to the Palestinian struggle. Despite this, though, the refugee issue can still rally immense political mobilization and support or, on the other hand, political condemnation. It remains the 'Holy Grail' of Palestinian politics.[36]

The shared experience of the Palestinian exodus, of refugeedom, exile, resistance and the deep and commonly held Palestinian sense of injustice, has since played a detrimental role in shaping Palestinian national identity.[37] Undeniably, the refugee issue is the most emotive one for Palestinians, refugees and non-refugees alike.[38] Though it physically divided them, refugeedom gave the Palestinian people a rallying point and therefore a greater sense of unity than they had previously experienced. And as a collective experience, it quickly morphed into a story about the dispossession of all: 'None were masters of their own fate.'[39] The refugee issue, then, as historian Rashid Khalidi puts it, 'cemented and universalized' a Palestinian national identity that had been evolving since before the First World War. Khalidi divides the evolution of a Palestinian identity into three phases, the first of which starts with the period under Ottoman rule. The second stage, the mandate years, saw a deepening sense of identity taking shape among different layers of Palestinian society. The 1948 War and its consequences erased all remaining internal differences and conflicts and gave all Palestinians a sense of common identity.[40] *Al-Nakba*, the Palestinian catastrophe – as the 1948 exodus is commonly referred to – lies at the very core of Palestinian collective memory.[41] Throughout the spring of 2018, Palestinians in the Gaza Strip staged consecutive protests under the banner 'The Great March of Return', marking seventy years of displacement, once again proving the political dynamite that the refugee issue continues to hold in Palestinian society, as well as the centrality of the issue in the Israeli–Palestinian conflict.

Further complicating the matter is the fact that the Palestinian Nakba is inherently intertwined and ultimately inseparable from the Jewish–Israeli celebration of independence.[42] That one peoples' catastrophe is so intimately connected to the other peoples' saviour (the birth of the nation) – undoubtedly a key story to the larger Israeli collective memory – entails that the refugee issue also lies at the core of the so-called 1948 debate and in the ongoing 'conflict of narratives' between Israel and the Palestinians.[43] The traditional Zionist narrative regarding the reasons for the Palestinian exodus has always been that the Palestinians left the country on orders from Arab leaders so that they would not come to harm during the Arab states' invasion of the fledging Jewish state. Since 1948 this story has been largely accepted by the Israeli public, and its stamina, despite that it has been solidly debunked by several scholars, must be seen in relation to the instrumental role of official Israel in it.[44]

In the Israeli society's 'ethos of conflict', it is undeniably *security* that stands out as the 'cultural master symbol', and this is clear in the Israeli view of the refugee issue.[45] When Israel argues that it cannot, under any circumstances, allow the Palestinian refugees to return, it is most often under the banner of 'security concerns'. Israeli leaders have a long history of exploiting this doomsday scenario for the Israeli public: already in August 1948, then foreign minister Moshe Sharett warned from the Knesset podium that returning the refugees would be none other than 'an act of suicide by the state of Israel ... like stabbing a knife into our chests with our own hands'.[46] And since the summer of 1948, 'no-return' has been the Israeli policy.

But the Palestinian refugee is also, together with the status of Jerusalem, a matter of greater extent than the parameters of the bilateral conflict between Israel and the Palestinians. It is a core issue also in the regional context. History has shown that the problem can pose a grave threat to regional stability, and it remains today, therefore, an issue with multiple regional stakeholders. The first and second Palestinian *intifada* and the tension on the border between Israel and the Gaza Strip (where about two-thirds of the population are registered refugees) illustrate that the combination of poor camp conditions and rising militancy can have lethal consequences. Moreover, during six decades of conflict in the Middle East, Palestinian terrorist or guerrilla incursions into Israel have likewise had a hand in triggering at least three Arab–Israeli wars – in 1956, 1967 and 1982 – and at least two civil wars – Jordan's 'Black September' in 1970 and Lebanon's civil war of 1975. Palestinian terrorism against international aviation throughout the 1970s and 1980s was additional proof, not just to the region's population but to the entire world, that the Palestinian refugee problem is a matter whose ramifications stretch well beyond the Israeli–Palestinian frontlines.[47] These are among the reasons why several scholars refer to the Palestinian refugee problem as 'the single most important' issue in the Middle East peace process.[48]

Despite its centrality in the region's conflicts, though, the Palestinian refugee issue has been far removed from the negotiating table in the years of the so-called peace process. In the era of the peace process, which spanned from the end of the Cold War and the Madrid conference in 1991 to the violence of the Second intifada in 2000, the matter was labelled a 'final status' issue. Final status issues were to be left for future negotiations, at a later stage in the process when sufficient progress on security and mutual trust was established. Although it was discussed at Camp David II, at Taba in 2001 and in the Olmert-Abbas talks of 2008, there is nothing to suggest that the refugee issue has been a dominating theme in any of the talks in the period since the Oslo Accords and after. The thorniest issues, the fate of the refugees and the future status of Jerusalem, in other words, were not lifted and given priority; rather, they were to be dealt with the last. But this sequencing logic was not always the prevailing view.

In fact, the current (in)action and the assessment of what role the refugee issue should have in the peace process, or its ranking in the hierarchy of problems, stands in great contrast to the international community's initial reactions and thoughts about the matter. In 1948, Count Folke Bernadotte was appointed the first UN mediator to the Arab–Israeli conflict. The refugee problem quickly became the Swede's principal worry.

Bernadotte, a man solidly supportive of the humanitarian dictates of the Red Cross, was genuinely, and increasingly, worried about the health of the refugees, and this issue was his number one priority. After encountering the refugees in Ramallah, Bernadotte noted in his diary that he had never seen 'a more ghastly sight'.[49] Speaking to the UN Security Council in August 1948, Bernadotte told the member states that he thought the danger to Israeli security was 'slight' and that he therefore urged that the refugees be allowed to return to their homes 'at the earliest practicable date'.[50] At that time, Bernadotte estimated that the refugees numbered around 250,000 to 300,000 people.[51] As time passed, the war raged on, and the scope of the refugee problem continued to grow, so did Bernadotte's concern.

On 17 September 1948, the Count's mediating mission came to a bloody halt, as Jewish terrorists shot and killed Bernadotte as he drove to his offices in West Jerusalem. The bullets could not kill the ideas that he carried, however, and Bernadotte's imprint on the Middle East had already been made. Only the day before his assassination, on 16 September, Bernadotte had delivered his report to UN's secretary general Trygve Lie.[52] In the report, and the letter attached to it, Bernadotte reiterated his genuine concern about the refugees' plight and strong support of their right of return to their homes 'at the earliest practical date'.[53]

In Bernadotte's view, there could be no lasting peace between Israel and the Arabs without a resolution to the refugee question. The so-called second Bernadotte plan, with its 'doctrinal' postulate that the refugee should be allowed to return to his home and his land as soon as possible was later adopted by the United Nations General Assembly in Resolution 194 (III) of 11 December 1948.[54]

To this day, Resolution 194, adopted on 11 December 1948, remains the single most important resolution passed by the UN concerning the Palestinian refugee issue. Echoing Bernadotte's words, Resolution 194's paragraph 11 stated,

> That the refugees wishing to return to their homes and live at peace with their neighbors should be permitted to do so at the earliest practicable date, and that compensation should be paid for the property of those choosing not to return and for loss of or damage to property which, under principles of international law or in equity, should be made good by the Governments or authorities responsible.[55]

With Resolution 194, the UN member states also established the PCC, which was instructed to 'take steps to assist the Governments and authorities concerned to achieve a final settlement of all questions outstanding between them'. Specifically, the commission was instructed to 'facilitate the repatriation, resettlement and economic and social rehabilitation of the refugees and the payment of compensation'.[56] Resolution 194 and the establishment of PCC translated into what emerged to become a consensus in the Western world, namely that the refugee problem was the most important problem to tackle, if the hope and desire for regional peace was to materialize. This was Count Bernadotte's immediate legacy in the Middle East.

In the months after his assassination, Bernadotte's reasoning found much support among key actors within the UN and the UK and US foreign policy establishment in Washington, D.C. Historian Matthew Jacobs refers to a 'network' of Middle East specialists, academics, businessmen, government officials and media personalities, in Washington, D.C., and shows how they interpreted and shared their perceptions of the Middle East in general and the Israeli–Palestinian conflict in particular. Among them there was a shared understanding that the refugee problem had a dramatically destabilizing effect on the region, and that its solution was key to both reducing violence and border clashes as well as the conflict as a whole.[57] At the US State Department, Dean Rusk, then the director of United Nations Affairs office, concluded that the refugee problem indeed was the 'key to war and peace in the Middle East'.[58] Already subsumed by the logic of the Cold War, the United States feared the consequences of hundreds of thousands of Palestinian refugees scattered throughout the region, with no solution to their plight in sight. The situation was a fertile breeding ground for communism in the view of American policymakers. The United States had to make sure, argued then Defence Secretary James Forrestal, that the Arab world remained oriented towards the United States. The fact that the refugees constituted a potentially devastating destabilizing element, in a geo-strategically very important neighbourhood, meant that alleviating the conditions of the refugees could be seen to be in Washington, D.C.'s primary *strategic* national security interest to solve the problem.[59]

The contrast between this approach and the current international take on the refugee issue, where the matter is hardly ever debated let alone payed attention to in international mediation efforts, is evident, and it begs the question: How, and why, did the Palestinian refugee problem go from being recognized as the key to regional peace to being in its current position, more or less completely off the international agenda? What characterized the initial international diplomatic response to the refugee problem – and how did it evolve?

Structure and content of the book

While there is an extensive body of literature that deals with how the future solution to the refugee problem might look, it has not, in any comprehensive way, engaged with the earliest efforts to address the problem. Moreover, in the scholarly contributions that *have* taken a historical approach and have studied the international efforts to reach Arab–Israeli peace in this formative period, the refugee problem has mostly been dealt with in a superficial way, as one among several challenging issues. Focus on the refugee question was, in other words, sacrificed for the benefit of a more general overview. When the refugee problem has been the focus of academic studies, this has either been on a limited, episodic, basis and/or with a singular perspective, be it Israel's or the Americans'.[60] A systematic analysis of the treatment of the Palestinian refugee problem throughout the entire first formative phase of the conflict, based on primary records from multiple archives, is thus both timely and necessary.

It is worth mentioning that this book does not unveil a trove of undiscovered 'raw' material. Instead, the archival material has been declassified for some time, and most scholars with an interest in Middle East history know of its existence. In fact, much of the primary material used here is shared with other scholarly works that cover either the same time period or, alternatively, a common topical interest. This book's originality is not in the pool of material upon which analysis is based – although portions of that pool have never been used and are grossly underutilized in the existing literature – but rather in its approach to that primary material: its unprecedented range in terms of time, its multiple levels of analysis and ultimately the guiding research questions that constitute its point of departure.

In addition to the primary sources, there is a wide array of existing secondary literature on the topics that this book touches on. Within the literature on the Palestinian refugee problem, the most dominant aspect has been the debate about 1948 in the historiography of the Arab–Israeli conflict. Indeed, this part of the literature has developed into somewhat a genre of its own. In addition to what one might lable 'origin literature' (as discussed in detail above), the literature on the refugee issue can be grouped into two broad categories according to general focus: 'identity literature' and, secondly, work that addresses the refugees' claims and is oriented towards policy recommendations for a future solution. Several works detail and explain the development of a (modern) Palestinian identity. Closely connected to origin literature, they show that while the world was slow to realize the Palestinian dimension of the Arab–Israeli conflict, Palestinian identity was not a recent invention and was part of the story all along. The identity-oriented literature displays a distinctly Palestinian dimension to the Arab–Israeli conflict in this formative early phase of the Arab–Israeli conflict.

A second subcategory of relevant exiting literature can be labelled as 'claims literature'. It deals with the mapping of the Palestinian refugees' claims dating back to 1948 and before and was, broadly speaking, born in the aftermath of the Madrid conference and the Oslo process. As Michael Dumper observes, these works, often funded by governments invested in the process (like Canada and Norway), generated 'policy-relevant' research.[61] To the extent that this body of work deals with the refugee issue in the context of peace negotiations, they do so by focusing on the peace efforts of the 1990s and onwards. While there is most often a chapter or a section addressing the origin of the problem, this literature rarely looks further back than the beginning of the Oslo process, let alone to 1967 or 1948.

In the general literature on the Arab–Israeli conflict and peacemaking efforts, an extensive body of scholarly works, the refugee problem has claimed a tiny portion. In academic works in which it has played a role, it has been either one issue among many or an isolated aside that has failed to accumulate any sense of analytical continuity or larger perspective. This book combines the focus on the refugee issue that is typical of the origin-/identity and claims literature and the traditions of diplomatic history studies typical of the general works on the Arab–Israeli conflict.

The research for this dissertation has been conducted in multiple archives, primarily in three different countries: Israel, the United States and the UK. As a supplement to this primary material, I have also consulted the relevant edited volumes on US and Israeli foreign policy documents, the *Foreign Relations of the United States* (FRUS) and *Documents on the Foreign Policy of Israel* (DFPI), respectively. The lack of available Arab archives is a well-known methodological challenge for most scholars of Middle East history, politics and society. One is left to trying to piece together a picture of the Arab side of things from other available material, such as communications (on various levels) to and from the Arab states to the United States and the UK; memoranda of conversations with Arab delegates and leaders; the Western powers' regional embassies' assessments of the state of things in the Arab world; and of course any relevant secondary literature.[62] As a source of insight into internal Arab deliberations, however, these options comprise a pair of binoculars where a magnifying glass is in order. Regrettably, and predictably, this forces the research to gravitate towards the Israeli and Western material.

The lack of access to Arab sources is exacerbated when it comes to material shedding light on the explicitly Palestinian side of the story. One of the great paradoxes of this study about the treatment of the Palestinian refugee issue is that the refugees themselves are virtually absent from it. The lack of official institutions and overall organization that statelessness entailed makes this problem even more intractable than archive access in the case of the Arab states – for Palestinians no overall structure with which to keep records of events existed. The lack of Palestinian sources is not, however, the main reason why the refugees themselves seem to have disappeared from this story. As the following text shows, the Palestinians are, with a few notable exceptions, voiceless actors in the negotiations and initiatives surrounding their plight.

The subsequent chapters follow a stringent chronological line, with some small exceptions. Chapter 2 is primarily concerned with the first round of efforts to find a solution to the problem, led by the PCC, namely the 1949 Lausanne Conference. Chapter 3 engages the role of the refugee problem in the top-secret Anglo-American effort – the Alpha project – in 1955. As Project Alpha was about to wither out, the Suez Crisis broke out in 1956. The ensuing near continuous tension on the borders between Israel and its Arab neighbours prompted the US State Department to once again draw up suggestions for new US policy in respect to the refugee issue. This effort and the thinking and analysis that shaped it and came out of it is detailed in Chapter 4. At the tail end of the 1950s, there was a push to reawaken the by then dormant Conciliation Commission. The ensuing three chapters, Chapters 5 through 7, pick up where Chapter 4 left off, charting a largely unexplored diplomatic initiative, namely the 1961–2 mission of Joseph Johnson. Johnson operated as President John F. Kennedy's special representative, and the Johnson mission represented the last serious push to find a way forward on the refugee question. Chapter 8 brings us to the watershed year of 1967 when Israel and the Arab states ventured into their third war. Though the war was short, it cast long shadows. The 1967 War forever changed the Middle East, and it also changed Arab–Israeli peacemaking. The Palestinian refugee problem increased in scope and complexity as a result of the 1967 War, but when the guns fell silent and the dust settled in June 1967, the diplomatic efforts took to focusing on territorial issues, not the refugee problem.

If there was a period in which a deal could have been struck involving the repatriation of a significant number of refugees, it was very early on. That it did not happen was due to several factors, which are discussed in the final chapter of this book. Although there were individual actors who perceived the Palestinian refugee problem as political in nature, this gradually developed into a general tendency of think of it in a mainly humanitarian framework. And in a post-Second World War reality, one marked by postcolonialist processes and the Cold War's bipolar balance of power, the Palestinian refugee problem was not the most acute issue.

As the book also clearly shows, if something were to have created movement or any form of progress on the refugee question, it would have been a process led by the United States. But over the course of the three different US administrations detailed in the following text, there was never really any genuine political effort to become engaged in solving the problem. And in the absence of sustained presidential leadership, existing US policy initiatives in this regard were too easily undermined by, first and foremost, a determined Israeli leadership and diplomatic corps but also key figures (Israel's 'friends') in the Jewish American community. In this political climate, the White House always let domestic political considerations trump strategic calculations. In sum, the main actors – the Arab states, Israel, the United States and the UN – agreed on very little when it came to the treatment of the Palestinian refugee problem. Collectively, they thus managed to produce very little for the Palestinians, save for a bucket of their crocodile tears.

From principles to practicalities: Repatriation versus resettlement

'Listen, I can get a million sons of bitches to make war tomorrow, can't I get one son of a bitch to help me make peace?'[1] With these words, US president Harry Truman enlisted Mark Etheridge as the American delegate and chairman of the newly established Palestine Conciliation Commission (PCC).

Throughout the winter and spring of 1949, there were two more or less simultaneous negotiation tracks, both rooted in the UN system, and their relationship was neither supportive nor mutually beneficial. Several authors mention alleged jealousy regarding a plane that American diplomat Ralph Bunche had at his disposal, as well as the attention Bunche received both in Washington and at Lake Success, as parts of the explanations for this.[2] On the first track, there were the armistice negotiations between Israel and its neighbouring Arab states, conducted mainly on the Island of Rhodes.[3] These started in January 1949 and were led by Count Bernadotte's 'heir' and former assistant, the American diplomat Ralph Bunche.[4] At Rhodes, Bunche concentrated on reaching armistice agreements, which included the drawing of what were meant to be temporary borders.[5] The Rhodes negotiations were 'very specifically *not* a peace conference', and Bunche did not allow complicated political issues into the discussions.[6] These issues were left to the second track, the PCC, which was meant to concentrate on 'nonmilitary subjects' – refugees and Jerusalem predominantly.[7] The man tasked by Truman to head these talks was Mark Etheridge.

Etheridge was a southerner journalist, who ran newspapers in Louisville, Kentucky. This was a world far away from the conflicts of the Middle East, and initially Etheridge was not interested in taking on the assignment. He was unable to resist the Oval Office, however, once President Truman 'put the heat on'. According to Etheridge's own description, he 'got stuck' on the Palestine commission, and with this reluctant start, and after getting 'one day's brief for each thousand years of Palestine history', he was flown to Jerusalem to join his commission peers.[8]

The PCC was tripartite by design, with delegates from three different UN member states: Turkey, France and the United States.[9] Originally, the commission was intended to be 'superpower free'; neither the United States nor the Soviet Union was supposed to be on it. Great Britain, however, recognizing that any permanent settlement would *have to* be under US supervision, argued that it was only natural that the Americans would have a delegation seat on the PCC. France was chosen mainly because it was deemed unfavourable to have two Anglo-Saxon states on the commission, and because France was big enough to dispel fear of utter US domination. Turkey was a Muslim state that had granted recognition to the new state of Israel. The chosen Turkish member of the PCC, Hussein Cait Yalçhin, was an elderly man with a background in journalism and well known for his anti-Soviet views. The French delegate, Claude de Boisanger, was described as a highly esteemed and able career diplomat, quick-witted, intelligent and objective. The Israeli diplomats viewed him as 'the protector, father confessor and guardian angel of the Syrian and Lebanese'.[10]

To assist Yalçhin, de Boisanger and Etheridge with their enormous task, the PCC was also equipped with a secretariat, headed by Spanish Dr Pablo y Flores de Azcárate.[11] Because of the undeniable political power of the United States, all parties in the negotiations looked to the US delegate for leadership, and Etheridge soon became the driving force of the PCC.[12] The refugee question would become the main defining feature and a front-line issue for the negotiation process Etheridge was to lead.

The Palestine Conciliation Commission: Early days, lost chances

From Israel's perspective, the ideal solution to the refugee problem was to solve it via resettlement in neighbouring countries. Their return to Israel was out of the question.[13] Meanwhile, in Damascus, Cairo, Baghdad and Beirut, where Etheridge led the PCC in pre-negotiation consultations, the Arab leaders met them with a near unanimous demand for unqualified refugee repatriation, as well as a point-blank refusal to enter into separate negotiations with Israel.[14] The return of the Palestinian refugees to their homes, in the minds of the Arab leaders, was *the* essential condition for the negotiation of other outstanding issues between them and Israel, including borders, security and Jerusalem.[15] This tension between repatriation and resettlement would dominate all the coming international efforts to approach the refugee problem. And as the parties positioned themselves for the expected negotiation effort they all dug their heels in: the Arab states calling for full repatriation, the Israeli leadership for full resettlement.

The commission soon decided that the Arab regimes were presenting what the PCC deemed to be an utterly unrealistic condition, from which they would have to be dissuaded.[16] If they could 'succeed in diverting the Arabs from their strong stand that *all* refugees must return', it would present substantial progress for the commission, Etheridge argued.[17] Nonetheless, they recognized that the repatriation of refugees was *the* main issue for the Arabs and that it was therefore urgent, if peace talks between Israel and the Arab states were to materialize at all, that Israel had to provide some kind of conciliatory statement or gesture on the refugee issue.[18] But with the Israeli cabinet's decision not to make any conciliatory statement or gesture on the refugee issue outside the context of a larger peace settlement, the PCC's assignment was made nearly impossible.[19]

The concessions the PCC asked of Israel were, according to Etheridge, nothing that would jeopardize Israel's position in the peace negotiations: in fact, Etheridge thought it was 'astonishing' and 'pure rubbish' that Israel had failed to give anything at all on the refugee issue to that point. He had been convinced from as early as March 1949 that the Israeli government had already decided how many refugees they would allow back and under what circumstances this would happen.[20] US secretary of state Dean Acheson supported the PCC and joined the commission in repeatedly pressing for an Israeli gesture but to no avail.[21]

Etheridge did not soft-pedal as to why he thought the PCC was getting nowhere: '[The] failure of [the] Jews' to make a conciliatory gesture regarding the refugee problem 'prejudiced [the] whole cause of peaceful settlement on this part of the world', he reported to Secretary Acheson.[22] In fact, in Etheridge's opinion, Israel's position on the refugee issue had 'stiffened rather than modified', since the commission first started its exploratory consultations.[23] Etheridge went so far as to speculate that the Israeli reluctance could be part of a larger strategy:

> I am more than ever of [the] opinion that if [the] Jews are not deliberately stalling peace negotiations until they can consolidate their position and grab off more land[,] as they seem to be doing in [the] triangle [i.e. the northern West Bank], they are being most short-sighted and making it difficult for themselves ever to have peaceful relations with their neighbors.[24]

Despite having so little success in their campaign for an Israeli gesture of conciliation, the members of the PCC decided that they would push ahead for more formal peace negotiations nevertheless. They were partly emboldened to do so because of the progress they had made on the Arab side of the table. The commission had managed to get the Arab states to drop their initial demand for full repatriation ahead of the commencement of any talks. In what Etheridge described as a 'real concession', the Arab states, at the Beirut summit, had agreed to proceed with further talks at a neutral location, thus the PCC decided to move the warring parties to Lausanne, Switzerland, for more formal peace talks.[25]

Before the main delegations were properly settled in at the lavish Beau-Rivage Palace on the banks of Lake Geneva, events in another diplomatic arena were fast dispelling hope for any progress in Switzerland. In New York, at the UN temporary headquarters at Lake Success, Israel was preparing to fight another major diplomatic battle: to gain admission to the UN. Though geographically far apart, Lausanne and Lake Success became closely interlinked. Briefly put, progress at the peace negotiations at Lausanne was held hostage by the Israeli delegation fighting for Israeli UN admission at Lake Success.

Chasing an Israeli gesture

Within the Israeli leadership, and especially within parts of its foreign policy leadership and the country's diplomatic corps abroad, considerable importance was placed on Israel's efforts to join the so-called family of nations.[26] At the time of its initial campaign to obtain UN admission at the end of 1948, however, Israel was still in the midst of several unresolved political problems with international ramifications: Israel's borders remained undefined, the future status of Jerusalem was undecided and the Palestinian refugee problem was growing on a dramatic scale. Because of this, Israel's first admission application met with a negative vote in the UN Security Council on 17 December 1948, following staunch opposition from both the UK and France.

Since the first failed attempt, however, Israel had signed an armistice agreement with Egypt at Rhodes, and agreements with the other Arab states were soon to follow.[27] This improved Israel's position at the UN tremendously, and on 4 March 1949, the Security Council passed an affirmative vote on the Israeli application, moving the matter to the General Assembly, where potential new member states needed a majority vote.

To the PCC, Israel's UN application represented a golden opportunity. Etheridge had long thought that the United States needed to develop a tougher policy towards Israel on the refugee problem, and there was leverage in the fact that the UN and the international community controlled something that Israel really wanted.[28] Since negotiations were getting underway in Lausanne at the very same time, the PCC pressed its advantage in the hopes that Israel would finally produce the conciliatory statement or gesture that the PCC and the United States already sought for a couple of months. Etheridge hoped that if Israel had 'the world public opinion brought to bear upon her through [the] UN', things would change in Lausanne.[29] But the Israeli delegation soon made it clear to the PCC that they did not intend to discuss refugees or Jerusalem while admission to the UN was under debate at Lake Success.[30] In the end, it became evident to all that so long as the admission question was undecided, progress in Lausanne was out of the question.

Though Israel had emerged from the March vote in the Security Council with great confidence, it now had to recalibrate and prepare for a new fight leading up to the General Assembly debate and vote. In early April 1949, Israeli foreign minister Moshe Sharett was summoned to a meeting with US secretary of state Dean Acheson on the grounds that the Israelis were being 'un-cooperative' regarding refugees and 'defiant' regarding Jerusalem.[31]

In fact, the Americans were becoming increasingly annoyed by the Israeli policy regarding Jerusalem. During the spring of 1949, the Israelis had taken steps that exposed their determination to gain permanent control over the disputed city, including the transfer of certain governmental offices from Tel Aviv to Jerusalem in clear violation of previously passed UN resolutions.[32]

To the Israelis, the April memo from Acheson was a signal that perhaps UN membership should not be taken for granted. They expected that Secretary Acheson would most likely use Israel's application for UN membership to exert pressure regarding the matters of Jerusalem and the Palestinians refugees.[33] Soon enough, the Israelis were proven right – the Americans reversed themselves by deciding to endorse a proposal that the Israeli admission application ought to be subject to extra deliberation in the UN's Political Ad Hoc Committee before the General Assembly vote.

The suggestion to move the admission discussion to the Ad Hoc Committee came from UN mediator Ralph Bunche. Though Israel's signing of an armistice agreement with Egypt had tipped the March vote in their favour within the Security Council, Bunche, the man closest to that agreement, voiced significant reservations regarding Israeli membership in the UN. Bunche had emerged from the Israel–Egypt negotiations on Rhodes with a strong dislike of the way Israel had behaved during the talks.[34] In late April, then, he urged the US UN delegation that at before being admitted, Israel should have to 'come clean' on four issues: the unsatisfactory nature of the report on the assassination of Count Folke Bernadotte; its attitude towards the refugee problem; the future status of Jerusalem; and the various existing boundary demands.[35] Bunche's approach was almost diametrically opposed to the designs of his boss, UN secretary general Trygve Lie.[36] Lie had even suggested that Bunche lobby for Israel's admission, but Bunche saw this as a highly 'inappropriate' move from the acting mediator to the conflict.[37] Of the four concerns raised by Bunche, Jerusalem and the refugee issue would emerge as the two main hindrances to Israel's UN admission.

During the week leading up to the meeting of the Ad Hoc Committee, it became increasingly clear to Israeli diplomats that an Israeli declaration entailing a 'constructive approach' to the refugee problem had become a 'point of honour' for the United States that was 'affecting [the] whole relationship' between the two countries. If the matter were to be simply 'brushed aside', it would be considered a serious snub towards the US secretary of state, who on numerous occasions had appealed directly to Israel for a conciliatory gesture or statement.[38] This sensitivity put Israeli leaders in a difficult position. The Israeli cabinet had already agreed on a strict policy of no return for the Palestinian refugees in the previous summer (of 1948) and remained unwilling to budge on this point. Even Eban, perhaps the strongest force behind Israel's drive to achieve UN membership, did not think that it was a goal worth the surrender of Israel's 'vital rights and interests'.[39] Still, the Americans had made it clear to Israel that the way to gain the active support in the unfolding admission process was to give a numerical commitment to repatriation or, at the very least, a commitment in principle on the refugee issue (or on Jerusalem). Eban therefore found that he had to balance on a knife-edge, to devise a statement that would concede enough to please the sceptics at the General Assembly but keep from causing problems for the Israeli delegation at Lausanne. Eban and his team of diplomats began to search for the formula that would secure the US support. The Israelis presented the American diplomats with several drafts of Eban's potential speech to the Ad Hoc Committee, but up to the day before the Americans remained unimpressed, regarding Eban's statements as too 'evasive'.[40]

In the end, it was on the issue of Jerusalem that the Israelis found a way forward in New York. Though the refugee question bedevilled the PCC and the Americans, Eban found it 'raised little echo' within the General Assembly itself, while the 'Jerusalem theme' was 'very strong'.[41] Eban understood, as well, that the most important thing in this regard was to avoid open conflict with the Vatican's interest in the Holy City's future.[42] While the Vatican did not have a formal vote within the General Assembly, its influence on the Catholic Latin American bloc – at that point the largest within the assembly, in numerical terms – was considerable. Eban's larger aim for his speech was therefore to 'placate' the Ad Hoc Committee 'without substantive changes [of] our principles'. What Israel needed to do, he thought, was provide what he referred to as 'conciliatory formulations'.[43] By keeping the United States and the Vatican happy on the topic of Jerusalem, Eban hoped to evade conceding anything at all on the refugee issue.

Together with Israel's position on the refugee issue, the future status of Jerusalem had been a point of tension in the relationship between Israel and the United States.[44] As the Israeli records show, it was Chaim Weizmann's personal interference with President Truman that swayed the US position. It was common knowledge within the Israeli leadership and within the Zionist movement in the United States that Truman had a weak spot for Weizmann. Their relationship had been utilized with great success at critical points in the period between 1947 and May 1948.[45] Prior to Eban's speech, Israel's president Chaim Weizmann thus wrote letters to President Harry Truman regarding the future of the Holy City. These letters 'greatly impressed' Truman and prompted him to 'discuss [the] matter [of UN admission] favorably with Acheson'.[46] Two of Truman's close advisors, David Niles and Clark Clifford, disclosed to the Israelis after the admission was a fact that it had been Weizmann 'more than any other single factor' that had influenced Truman's decision to support them.[47]

Eban was therefore able to address the Ad Hoc Committee in whatever manner he chose with great confidence: he knew that the White House was already satisfied by Weizmann's letters, and American support regarding Jerusalem would anticipate a blessing from the Vatican as well and, in turn, the numerically important Latin American bloc. Israel's ambassador to the United States, Eliahu Elath (previously Epstein), could therefore assure his colleague that even though the 'refugee problem [was] still unsettled' between the United States and Israel, Israel's chances for admission were 'greatly increased'.[48] In other words, there was no reason for Israel to concede anything on the refugee issue. Eban could make a statement at the General Assembly that offered little more than a reiteration of declared Israeli policy since the summer of 1948: no return for the Palestinian refugees.[49]

It appears that Truman believed that what had been practically impossible to obtain from Israel while it remained outside the UN would be more attainable once it was a full-fledged member state. The American decision to co-sponsor the UN General Assembly Resolution 273 (III) of 11 May 1949, which admitted Israel as the fifty-ninth member state of the UN, was ultimately based on pragmatic *realpolitik*.[50] The final vote was thirty-seven in favour and twelve against, with nine abstentions. The twelve votes against came from the Arab/Muslim bloc of countries, while the UK, Belgium, Brazil, Denmark, El Salvador, Greece, Siam, Sweden and Turkey all abstained. In a situation where the United States and the international community at large proved to have a very limited influence on Israeli policy, cooperation on Jerusalem was deemed to be of more importance than a concession on the refugee issue. The American delegation at the UN and the diplomats at the US State Department had come to understand that they could not get Israel to move on both issues. And for Truman, Jerusalem held a higher symbolic and political value than did the refugee issue.

The US decision to back Israel's admission notwithstanding its non-compliance on the refugee issue deeply discouraged PCC chairman Mark

Etheridge. Etheridge had accepted his PCC mission based on the belief that the Oval Office had his back – Truman had personally told Etheridge that he was prepared to apply pressure 'when and where necessary'. Etheridge had conveyed as much to Ralph Bunche in a confidential brief upon his first journey to the region.[51] After the UN admission episode, he felt betrayed by the administration that had tasked him to do the job but removed the tools needed for him to succeed. Several years later, Etheridge commented,

> I recognized that Israel was going to be very tough to deal with and Israel was desperately trying to get into the U.N. I got a promise out of the President that we would withhold recognition of Israel in the U.N. Hell, I hadn't been out there [negotiating] a month before we moved for recognition of Israel in the U.N. *We* moved it. We just didn't *vote* for it, we *moved* it.[52]

The US sponsorship of the admission resolution 'has weakened our [PCC] position and muffled my voice', Etheridge wrote with indignation to Acheson after the admittance was a fact. To counter the negative reports Etheridge sent to the Truman administration, Eytan asked Eban to 'mobilize all Frankfurthers [and] Cliffords etcetera'.[53]

Indeed, the only thing that the PCC managed to get Israel to accept in the spring of 1949 was the signing of the so-called Lausanne Protocol. As Israeli archival material clearly indicates, however, even this was merely a tactical manoeuvre to keep the Lausanne negotiations quiet during the Israeli admission campaign at Lake Success.[54]

It would soon become obvious that President Truman had been wrong in his somewhat hopeful calculation: Israel as a UN member state would not be easier to deal with in the context of the UN peace process. In fact, the Israeli delegations returned to Lausanne with instructions from their foreign minister to go back with a 'stiffened neck'.[55] Despite reports in the immediate aftermath of Israel's UN admission, the Egyptian government had instructed their Lausanne delegation to go ahead and discuss territorial issues, provided the Israelis accepted the *principle* of repatriation – a reversal of their previously held position – the talks remained paralyzed by the same 'horse-and-cart' dilemma that had existed since the pre-negotiation phase.[56] Israel continued to insist that any solution to the refugee issue would only arrive as a natural consequence and integral part of a full peace agreement. Conversely, the Arab states maintained that the refugee was *the* most important issue and insisted that it had to be settled *prior* to any move towards a full peace agreement.[57]

To an extent, the commission shared the Arab states' position that the refugee issue was at the 'top of the "hierarchy"'. They objected, however, to the notion that this automatically implied 'head of the "chronology"' as well.[58] The Arab states felt that Israel was using the refugees' suffering to pressure them into a settlement based on the status quo.[59] The Israelis, on the other hand, claimed that the Arab leaders were only using the refugees to push their own respective national interest and agendas, and that their refugees-first policy was a 'purely tactical' stance.[60] The rise and fall of the so-called 'Gaza Plan', Syrian president Husni Zaim's scheme to resettle 300,000 refugees in Syria, and the Israeli 100,000 offer indicate that there was something to the misgivings of both Israel and the Arab states.

Truman's anger and frustration over the lack of Israeli compliance in the negotiations after its UN admission manifested itself as a diplomatic row between the two nations. The subsequent memorandum from Truman to the Israelis was described by Sharett as the 'stiffest ever delivered'.[61] The tension did not, however, produce a real shift in policy or positions on behalf of Israel.

An offer everyone could refuse: The Gaza Plan and the 100,000 offer

With the initial Gaza Plan, Israel proposed that the Gaza Strip (including all of its residents), which had been controlled by Egypt since the war broke out in May 1948, would be placed under Israeli sovereignty.[62] The Gaza Plan and the discussions surrounding clearly demonstrate that support for an independent Arab state in Palestine was not an option that received much attention at the peace talks, nor was it on anybody's agenda as such. For both Jordan and Egypt, the important thing in the negotiations with Israel was land, not refugees, and this was true for Israel as well.

Though there have been some conflicting narratives on the origins of the plan, the primary sources leave no doubt that the plan can be traced back to Israeli leadership circles.[63] It was Walter Eytan who observed that Egypt had 'no territorial ambitions in Palestine' and that they indeed were 'anxious to get rid of the Gaza strip'.[64] Britain and the United States favoured a solution where

Gaza would be annexed by Jordan.[65] Jordan on the other hand, noted Sharett, would prefer to see the strip go to 'Israel or Satan' rather than Egypt, if it were not able to secure Gaza for itself.[66]

Israel was thus well aware of the disagreement and indecision surrounding the fate of Gaza. This leeway prompted Eytan to urge the Israeli leadership to start 'hammering out' a policy on what he saw as a central issue.[67] If Israel had 'a clear line [on Gaza], one way or the other we could, such is the confusion in men's mind, get our way', Eytan wrote to Foreign Minister Sharett.[68] They needed to move fast, he insisted, before the international community and the Arab world settled on a Gaza policy. Sharett and Prime Minister David Ben-Gurion got the message, and the very next day the cabinet made its decision regarding the Gaza Strip: Israel would offer to incorporate the entire Gaza Strip and all its local population.[69]

The territorial dimension – the physical incorporation of the Gaza Strip – was, in Sharett's view, a strategic asset for Israel. Offering to absorb these refugees, moreover, could be depicted as a 'major contribution' to the refugee problem as a whole and perhaps free Israel 'once and for all' from UN pressure on the matter.[70] And this win-win situation for Israel was not merely wishful thinking on Sharett's part. Etheridge had confirmed that if Israel made this offer, it would satisfy the US government's 'sense of fairness' on the matter.[71]

In the official proposal sent to the PCC on 29 May 1949, Walter Eytan stressed that, for Israel, the incorporation of the Gaza Strip and its residents would be an economic liability. However, Eytan wrote, Israel was willing to accept it because 'it was felt that it was here that [Israel] could make a really constructive large-scale contribution to the refugee problem'.[72] But it was a take it or leave it kind of proposal. When the PCC pressed Israel to clarify how many refugees it would allow to return to within its borders, if the original Gaza Plan fell through, Eytan wrote to Etheridge, 'No alternative, even on a much smaller scale, readily presents itself to the mind.'[73]

The Gaza Plan got a mixed reception in both the United State and Britain. The Americans would only back the plan if the Egyptians consented to it, meaning that Israel would have to cater to any additional demands Egypt might have.[74] The British were rather looking for a plan that was more in the interests of their regional ally Jordan and King Abdullah. The Jordanian monarch wanted Gaza under his own control. Because the British had troops stationed in both Jordan and Iraq, they were also very interested in securing easy access to the Mediterranean. They therefore suggested a land bridge between Jordan and Gaza that of course required the strip to stay Arab.[75] The British suggested it was better if Egypt kept Gaza and Israel took 'another 150,000 refugees from elsewhere'. The British policy should perhaps be seen as part and parcel of what Ilan Pappé has referred to as the British' 'Palestine syndrome', an illness where symptoms included a reluctance to assume any actual responsibility.[76]

The British suggestion regarding which among the refugee population that should be prioritized was also one that was more in the interest of King Abdullah. If the original Gaza Plan materialized and all those living there came under Israeli rule, Egypt would be more or less freed of her refugee burden. But for the other Arab states, notably Jordan, nothing would change, and their burden would remain. While Jordan might have been willing to resettle a lot of refugees, such an eventuality would have to entail some kind of financial aid package or regional development plan to the country's benefit. In the same vain, the British also proposed to include in the Gaza Plan some sort of territorial compensation to the Arab states (and particularly Jordan), via a corridor in the Negev desert and access to Mediterranean ports in Gaza and Haifa. But with Israel's Gaza Plan, none of this would happen, and Egypt would be the only Arab state that benefited.[77]

Over the summer, the Gaza Plan gradually faded from the scene. One obvious reason for this was Egypt's emphatic rejection of it, and British and American reluctance played parts as well. Yet it seems unlikely to been ratified and implemented in any case, because Israel had been getting cold feet. First of all, Israel found that it had underestimated the number of people living in the Gaza Strip when the initial offer was made. When newer calculations pointed to about 275,000 to 280,000 inhabitants – over 100,000 more than Israel had anticipated – Israel claimed that absorption would be impossible. Israel also feared that refugees from Lebanon, Syria and Jordan would exploit the opportunity to move to the Gaza Strip and use this as their springboard out of the refugee camps they were currently living in. The fact that Egypt instigated a mass transfer of Palestinians from Ismailia to the Gaza-Rafah border in August 1949 demonstrated the viability of this particular Israeli concern.[78] What troubled the Israeli leadership the most, however, was their realization that their Gaza Plan appeared to indicate their willingness and capacity to absorb into Israel a considerable portion of the Palestinian refugees, and that pressure to allow repatriation outside of the Gaza context would promptly ramp up.[79] And this was precisely what happened.

To the Americans and the PCC, it was very difficult to reconcile Israel's willingness to take Gaza and over 300,000 Palestinians (refugees and inhabitants) with the same nation's refusal to commit to absorbing an absolute number of refugees, *without* Gaza as part of the equation.[80] According to Israeli intelligence, Etheridge would have been happy with a commitment of 200,000 people (including the family-reunification schemes that were already underway as well as those Arabs who were already living in Israel), and he was incensed that Israel refused to state a number outside of the Gaza context.[81] But Israel's adamant refusal to even consider this demonstrated that it was mainly territorial interest that had been the driving force behind the scheme.[82]

Israel's backtracking should also be understood in light of the growing domination of a school of thought in Israel that saw advantages to the state if it simply allowed matters to drag on. Israel did not need a formal peace with the Arabs, or at least it needed it less than the Arab states did, according to this line of reasoning.[83] It was a school of thought led by Prime Minister Ben-Gurion that picked up momentum throughout the winter and spring of 1949, as Israel concluded armistice agreements with one after another of their neighbouring Arab states. Ben-Gurion saw no need to rush anything: 'If Israel appeared over-eager', historian Avi Shlaim notes of this period, 'the Arabs might demand a price'.[84] In this context, the Israeli leadership thought it better to 'wait a few years' and elude some of the outside pressure that was then being applied to finding a solution to the refugee issue.[85]

This reasoning also helps to explain Ben-Gurion's strong reluctance to engage with the Syrian prime minister Husni Zaim when the latter proposed that Syria should resettle 300,000 Palestinian refugees.[86] Zaim's plan was motivated more by aspirations for modernizing and developing the northern Syrian countryside in the Jazirah region than by a humanitarian drive to alleviate the plight of the refugees. As Shlaim aptly describes it, the offer was one of 'enlightened self interest'. Jazirah was characterized by its fertile land, but it was sparsely populated, making it an ideal possibility for large-scale resettlement of refugees. Zaim also hoped that by agreeing to resettle as many as 300,000 people, he would attract international development aid, which again would benefit the Syrian infrastructure and raise the standard of its agricultural sector.[87]

The alternative view was promulgated by Foreign Minister Sharett and held that Israel would be better off hastening its search for a solution to the refugee problem, because Israel *was* suffering (both economically and militarily) from the lack of a formal peace with its neighbours. Sharett advocated finding out how many refugees would want to return before deciding what to do with Israel's now-empty Arab villages, and if Husni Zaim was offering to resettle as many as 300,000 of them, this was a proposal worth exploring.[88] However, Sharett was not Israel's strong man, and Ben-Gurion refused to meet with Zaim. The prime minister was solely focused on the territorial issue and persuading the Syrians to sign an armistice agreement; since Syria posed little military threat to Israel, there was no incentive for him to change his mind.[89] The refugee problem therefore remained unremarked as the Gaza Plan and the offer from Syria's prime minster Zaim faded away under the auspices of Ben-Gurion's favoured approach.[90]

In early August 1949, however, something happened that seemed to suggest that Israel had decided to break from this position: an Israeli offer to repatriate 100,000 refugees suddenly surfaced. In her 1983 study of the '100,000 offer', Israeli scholar Varda Schiffer showed that it was in fact a mere tactical position 'designed to ease American pressure and improve Israel's image both in Lausanne and at the UN'.[91] Despite some other scholars' continued insistence that this was a genuine Israeli concession, closer scrutiny of this episode confirms Schiffer's claim.[92] Moreover, the situation with this so-called offer is noteworthy because it sheds light on how Israel manoeuvred in relation to US pressure – in particular by playing the State Department and the White House against each other.

The political driving force behind the 100,000 offer was Israel's foreign minister Moshe Sharett. Together with Eban, Sharett had long felt that it was necessary for Israel to do something that would ensure that its standing in the international community did not weaken any further, and the refugee issue was putting a very unhelpful strain on US–Israel relations.[93] Perhaps unsurprisingly, Sharett's initial proposal in this regard – to offer repatriation for 100,000 Palestinian refugees – met tough opposition from Prime Minister Ben-Gurion. Interestingly, Ben-Gurion thought that 100,000 were both too many *and* too few refugees.[94] As to the former concern, that many people were not in keeping with Israel's security parameters. As to the latter, Ben-Gurion had no faith that an offer to return 100,000 refugees would carry enough weight in Washington – after all, it was less than half of the 250,000 refugees the Americans had asked the Israelis to allow back. Domestically, Ben-Gurion also knew that the opposition parties in Israel were strongly opposed to any repatriation, as had been underlined during the Knesset debate on the 100,000 offer.[95]

And even if the Americans acquiesced and supported it, Ben-Gurion was certain that the offer was a long way from what the Arabs were expecting. Though Arab leaders in private had scaled down their demand for full repatriation, 100,000 people was barely one-seventh of the total refugee population. In the end, though, Sharett managed to get the Israeli cabinet's support for his plan and was given the green light to take the idea to Washington. He was only authorized to make a formal offer if the Americans welcomed the idea.[96] Again, the leading Israeli politicians recognized the value of having US support for a proposal or an initiative and always did what it could to ensure that this was within reach before committing to anything at the negotiating table.

Naturally, it was Ambassador Eban who was instructed to sound out the Americans. His instructions were to do so both on his own, as well as via other more discreet channels, such as Israel's 'friends' with access to the Oval Office.[97] Israeli archival records repeatedly refer to 'our friends'. Whom these friends are, is never spelled out, but most likely they include men such as Major General Hilldring, one of Truman's advisors on the US delegation to the UN General Assembly; presidential advisors David Niles, Clark Clifford and Ben Cohen; the businessman Abraham (Abe) Feinberg, who was central in the financing of Truman's re-election campaign; the lawyer Max Lowenthal, who gave legal advice on the Palestine question; and perhaps, most influential of all, Eddie Jacobson, Truman's close personal friend, who many times was used to promote the Israeli agenda in the Oval Office.[98]

The first man Eban chose to see was Andrew Cordier, a senior aide to UN secretary general Trygve Lie.[99] Sharett had given Eban free reins as to which channels he would use to sound out the proposal, suggesting that he go to either Hilldring, Bunche or Cordier. When Eban chose Cordier (although Cordier was a UN man), it was reportedly because of the latter's good access to authorities in the State Department. Cordier's initial personal reaction to Eban was that such an offer would be 'extremely helpful'.[100] He thought that many in the State Department would share his view, and he volunteered to float the idea and provide the Israelis with a quick reply. After one more consultation, this time with George McGhee, Eban reported back to the ministry that the 100,000 offer would possibly have a 'very deep effect' on Washington.[101]

But when Cordier returned to Israel four days later with the verdict from the State Department, he had to admit that his own take on the offer had been overly optimistic. The State Department found the figure to be 'too low'.[102] The Gaza Plan, proposed only a few months earlier, appeared to undermine Israel's claim that it could not accept more than 100,000 returnees. The US State Department then tried to enhance the Israeli offer, as sought to engage Jacob Blaustein of the American Jewish Committee to influence Israel to accept 250,000 refugees and give up a part of the southern Negev. This plan came up short, however, when Blaustein quickly called Israel's attention to the State Department's planned move and promised the Israelis that he would give his 'full cooperation' to obtaining the White House's support for the initial Israeli proposal.[103]

That the State Department's reaction was critical mattered less to the Israelis, though, once their White House contacts reported President Truman was 'extremely pleased' with the 100,000 offer.[104] This news came to the Israelis from Major General John Henry Hilldring, a man handpicked to be on the US delegation at the UN General Assembly session on Palestine by presidential advisor David Niles under the pretext that he was the one individual advisor in whom both Truman *and* the American Jewry could have 'complete confidence'.[105] This revelation to the Israelis was reportedly made in direct defiance of the president, who had specifically asked Hilldring not to disclose this news to the Israelis, in case there was still a possibility of bargaining over the final number. Thanks to Hilldring, Truman's hopes were dashed.[106] Hilldring later insisted to Secretary of State Acheson that he had not told the Israelis anything about Truman's reaction to the offer, but the Israeli archival sources clearly tell a different story.[107] It was confirmed to Israeli diplomats in additional meetings through the course of the next two days that the 100,000 offer would be viewed favourably in the White House.[108] Knowing that Truman already approved of the offer, the Israelis in turn felt confident enough to formally present it, despite the negative reply expressed via Cordier, from the US State Department, and despite the PCC's negative reaction. The PCC considered 100,000 refugees to be inadequate but promised to take the offer to the Arab delegations the next day.[109] In essence, it did not really matter to the Israeli leadership what those entities thought of the offer, because Israel's main objective had never been to actually implement the plan but instead to ease Israel's strained relationship with the White House. In this, they were successful.

About three weeks after General Hilldring informed the Israeli diplomats of Truman's reaction to the 100,000 offer, the news of this meeting and its leaks reached Secretary of State Acheson.[110] He was not pleased, and in a letter dated 9 August 1949, he used very candid words to make it clear to the Israelis that, despite reports to the contrary, the policy of the United States on disputed territories and the refugee question, which had been stated repeatedly, remained unchanged.[111] Israel 'sh[ou]ld be left under no illusion', he wrote, that the president, the State Department and the US delegation at Lausanne stood together in these matters.[112] This, of course, was only partly true, as there were clearly substantially different views on what could and should be asked of Israel in this unfolding process. In contrast to the State Department and the US career diplomats at the UN, Truman needed to calibrate his Palestine policy with an eye to the domestic audience. Acheson's indignation had little noticeable effect on the Israeli diplomatic corps. Elath simply noted dryly that, in the future, it would probably be more appropriate if the US State Department learned about the US president's positions from the president himself, rather than Israeli diplomats.[113]

Despite this small diplomatic hiccup that Acheson's letter signalled, Israel had to be satisfied with how things had played out. Walter Eytan, Israel's chief negotiator at Lausanne, acknowledged that 'the 100,000 scheme was a matter of immediate tactics', and that it had served its purpose well.[114] Foreign Minister Sharett agreed with his chief negotiator, noting that the offer had 'vastly improved' Israel's 'tactical position' vis-à-vis the United States and the Arabs.[115] In a Knesset debate on foreign relations, Sharett later boasted that with this scheme, Israel had managed to 'discard' the repatriation issue and likewise guarantee that the refugee question would be forever directly linked to an overall peace agreement.[116]

Sharett was right to conclude that something had changed in the international community's approach to the refugee issue. The waning diplomatic belief in, and focus on, repatriation as the solution to the refugee problem was reinforced by developments on the ground. In addition to the measures taken in order to inhibit those who had already fled from starting to return, Israeli authorities also decided that, for military strategic reasons, they had to 'clear' the new state's borders of Arab communities.[117] Throughout 1949, the IDF 'transferred' and expelled, by soft and hard means, at least 20,000 Palestinians in 'border-clearing operations'.[118] The overall picture emerging was that, with each passing day, the facts on the ground gradually changed to the benefit of the newborn state of Israel. A Palestinian return to this territory became gradually harder to envision.

In some ways, the period from 1950 through 1954 represents an interlude in the efforts to create peace in the Middle East. After Lausanne, yet before the top-secret Anglo-American Alpha Plan, no wars or major peace initiatives arose during these years. In 1951, efforts were directed towards a peace conference in Paris that never made it past the preliminary stages of negotiation. In November of that year, the PCC was forced to admit that the Paris conference was yet another failure. The General Assembly of 1951 gave only a superficial consideration to the Paris effort, and its main Palestine resolution of that year mentioned neither refugees nor compensation specifically.[119] The only outcome of the Paris effort that stuck was the PCC's decision to initiate a separate process to aid the release of the so-called 'blocked' – that is, frozen – Palestinian bank accounts in Israel.[120] For the PCC, this was an effort to see whether progress on the more technical parts of the refugee problem would propel progress on other, more substantial aspects. For Israel, the PCC's request to engage in talks to release the blocked accounts, like the issue of compensation, represented a golden opportunity to improve its image on the international diplomatic stage.

As historian Neil Caplan has aptly noted, the PCC moved from conflict *resolution* to conflict *management*.[121] Throughout these years, the approach to the Palestinian refugee problem was substantial reframed.

In 1948–9, the refugee problem had been treated mainly as a political issue. It was seen as principally important that those refugees who wanted to return were so allowed. As the new decade dawned, however, there was an increasing tendency to view the problem through a practical lens. Gradually, the efforts that were undertaken sought to dissolve – rather than solve – the Palestinian refugee problem.

Two examples of this occurred already towards the end of 1949. First, the so-called McGhee plan was launched, a scheme that stipulated spending about $200 million to develop the region, with 30 million intended for Israel and the remaining amount for the Arab states.[122] Next, the initiative called the Economic Survey Mission – commonly referred to as the 'Clapp mission', led by Gordon R. Clapp – was tasked to inquire about resettlement options in the region. The mission was initiated on 23 August 1949. Right away, it met with serious opposition from the Arab world, including the refugees themselves, who feared, with good reason, that the mission's real purpose was to move towards resettlement of the refugees in the Arab world. Reports of opposition came from both Syria and Lebanon, while Jordan, true to tradition, was apparently more cooperative.[123] There was little promise in both, as they were never linked to any political pressure. Essentially, these initiatives amounted to slapping an economic Band-Aid on a political wound.[124]

While these initiatives failed to break the refugee deadlock, it did manage to give birth to an organization that since has become one of the conflict's permanent features: the United Nations Relief and Works Agency (UNRWA).[125] The establishment of UNRWA represented the ultimate illustration of the decisive shift in the international community's approach to the problem. In less than a year, the international call for refugee repatriation had moved, from the discussion of substantial to limited repatriation, to a near complete focus on large-scale resettlement and economic development schemes.

A beautiful dream:
The rise and fall of Project Alpha

UNRWA had been established to 'prevent starvation and distress and to further the conditions for peace and stability'.[1] The Palestinian refugees with this became the only refugee population with a UN agency of their own – the world's other refugee problems remain to this day under the purview of the UN High Commissioner for Refugees (UNHCR). As historian Jacob Tovy remarks, this reflected the 'complexity' of the conflict and the 'political, religious and emotional powder keg' that the refugee issue had become internationally.[2]

The UN had no own money to finance such a big operation. The establishment of UNRWA thus meant that the international community had to step up its financial support to the Palestinian refugees. Seventy per cent of the organization's funding was given by the United States, allocated by Congress under the so-called Mutual Security Act.[3]

For the Americans, the Palestinian refugee issue was one closely connected to the fear of the spread of communism in the Middle East and the world. The poverty and despair of the refugee camps could easily be taken advantage of, US diplomats and policymakers feared. Several hundred thousand refugees living in dire conditions, having lost their land, homes and livelihoods, meant dangerously fertile ground for the planting of communist seeds. In 1949, Gordon Clapp of the Clapp mission had warned that if the refugees remained refugees, their sense of hopelessness and bitterness would only increase.[4] Although many of the refugees fared better than much of the local population around them, in terms of health and education services, these were urban people from the Palestinian middle class now, living in leaky tents in their Arab host states. These tradesmen and farmers were 'drowned in the boredom and frustration which the camps bred', and they were viewed as a clearly destabilizing element in the region.[5]

The 'real key' to the region's problems is the refugee, wrote the American consul general back to the US State Department in January 1953. The refugee is going to be a 'festering sore in Arab Palestine', and, he lamented, there is 'no immediate prospect of effective treatment of him'. The refugee 'now resembles a boil, which is ready to burst when prodded', he warned the department.[6]

This had been the consistent line of thinking within the US State Department since 1948. Repeatedly, US officials and diplomats linked the refugee situation with the increase in border clashes and a general negative impact on regional stability.[7] Ralph Bunche, the chief architect behind the only successful Arab–Israeli negotiations (in 1949), held the opinion that it was precisely the failure to resolve the refugee problem that explained why his armistice agreements had not translated into a full peace.[8] For the Eisenhower administration this view became reinforced after Secretary of State John Foster Dulles's returned from his first tour of the Middle East in May 1953.[9] The open question remained: What could be done to improve the situation? Could the United States take lead in efforts to find a solution to the problem?

Establishing the Alpha Plan

When General Dwight D. Eisenhower came to the presidency in 1952, it was with little or no desire to get involved in the Middle East. While foreign policy made up most of his inaugural address on 20 January 1953, the Middle East as a region and the Arab–Israeli conflict were unremarked. Much like his predecessor, Eisenhower's main foreign policy doctrine focused on keeping the communist ideology from spreading. The operative conviction was that world peace hinged fully on the ability of the United States to contain the Soviet Union. Furthermore, the new administration sought to distance itself from its predecessor's Middle East policy and instead approached the region with 'friendly impartiality'.[10]

While Eisenhower's administration harboured no outspoken ambitions of creating Israeli–Arab peace, the conflict had certain dimensions that were unsettling when viewed through the Cold War lens. One such dimension of them was the Palestinian refugee problem. Indeed, in July 1954, when the National Security Council (NSC) completed its first comprehensive study of

US objectives in the Middle East, it stated that, among all the problems in the region, the refugee issue was the main cause for concern.[11]

The American security establishment saw the solution of the refugee problem and increased regional stability as part of the state's national security interest. In addition, a worry in Washington, D.C. related to the Americans' relationship with the oil-producing Arab states. Secretary Dulles apparently felt that in its Middle East policy, the previous administration had 'gone completely overboard for purely domestic political purposes', and that the policy lines stipulated by the State Department had not been followed.[12] This had dangerously weakened the American position vis-à-vis the Arabs, and it needed to be corrected. In Dulles's view, a more balanced approach made for a more sensible foreign policy, even though he realized that this was going to make him 'damn unpopular' with the American Jewish community.[13] This approach, which was referred to internally as 'deflating Israel', was intended make a more 'reasonable' settlement possible.[14]

Across the Atlantic, a similar development was taking place in Britain. Israeli diplomats noted a shift in public opinion and among government officials after the Qibya raid in October 1953. On the night of 14 October 1953, a special military unit (Unit 101) of the Israeli Defence Forces led by Major Ariel (Arik) Sharon blew up forty-five houses and killed sixty-nine inhabitants of the village of Qibya in the West Bank, then under Jordanian rule.[15] Because the border of the 1949 armistice agreement zigged and zagged across the rocky hills of the territory in the West Bank, Palestinian refugees were often able to watch the new Jewish immigrants working what had once been their own means of livelihood. The hundreds of refugees who then crossed into their old territory to reap what they viewed as their crops, to steal irrigation pipes or to otherwise express their displeasure perpetuated the tension that eventually led to the Qibya raid.[16] The particularly violent Israeli response produced massive protests and sweeping condemnation internationally and inside Israel itself.[17]

In general, British influence and involvement in the region had dwindled since the termination of its mandate in Palestine in 1948. For a number of years, the country had been suffering from what Israeli historian Ilan Pappé called the 'Palestine syndrome'. This condition was characterized by a great reluctance to 'assume any direct responsibility' for the conflict that had cost so many British lives and so much effort and money during the mandate period. Yet there was still British interest in the region.[18] When the Free Officers, led by Colonel Gamal Abdul Nasser, took power in Egypt in 1952, this greatly worried the British.[19] They then became increasingly agitated about the situation in Egypt and particularly about the Suez Canal.[20] The enormous British base in the Canal Zone was, among other things, costly at a time when there was a strong domestic demand for substantial reductions in British defence expenditure.[21]

After negotiations between Egypt and Britain in the summer of 1954, an agreement was signed on 19 October 1954, which stipulated that the British army would withdraw from Sinai by June 1956.[22] And an Anglo-Jordanian treaty, signed in 1948, obligated Britain to come to Jordan's side if it were attacked. The continuing dance of border infiltrations and Israeli reprisals in the Jordan Valley had become a constant challenge for King Hussein and thus also for his British patrons. The Qibya raid had profound implications in this regard.

All of the above-mentioned factors help to explain the British decision to re-enter the field of Middle East peacemaking and to clarify why British foreign minister Anthony Eden dispatched his previous private secretary, Evelyn Shuckburgh, to the Middle East in the autumn of 1954. Shuckburgh was sent out to acquaint himself with the problems of the area and told by Eden to 'look out for any possibilities of an Arab-Israeli settlement'.[23] Shuckburgh returned with a report titled 'Notes on Arab-Israel Dispute' in mid-December 1954.[24] Its main points were as follows. First, the British should work in close cooperation with the United States in the area. Second, their shared approach should mainly target Egypt and Israel. Third, Israel needed to give 'visible' concessions on border adjustments and the refugee problem. Fourth, the signing of any such settlement would be rewarded with a security guarantee to both Egypt and Israel from the Western powers. Finally, Shuckburgh saw it as essential that the defining objective of the project had to be a settlement, not a full-fledged peace treaty.[25] It was Shuckburgh's report that would come to serve as the basis for the next round of Middle East peacemaking, better known as Project Alpha or the Alpha Plan.

Right before Christmas in 1954, a top-secret memorandum was sent to a few individuals in the US State Department. The memo informed them that the new joint Anglo-American effort to create a settlement in the Arab–Israeli conflict was underway, and that all information on the case was to be distributed as 'top secret' under the code name 'Alpha'.[26] It was believed, to start with, that an Israeli–Egyptian agreement might serve as a cornerstone for the establishment of a 'new regional strategic system'.[27] To reach such an agreement, the diplomats therefore would focus their efforts on two major problems that had been left unsolved by the 1949 armistice agreements: permanent borders and the Palestinian refugee problem.[28]

On 16 December 1954, during a dinner in Paris, Evelyn Shuckburgh presented his thoughts to Dulles.[29] Right away, Dulles agreed to give it a try, if the project moved ahead swiftly.[30] From Dulles's point of view, they had the next twelve months at their disposal, after which the next American election campaign would commence and make 'all action impossible'.[31] After 1955, that is, the Arab–Israeli conflict would again be back in US domestic politics, and Dulles noted ruefully, 'If the Republicans failed to offer measures acceptable to the American Jewry the Democrats would surely promise them.'[32] Dulles felt that this was the best time for the US administration to put some pressure on Israel. If Israel rejected a reasonable proposal, Dulles claimed, it would jeopardize not only their public US aid but also private aid.[33] Dulles had good reason to include this dimension in his analysis, because ever since the establishment of the state of Israel in 1948, support of, and for, the Jewish state had played a disproportionate role in American domestic policy. Dulles was in fact so concerned about this that he pursued a secret bipartisan agreement to keep the Arab–Israeli issue out of domestic politics. On 30 September 1953, Dulles and Eisenhower had discussed this possibility with the leader of the Democratic Party, Adlai Stevenson, seeking to enlist him and his party in a bipartisan Middle East policy that would 'protect the administration against pro-Israel dissatisfaction'. Their effort met with little success. According to Stevenson's report to the Israelis, he had refused to make any such a deal.[34] Although Dulles ultimately failed to banish Israel and the Arab–Israeli conflict from the domestic arena, he was happy with the administration's goal of obtaining a more balanced Middle East policy.

Dulles appointed American diplomat and former ambassador to Israel, Francis H. Russell, to team up with Shuckburgh of the British Foreign Office to start to hammer out a 'package' deal that they could eventually bring to the Israelis and the Egyptians. As the Americans' chief liaison to the project, Russell worked on Alpha under cover of being the new special assistant secretary for public affairs. President Eisenhower was informed about the effort and he gave his consent but no promise of any personal commitment.[35] Starting 21 January

1955, the British and the Americans meet for Alpha consultations twice a day in the US State Department's offices at Foggy Bottom in Washington, D.C.[36]

From the outset, the chief objective of Project Alpha was to terminate the state of belligerency between the countries. This served two main purposes: removing the basis for the Suez Canal blockade and the secondary Arab boycott and justifying to the US and UK publics and lawmakers the additional costs that security guarantees and aid packages would require.[37] Again, the Anglo-American assumption that Arab public opinion was not ready for full-scale peace treaties lowered the level of ambition of the project. The Americans and the British instead aimed to bring about, to the greatest extent possible, arrangements that were lasting and sustainable, and that would enable the 'substance, if not the form, of peace'.[38] What would this approach entail for the treatment of the Palestinian refugee issue?

Resettlement and repatriation in the Alpha Plan

Both Shuckburgh and Russell agreed that regarding repatriation, it was highly unrealistic to expect the Israeli government to make any kind of general statement endorsing the return of any significant number of refugees, let alone actually allowing them to return.[39] In general, Russell and the Americans were more sceptical than the British about the possibility of getting Israel to make any meaningful concessions at all. Shuckburgh connected this American scepticism to the fact that Russell had come to the Alpha Plan more or less straight from a position at the US Embassy in Tel Aviv, and that this allowed him to see Israel's point of view 'rather clearly'. This was a good thing, Shuckburgh thought, considering that the British themselves were 'rather short on Israeli experience'.[40] As to the likelihood of getting Israel to agree to any significant repatriation, however, the British were as grim in their outlook as the Americans. Repatriation was, in Russell's opinion, one of Israel's real 'trump cards', one that it would most likely refuse to play outside the context of a general settlement.[41] Shuckburgh agreed and argued that the United States and the UK therefore had to 'extinguish the [refugees'] hope of returning to Israel' and focus instead on how to best leverage compensation as an alternative to repatriation.[42] For the Alpha group, repatriation was reduced to merely a 'formality which must be gone through'.[43]

Asking Israel to simply acknowledge the principle of repatriation was in essence the same policy that had been employed since Lausanne. The difference between this new deal and Lausanne was that whereas the American diplomats in Lausanne had urged Israel to agree to limited repatriation for about 250,000 to 300,000 refugees, the number being asked of Israel had by this point decreased substantially. In the Alpha framework, it had dropped to 15,000 returnees a year for five years. If a year's quota were unfilled, in addition, the balance would not carry over to the next year. The Alpha Plan would ask Israel to pay compensation for the land that they had annexed. The grand total of 75,000 refugees who should be allowed to return to Israel was a cost to be covered by UNRWA. Russell thought 'was as far as Israel would go in accepting refugees'.[44] According to then undersecretary of state George Allen, Dulles's personal conviction was that a token number of 15,000 to 20,000 returnees would be sufficient.[45] In other words, Israel's hard-line position on the refugee issue was paying off. It would be Israel's red lines, not those of the Western powers or certainly not those of the Arab states, that defined the Alpha Plan's starting point. What the Palestinians themselves asked for or wanted was not on the international diplomats' radar.

The general understanding within the Alpha group was that the refugees would not actually be returned to their original homes, as envisaged in UNGA Resolution 194, because these homes were, 'in most cases, occupied by Israelis'.[46] At the US State Department, the belief that only 'simple farmers' would harbour a genuine willingness to return was dominant.[47] The general reading of the situation was that, for these Palestinians, return was all about their own particular 'five acres' of land, not Palestinian statehood.[48] Members of the business and merchant class, however, would in fact be frightened by the prospect of finding themselves repatriated to Israel, despite their 'ritualistic insistence upon return'. 'It is very doubtful', the Alpha proposal insisted, 'that the full 75,000 would want to return'. Though they had very limited intimate knowledge of the Palestinian position, this was the core understanding that the Alpha group came to share and that guided their next steps in trying to find a solution to the refugee problem.

What, then, about resettlement? With so few being potentially returned, resettlement options became a key point for the Alpha-group diplomats to develop.

According to the groups' rough estimates, Iraq held the best prospects for resettlement via economic development programs in the long run. A large number of refugees would also have to be resettled in the Jordan Valley (200,000, including those resettled by the proposed Johnston plan), Egypt (70,000, through the Sinai project), Syria (80,000), Iraq (60,000, initially) and Lebanon (40,000).[49] It would be easiest, some argued in one of the early Alpha meetings, to find a way to 'give the refugees some money' so that they could 'settle themselves'.[50] This idea, of course, was both impractical and politically problematic.

The British and Americans then worked out an internal agreement on five basic elements that would guide their approach to the compensation question: First, to be able to pay its part of a compensation deal, Israel would have to borrow money from friendly Western powers. Second, some kind of board would have to be created in order to handle all of the refugees' claims. Third, the amount to be paid to each individual claimant would represent only a limited percentage of the total amount claimed. Fourth, any individuals who received compensation above a fixed amount would have to relinquish all claims to UNRWA relief and assistance in their rehabilitation process. Fifth, the government of Israel should be asked to donate land to those refugees who would return, while the UNRWA would be responsible for financing the development of that land and the facilitation of the refugees' rehabilitation there.[51]

The decision to 'scale down' the individual claims had significant implications. If you happened to be a Palestinian refugee who, before 1948, had been well off in terms of owning property or having accounts that were now being blocked by Israel, your claim would, under the Alpha regime, be sacrificed to the greater good of your fellow refugees. But on a related point, the two delegations disagreed: while the British position held that compensation was separate from repatriation, meaning that even a returnee with a claim would be entitled to compensation for his or her losses, the US position was that the refugee's choice should be either compensation *or* repatriation. If the latter were chosen, the former would be off the table. It was a position that was designed to, in Russell's own words, 'deliberately ... discourage repatriation'.[52]

In addition to its points about the refugee issue, the final Alpha proposal called for territorial adjustments, an agreement regarding the supervision of and access to the holy places in Jerusalem, agreements on the sharing of ports and mutual overflight rights, as well as the restoration and/or construction of telecommunications facilities between the Arab states across Israeli territory.

Finally, it also aimed at ending the Arab states' secondary boycott of Israel. Both American and British companies were being targeted by the secondary boycott, so the resolution of this issue was in the Western powers' own (financial) interest as well.[53]

Securing regional acceptance of the Alpha Plan

The Anglo-American line on the refugee issue represented a further depoliticization of the Palestinian issue. By refocusing their efforts in this direction, by giving lots of attention to resettlement and compensation and little attention to a political solution to the refugee problem, Alpha contributed further to the reframing of the Palestinian refugee problem. This was clearly in the interest of Israel. Israel's position remained that repatriation was out of the question.

But not all elements of Alpha were advantageous to Israel. Notably, the plan's linking of the promise of a Western security guarantee to the signing of a settlement went counter to what Israel for some time had worked to achieve. Alpha contained a promise that, if the Egyptians and Israelis reached an agreement, they would both benefit from a US–UK security guarantee.[54] Israel, for its part, wanted a security guarantee to remain outside the context of an Arab–Israeli settlement.

Since its establishment as a state in 1948, Israel had made a point of its non-aligned positioning. Although Israel understood that everybody in Washington placed it in the Western camp, Israel's policy had been to never formally acknowledge any allegiance. There was great insecurity in the United States, regarding Israel's real alliance. Though they had good diplomatic relations, the fact remained that many of the inhabitants of Israel were Jews who had immigrated from the Soviet Union and Eastern Europe. But when Israel began pushing for a security guarantee in London and Washington, it was a signal of a significant foreign policy shift on Israel's behalf. In Israeli politics, the issue of a security treaty with the United States was a part of a larger debate regarding Israel's abandonment of its non-aligned policy from its early years of statehood. Concern about the independence of Israel's foreign and defence policy was widespread in Israeli leadership circles. The school of thinking that feared that a security treaty with the United States would pin Israel down was spearheaded by Moshe Dayan and Ben-Gurion, while Eban and Shiloah of the Israeli embassy in Washington, D.C. (and a reluctant Sharett), were the foremost proponents of pursuing the treaty.[55]

Foreign Minister Sharett, who was under a great deal of pressure domestically, complained to Dulles in mid-April 1955 that the Middle East was becoming 'a network of pacts from which Israel is excluded not only as a participant but even as a candidate for participation.'[56] This was spurred by the newly signed pact between Iraq and Turkey (on 24 February 1955), later to become known as the Baghdad Pact.[57]

Though Dulles refused to meet the Israelis in their request of a security guarantee, the very fact that Israel was campaigning to obtain such a guarantee reassured the Anglo-American partners that they held something that Israel really wanted and that this would serve as necessary leverage in their efforts to gain Israeli cooperation on the Alpha Plan. Dulles had in fact argued since the first stages of Alpha that the security dimension of the plan would be an 'immense attraction'. He was supported in this by the British foreign minister, Harold Macmillan.[58] The two agreed that the security guarantee was the 'biggest carrot' that the United States and the UK had, and that it 'would be folly to give this away until we had a general settlement agreed between the Arabs and Israel'. Given that the Arabs wanted protection against an expansionist Israel, and Israel wanted protection against aggressive Arabs, Dulles concluded that the security guarantee was the card to be played when agreement on the other issues was reached.[59]

Moshe Sharett held a different opinion. Sharett argued that the United States needed to give Israel the guarantee *before* there could be any hope of a peace agreement, not as a part of a larger settlement. That is, rather than viewing it as a carrot for cooperation, Israel asked for the security guarantee as a precondition to its cooperation with the Alpha partner's plans. This was a bargaining tactic Israel had made good use of previously, as the discussion of Israel's UN admission showed. In 1955, Sharett made it clear to his counterpart Dulles that Israel should be expected to move nowhere as far as concessions on the cessation of territory or the return of refugees.[60]

The Israelis pushed this same line of argument on both sides of the Atlantic. In London, as the British Labour Party was preparing for the upcoming British election, Shuckburgh noted in his diary on 13 April 1955 that 'the Jews are organizing every sort of pressure and propaganda to get a treaty guarantee of their present conquests, so that they shall not have to make any concessions'. Shuckburgh feared, and rightly so, that the Israeli 'pressure campaign' meant 'trouble' for the Alpha Plan.[61]

Despite Sharett's efforts, the two Alpha allies stuck with their initial analysis that providing Israel with such a guarantee would be unduly improving Israel's negotiating position and in fact removing one of the main incentives for Israel to enter negotiations with the Egyptians in the first place.[62] Though they agreed on this, dissonance was brewing within the Anglo-American alliance. Up until the summer of 1955, the whole plan had been shrouded in secrecy. From the beginning, the two partners had agreed on the importance of this, should the plan have any chance of succeeding. For the American administration, however, domestic factors were pushing for a changed tactic.

Allied discord over Alpha

Secretary Dulles had made no Middle East policy address during the first two years of the administration or during the period of the congressional elections in 1954. By summer 1955, however, Dulles felt that he had to get on the record with the American public on the matter. In the 1954 congressional elections, the Republican Party had lost eighteen seats in the US House of Representatives, which resulted in a Democratic majority in the House. Dulles feared that waiting even a few months longer before publicly wording the administration's policy could be very unfortunate.[63]

To the British, Dulles explained that if he waited any longer, the Alpha positions would gradually become 'untenable' and as the presidential elections of 1956 approaching, he would be 'forced into a declaration more favorable to Israel'.[64] Dulles was convinced that 'at almost any moment' Democratic leaders would soon be coming out with pro-Israel policy statements and thus 'plunge' into the campaign and American public debate with the Arab–Israeli conflict.[65] The announcement of the Alpha Plan would therefore be a perfect way to get ahead of the campaign circus and 'provide an answer to Jewish pressure groups' in the United States, the American diplomats reasoned.[66]

In addition, a public speech would contribute to the establishment of a set of specific objectives that the Western powers and the UN could then pursue. For Dulles, it was also important to ensure that the administration remained faithful to the position that he had promoted regarding Israel and the security guarantee. By stating it in a public speech, Dulles hoped to galvanize his government around the idea that such a guarantee would be provided only *after* a settlement. Dulles's idea was that by publicly committing the administration to a strong stance on this, the policy could withstand the fallout later on.[67] Dulles did expect that there would be 'some pressure' against this position inside the United States, but he maintained that it would be 'possible to stand up to it'.[68] If he did not give a statement, though, Dulles feared that Democratic leaders would seize the initiative by committing themselves to a position that was 'favorable to the Jews' and that would be hard to walk back.[69]

For the most part, then, these were the *American* domestic political reasons for going public with Alpha. It was a break with the allies' initial agreement that Alpha public should be taken public only as a last resort.

For the British foreign minister, Dulles's sudden interest in a public statement came as a surprise. Macmillan did not share the American's enthusiasm for going public with Alpha and wanted Dulles to refrain from giving the speech.[70] The British calculations differed from those of the Americans, since they, after all, had more commitments, both economic and military, on the ground in the region; Macmillan and the British cabinet felt that the UK would be the one bearing the most risk in going public with Alpha. The British had a defence treaty with Jordan and had troops stationed in the region. If violence erupted, the British feared that they would be tasked with keeping the situation under control. In the refugee camps in Gaza and Jordan, Macmillan feared that the refugees would get 'out of hand', and furthermore that demonstrations would erupt against British and American people and properties in the other Arab states and perhaps also in Israel.[71]

In addition, Macmillan feared that a statement at this point would endanger Iraqi prime minister Nuri al-Said. Al-Said, a loyal ally to the British in Baghdad, had long sought a defence mechanism for his country that would not leave him as exposed domestically as the Anglo-Iraqi Treaty of 1930 had done. In the Baghdad Pact, first signed by Iraq and Turkey on 24 February 1955 and then by Britain in April of the same year, al-Said had found his opportunity. The pact was al-Said's chance to elevate Iraq's regional position vis-à-vis its arch nemesis, Nasser's Egypt.[72] But if Dulles's Alpha statement was poorly received throughout the Arab world, the chances were that the domestic and regional opposition al-Said had been facing for years would only grow rather than subside. The Baghdad Pact was still a shaky structure, as well, and the British feared that if the Americans went public with Alpha it would wreck the new alliance (and throw the Iraqi ruler from his position) before it had time to solidify.[73]

Thus, Macmillan suggested to the Americans that to avoid the situation getting out of control in the Arab world, the statement should be a joint Anglo-American announcement. This would better reflect the actual background of the Alpha Plan, and the British would be better positioned to sell the ideas to the Arab world. A solo speech from the United States would only help to enlist Israel, Macmillan thought.

But when the American wheels were in motion, there was little the British could do to stop it. In fact, once the decision was decisive, the British came around to acknowledge internally that it could possibly bring some benefits to the future of Alpha. Macmillan thought it could very well be in the UK interest that American Middle East policy would be 'frozen' along the lines worked out through the Alpha process. And as Dulles himself had argued, there was no more efficient way for him to ensure that this became US policy – than to present it in an official policy statement.[74]

As part of the commonplace routine, relevant American embassies in the region were asked to provide input and comments to the content of Dulles's forthcoming speech. The US ambassadors in Amman, Baghdad, Beirut, Cairo and Damascus had one substantial and consistent comment: the speech needed to include a more specific reference to repatriation of the refugees as a part of the solution to the refugee problem. If this were left out, the ambassador in Amman warned, the Arab public's reaction would be more negative than first anticipated. All of the ambassadors in the Arab states expected 'negative' or 'unfavourable' reactions to the speech, and in Tel Aviv Lawson expected 'outright and vigorous opposition'.[75] This regional view from the US diplomats echoed the concern voiced by the British, who urged the Americans to include 'some reference to the possibility that some of the Arab refugees who formerly lived in Israel might be allowed to return to their homes'.[76]

Interestingly, the view from the US embassy in Israel was diametrically opposed. Repatriation had to be played down as an alternative solution. Since the idea of Dulles giving a speech on US Middle East policy had first surfaced during the early summer of 1955, the political scene in Israel had undergone some substantial changes. The ruling Israeli Mapai party had lost five of its seats in the 120-member Knesset in the elections on 26 July, most of them to the General Zionist list.[77] Mapai's loss was largely attributed to the dovish line connected with the premiership of Moshe Sharett. Upon being asked to form the next Israeli government in August 1955, David Ben-Gurion had demanded that he again become the chief decision maker in Israeli foreign and defence policy. In Ben-Gurion's view, the Defence Ministry should dictate policy, while the Foreign Ministry should simply explain this policy to the great powers and the *ooom-shmoom* (a derogatory expression for the UN, or *Om*, in Hebrew).[78]

The US ambassador in Israel argued consistently that any statement on Alpha should be put off as long as possible, so as to not throw a 'new ingredient' into the 'post-election-government-formation-pot'.[79] With Ben-Gurion back in the Israeli government, as well, Ambassador Lawson warned, Israel's position was likely to 'harden rather than soften'.[80] And in the case of the refugee issue, Lawson was especially clear: 'Resettlement [of] Arab refugees in Israel conflicts head on with Ben-Gurion's passionate Zionism and his policy of unlimited absorption [of] world Jews by Israel.'[81]

Dulles presented Alpha to the world on 26 August 1955, by giving a speech before the Council on Foreign Relations in New York. It was slightly altered regarding the topic of repatriation, to accommodate the suggestions from the regional embassies. Dulles' speech was general rather than detailed, suggestive rather than assertive and appealing rather than committing.[82] Dulles talked about the need to make more land arable in the interests of resettling some of the refugees and offered American support to Israel regarding the means to pay compensation to the refugees who would not be allowed to repatriate. Furthermore, he commented on the need to come to a territorial agreement that in turn would be rewarded with an international security guarantee.[83]

In general, after all the planning and consternation, the big debut of the Alpha Plan was somewhat anticlimactic.[84] This was not only due to Dulles's rather toothless statement, of course. Along the Israel–Egyptian border in the Gaza Strip area, the situation was becoming increasingly volatile.

On the eve of Dulles's speech, the border area saw yet another wave of violence.[85] And on 1 September, just a few days after the speech, Israel attacked an Egyptian police station in Khan Yunis in the Gaza Strip, killing seventy-two Palestinian refugees and Egyptian soldiers and wounding fifty-eight. It was the biggest attack since 28 February 1955.[86] With several incursions and several fatalities, it would be hard to imagine circumstances that were more hostile to the American secretary of state's message of peace and appeal for new negotiations.

It suddenly dawned on Dulles himself that this speech might not in itself be enough to produce any action. What would happen next, he wondered, if the Arabs and the Israelis did not follow his lead?[87] From the British side, one thing was perfectly obvious: having advised against giving the speech in the first place, the British was not about to save their American counterparts. Eden's instructions to the Foreign Office were clear: this was a problem of the Americans' own making, and it was not the job of the British to 'pull their chestnuts out of the fire for them'.[88]

In Cairo, Nasser never really gave a proper response to Dulles's statement. Later, Nasser claimed that he had underestimated the force of the Palestinian refugee question. The refugees' claim of a free right of return or of compensation had to be met, Nasser argued, for the refugees to even consider a settlement. And it did not matter, he continued, whether the Arab states agreed to the deal if the 900,000 refugees opposed it.[89]

From Israel, the reactions to the speech were mixed. Mostly, they focused on Dulles's mention of the need for border adjustments. Predictably, the Israelis also objected to the American insistence that a security guarantee would come about only as a result of an agreement.[90] When it came to the issue of the refugee problem, on the other hand, the Israelis welcomed Dulles's offer of a US loan to finance the refugees' compensation, and Eban further disclosed in a conversation with American diplomats that Israel, 'in due course', would be presenting to the Americans their own plan on the question of compensation.[91] Eban was referring to the work of the Horowitz Committee whose report proposed that Israel should move forward on the compensation question and to finance the scheme by using some of the German war reparations, a very controversial plan in Israel. Israel recognized that, in terms of the question of repatriation versus resettlement, Dulles's speech was a testament to the fact that the Israeli position had gained substantially in credibility since 1948.[92]

While general reactions from Israel and Egypt had been critical and unenthusiastic, there was one group that viewed Dulles's speech in a positive and welcoming manner: the Jewish American community.[93] American Zionists had received it with 'distinct pleasure' and 'a feeling of relief that Israel's problems were now taken care of', in the words of the executive director of the American Zionist Committee for Public Affairs, Isaiah Leo 'Si' Kenen.[94]

But that the American Zionists embraced the administration's policy did not go down well with the Israeli government. Most likely, this was because the Israeli leadership were unhappy that the sought-after Western security guarantee had been publicly linked to the country's cooperation in the diplomatic process. In any case, Abba Eban was dispatched to clarify the Israeli government's position to the American Zionists.[95]

Eban visited the Israel Bonds Conference in Washington, D.C. in September 1955 and 'made it clear' that American Jews had to understand that the 'battle had not yet been won'.[96] That Israel sent Eban to lecture its Jewish American supporters on what they should be thinking on US Middle East policy and how they should react to a speech by their own secretary of state illustrates the importance Israel's leadership attached to this group of people and exemplifies the one-way monologue that characterized the relationship between Israel and its supporters in the United States.

Either way, American Jewish community's initial positive reaction to the speech mirrored its general reception from the US public. According to Russell, it was a speech 'extremely well received', and the *Herald Tribune* thought that it reflected Secretary Dulles 'at his best'.[97] For Dulles, who had been so guided by domestic considerations in his decision to make the speech in the first place, the positive reaction at home must have been as important as the speech's reception in the region. This would explain why the secretary of state, despite the recent violent flare-up on the Gaza–Israel border, and the otherwise lukewarm regional reaction to his speech, still told President Eisenhower a month later that he was 'more than ever convinced that the move [i.e. giving the speech] was a good one'.[98]

Still and all, it was developments in the region that would ultimately bring Alpha to its knees. Any momentum that Dulles had hoped to create for the next phase of the plan was halted by escalating violence and destabilization on the ground. Lamenting the situation, Shuckburgh painted a bleak picture of the region and Alpha's future in a diary entry for 30 August:

> Open fighting on the Gaza border; strikes in Bahrain; rapid internal deterioration in Iran: mutiny in South Sudan; mass outbreaks of murder and pillage in Morocco and the sacking of General Grandval; Soviet activity in Syria. Alpha seems like a beautiful dream.[99]

When Nasser, on 27 September 1955, announced that Egypt had signed an arms deal with Czechoslovakia, it was yet another obstacle for the Alpha Plan.

The Czech arms deal signified the de facto entrance of the Soviet Union into the Middle East, the first definite step down the road towards a regional arms race and towards the region becoming another playing field for the Cold War.[100] Another consequence of that move was that Israel shifted its quest for a Western security guarantee to a quest for US arms.[101] This, too, in in some ways altered the foundation upon which Alpha had been built.

In a brief to the Senate Foreign Relations Committee in late February 1956, Dulles reiterated that he still stood by the statement he had made in August 1955 – that in order for peace to be achieved, three main issues had to be resolved: the problem of the Palestinian refugees, the mutual fear between Israel and the Arab states and the absence of permanent borders in the region.[102] The dispatching of the American diplomat Robert Anderson to the region in January 1956 was a '"last shot" effort' from Dulles's State Department to make progress on these issues.[103]

Bringing with him what Russell later described as a plan of 'considerable detail', Anderson was to get the parties to enter discussions on border adjustments and the resettlement and compensation of the refugees.[104] Like Alpha, the Anderson mission ultimately failed to deliver. A combination of negative factors including bad timing, Israel's rejection of Anderson's mediation and the eventual decline of Anderson's own motivation have all been attributed to the Anderson mission's failure.[105]

Any momentum that Anderson might have had was effectively stopped when yet another wave of violence broke out in the Gaza Strip. Benny Morris has argued that Ben-Gurion and Dayan, as a reaction to the announcement of the Czech arms deal in late September, tried to provoke war with Egypt by striking hard against Egyptian targets. The biggest attack was on the night of 2/3 November, when an Israeli paratroop battalion killed eighty-one Egyptian soldiers and captured fifty-five.[106] Next, on 29 October 1956, Israel invaded Sinai and on 5 November, as prearranged, Britain and France intervened.[107] With the Suez War, the Anglo-American unity from the Alpha days came to a bitter end. As historian Keith Kyle writes, the British attack on Nasser signalled the 'dethronement of Alpha' from its previously prioritized position within the British Foreign Office.[108]

Alpha had not placed any particular emphasis on the refugee problem. While this problem was seen as an important explanation for the continued destabilization of the region, the project was not borne out of a specific desire or perceived need to solve the refugee issue in particular. Any talk about repatriation was window dressing for the Arab audience. Although they had done no research and thus had no data to back it up, the Western powers had by 1955 cultivated the firm belief that the refugees had no real desire to return.[109]

Indeed, one could make the case that one of the major flaws of Project Alpha was that Shuckburgh, Russell and their respective diplomatic teams failed to recognize just how closely connected the refugee issue was with the regional security issue. The lead-up to the Suez Crisis had once again confirmed that the refugee problem was a directly destabilizing factor in the region: *Fedayeen* operations targeted Israel from Lebanon, Jordan and the Gaza Strip.[110] At the US State Department, it was acknowledged that the refugee problem would only cause 'increasing difficulty'.[111] How the United States could and should deal with this difficulty, however, remained a point of continuous discussions among the foreign policy establishment in Washington, D.C.

The United States and the Palestinian refugee issue

Inside US administrations, the thinking about how to approach the refugee issue followed a cyclic pattern: the pendulum swinging back and forth between two alternative analyses.[1] One represented a piecemeal approach, solving the issues one by one, the other a package approach, a sort of grand bargain idea. Initially, after having returned from his first visit to the Middle East in May 1953, Secretary of State John Foster Dulles had favoured that Arab–Israeli peace was pursued directly through the Palestinian refugee problem. This piecemeal approach guided most efforts before 1955 – the Palestine Conciliation Commission's (PCC's) efforts in 1949, the Clapp Mission and Eric Johnston's mission to deal with the development of the Jordan valley in 1953. Then, came the 1955 Anglo-American Alpha Plan, which represented a break with this and gave way to the 'package' approach. This line advocated that the refugee problem should not be singled out but rather be approached as one element in a larger package in a general Arab–Israeli settlement. When Alpha failed and the dust from Suez had settled, US diplomats and policymakers again returned to the piecemeal position, again focusing directly on the refugee problem.

The need to reassess the situation was also prompted by the fact that UNRWA's mandate was about to expire in the summer of 1960. During the previous year's UNGA session, there had been considerable discussion about the future of UNRWA.[2] Should the organization be broken up or renewed? If the former, what would need to be done to take care of the refugees? If the latter, should UNRWA's mandate be simply reiterated or should it be developed further? And if so, who should pay for the renewed operations? Since UNRWA's inception, the United States had been paying about 70 per cent of the organization's costs. Could it afford to continue to pay this much to

UNRWA? On the other hand, could it afford to stop? As the largest donor, the United States obviously had great stakes in this debate and, consequently, in the international community's search to find a solution to the refugee problem.

There was a rising awareness within the State Department of the growing impatience of the US Congress, which allocated the US contribution to UNRWA under the Mutual Security Act of 1954. Specifically, Congress did so under Section 407 of that act, which dealt with the Palestinian refugees. In 1957, however, an amendment to Section 407 had been attached, which dictated that before allocating any more financial support to the Palestinian refugees, the president should take into account whether Israel and the Arab host governments were 'taking steps toward the resettlement and repatriation of such refugees'.[3] In the debate about the department's priorities for the fiscal year 1958, this was again emerging as a serious obstacle. If no steps were taken, the presumption was that Congress might enforce a cessation of US contributions throughout the remainder of UNRWA's mandate.[4]

It was this overall situation that prompted Secretary Dulles to establish a working group in the spring of 1957, tasked with coming up with a policy that would lead to a 'solution' to the refugee problem, 'as soon as possible'.[5] Henry S. Villard led the working group, and the report that it eventually produced became known as the 'Villard study'.[6]

The Villard study

Villard's working group delivered its first report with recommendations addressing the various elements that were seen as key to progress on the refugee question. They had proposals regarding UNRWA's future, repatriation, compensation, the unified development of the Jordan valley, the resettlement of refugees in Iraq, action at the UN and the financial implications this would have for the United States.

The overall assessment was that resettlement of the refugees remained the most feasible approach to the problem. Total repatriation was and would remain 'completely impossible', as the study maintained that no more than 100,000 refugees could in fact be expected to repatriate to Israel. This was a number slightly higher than the 75,000 that the planners of the Alpha Plan had stipulated.[7]

For Henry Villard, the reason for the failure of the previous US and PCC initiatives was, to a large degree, these proposals' failure to provide the refugees with a choice and/or the means to exercise it. This was new thinking in the department, and the Villard study's focus on the need for so-called 'free choice' between repatriation and resettlement set it apart from previous diplomatic initiatives. Still, it is important to note that even Villard's emphasis on free choice rested upon the belief that there was little actual desire among the refugees to pick repatriation. As before, the prevailing logic at the US State Department was that the refugees would not oppose resettlement if they were paid enough.

The working group's report argued that it would be crucial to 'quietly' approach Israel first. Israel should be asked to agree on a repatriation program, 'in the spirit' of Resolution 194, and 'establishing a refugee's right of a choice between repatriation and compensation'. Israel was expected to accept 'in principle' the 'right of all refugees to repatriation', subject to certain qualifications that it would have the right to develop and apply as it saw fit. The Villard study clearly stated that Israel had to have this prerogative, the main purpose of which was to 'discourage' repatriation as an option for many of the refugees.

Still, to make sure that the number of refugees choosing repatriation would be kept to an absolute minimum, Villard and his team suggested setting up what they called an 'indoctrination program'. Developed and realized with the help and support of the Arab states, this indoctrination program's main aim would be to educate the refugees about the incentives favouring compensation (and, implicitly, resettlement) that would have to be part of the program. The repatriation angle, in contrast, while being kept 'fair in spirit', would have to be 'sufficiently unattractive' to most of the refugee population.[8] The Villard group did worry, and rightly so, that the suggested compensation program would be criticized for being 'a bribe not to repatriate'.[9] The question was how to fend off this criticism. The study suggested that the United States would need to point out that for the refugee families, this compensation equalled up to four years of UNRWA rations, and that one hundred US dollars per refugee would be well above what most of their individual claims would amount to.

Alongside the repatriation program, it was recommended by Villard and his team that Israel should be asked to make a public statement stating its policy on repatriation. It was suggested that Israeli concessions should be attached more directly to US aid. Israel was still in difficult economic circumstances and was already seeking this money from the Americans, a request that had already been turned down once.[10] Villard and his group saw a great potential leverage in this. The last time Israeli finance minister Levi Eshkol had asked the United States to increase its aid to Israel, Dulles had told him that Israel should rather contemplate applying for a loan from the US Export–Import Bank.[11] No such loan had yet been granted, and the Villard study's recommendation was for the United States to refrain from making any new financial commitments to Israel before the issue of the refugee problem had been taken up again.[12]

Upon being presented with the working group's recommendations, Dulles expressed scepticism regarding the chances of getting Congress on board for anything less than a full-fledged peace accord. Specifically, he questioned the feasibility of asking Congress to pay for the implementation of resettlement and the compensation loan to Israel, if it did not receive a permanent solution to the conflict in return.[13] Nonetheless, Dulles gave the working group his reluctant blessing to continue its work.[14] Before any further steps were taken, though, the region was once again overtaken by events that threatened to cause regional upheaval and, as a consequence of that, caused division within the ranks of the Villard working group.

Regional turmoil and internal US division

In mid-August 1957, a diplomatic crisis erupted between the United States and Syria. In response to Syria's expulsion of two US diplomats and the military attaché, the Americans declared the Syrian ambassador to the United States and the second secretary at the embassy persona non grata.[15] The diplomatic fallout marked the beginning of a longer period of regional upheaval, and as a consequence, disagreement spread within the group of US State Department officials that had been engaged in the Villard study. The diplomats no longer agreed on the next move, and somewhat ironically, Special Assistant Villard himself became the loudest voice of opposition to the steps that had been recommended in the study carrying his name.

Writing to Dulles in September, Villard made the case that the Syrian situation had changed the atmosphere in the region so much that the moment was no longer ripe for an American initiative to solve the refugee problem.[16]

Villard had conferred with the UN secretary general Dag Hammarskjöld on the matter, and it turned out that the two were in complete agreement.[17] As things progressed, it became clear that their objections to the idea of pursuing an American initiative to resolve the refugee problem were not only about the ripeness of the regional situation but also about an altogether different take on how the refugee issue was best solved. Both Hammarskjöld and Villard came to promote a position that questioned whether the matter should at all be approached through political negotiations between Arabs and Israelis.[18] The better alternative, Villard's new position held, was to approach the refugee problem via the 'back door' instead.[19]

This 'back door' approach, in brief, meant solving the problem by giving the refugees economic opportunities and resettling them in the Arab states in so-called 'areas of employment'.[20] Economic development was not just Hammarskjöld's recipe in the Arab–Israeli context, as secretary general he had always maintained the view that to promote such schemes was the UN's 'most important role'.[21] He noted that the refugee demography was changing as the proportion of young refugees increased. If these people could be given job opportunities, their desire to return to their families' place of origin would quickly diminish. Villard supported this line of thought; he remarked that the young refugees had, in contrast to their parents and grandparents, 'few personal ties to Palestine' coupled with growing concern for their financial futures.[22] While economic despair certainly was part of the Palestinian plight, the economic approach failed to take into account that for most of the refugees the struggle was about something bigger than financial security.

Villard's new line of thinking was contested within the department and within the original Villard working group. Francis O. Wilcox, who, in his capacity as the assistant secretary of state for international organization affairs (IO) had been a member of the group who wrote the initial study, quickly wrote Dulles to oppose the new recommendations from Villard.[23]

First, Wilcox did not agree with Villard that the timing was bad. Second, and more importantly, Wilcox objected to the assumption that the refugee problem could not be separated from the overall conflict. He argued instead that the refugee issue was 'almost totally political'.[24] While he acknowledged that a solution to the issue was inextricably linked to an overall solution to the conflict at large, he did not think that this meant that the refugee issue could not be solved in isolation. Rather, he argued that progress on the refugee issue could pave the way for agreement in other areas of the conflict. Last, Wilcox thought that Villard painted an inappropriately negative picture of Israel's willingness to budge on the issue. Villard had stated that there was nothing that indicated that Israel would be willing to accept the repatriation principle. Wilcox thought that talks with the Israelis suggested that they actually had 'considerably more flexibility' on the matter.

He furthermore warned against the idea that the refugee issue would 'in time solve itself' and insisted that the current approach, channelling millions of US dollars through various UNRWA projects, was the 'most wasteful method' for dealing with the problem. The congressional reticence that this approach was likely to face, Wilcox wrote to Dulles, was 'much more serious' than what had been indicated by Villard. Wilcox had come to the US State Department after having worked as chief of staff of the US Senate's Foreign Relations Committee and therefore had an insider's knowledge of the issue of UNRWA funding and the process surrounding it. Wilcox told Dulles that when the time came to ask the Congress for more support to UNRWA, critical questions would be posed, and good answers would have to be given. And these answers, Wilcox warned, would have to 'contain the prospect of real progress – not just infinite continuance of the status quo'.

Wilcox, in other words, remained unconvinced by the 'back door' logic put forth by men like Hammarskjöld and Villard. He acknowledged that an 'indirect approach' could have some merit, but he did not think that it could ever provide a real answer to the problem. If one accepted that the problem at its root was political, then its solution also had to be found in political negotiations, Wilcox argued.[25] His recommendation, simply put, was to approach the refugee problem head on – through the front door.

While there had been little evidence to suggest that the United States held any great political power over Israel in the period since the establishment of the state, its *economic* power over its Middle Eastern ally was substantial. If the political willingness were there, power could be wielded to influence or manipulate a situation – and present a further opportunity for conflict resolution. And in the autumn of 1957, Dulles decided to put this to the test. The United States had tried to use economic pressure, unsuccessfully and somewhat half-heartedly under President Truman in 1949. At the time, it had resulted in little other than embarrassment for the US State Department. Under pressure from Israel's 'friends', Truman had intervened against the advice of the US State Department and the PCC chairman Mark Etheridge and signed off on the loan application from the Export–Import Bank. But President Eisenhower was not Truman – indeed, his administration took pride in being different from Truman's and framed Eisenhower as freer from those domestic constraints that had influenced Truman's decision-making on US Middle East policy. But did this mean that Dulles and Eisenhower would be able to use this economic leverage more efficiently than their predecessors?

The United States' limited influence

Israel was, for several reasons, a state in financially dire straits. In June 1957, Finance Minister Levi Eshkol described the Israeli economy as being only 'halfway along the road to self-sufficiency'.[26] Since its establishment, Israel had received hundreds of thousands of Jewish immigrants, and integration and caretaking of these into the state was a challenge both socially and financially. To support its economy and boost its capacity to receive a growing number of Jewish immigrants, Israel therefore, in March 1956, applied for a loan of 75 million US dollars, from the US Export–Import Bank to pay for water development projects in the Jordan Valley.[27] Among the Jordan Valley water irrigation schemes Israel intended to finance with the loan was the so-called Benot Yaaqov project, which sought to divert water from the Jordan River to the Negev desert.[28]

For several reasons, chief among them the Suez Crisis, a US decision on this application had been postponed.[29] The original loan request had been for 75 million US dollars. In 1957, it was scaled down to a loan request for 48 million US dollars from the Export–Import Bank.[30] This new application represented Dulles's opportunity.

Secretary Dulles suggested that the granting of this loan should be tied to their compliance on matters that the Americans were pursuing.[31] Dulles thought that if Israel were to be granted this loan, they should then be pressed to use the money to increase their capacity to accept Palestinian refugees back as well and not just the resettling of Jews immigrating to the country. He wanted to communicate to the Israelis that they could not expect to get more American aid for the purpose of settling more immigrants without some acknowledgement of the continued existence of the refugee problem.[32] The excessive immigration had been the topic of several bilateral consultations between Israel and the United States, and the Americans had also discussed it with their relevant counterparts at the British Foreign Office.[33]

In July 1957, the Export–Import Bank visited Israel on an investigative mission.[34] After that visit, the bank had told Israel that it viewed their projects in a favourable light. This was not a formal approval, however, and after further internal deliberations, the bank found that it was not comfortable signing off on the loan. The stated cause for this was that the bank did not want to place a disproportionate amount of its money in one country. As is customary in such cases of doubt, the bank therefore turned to the US State Department: in a conversation with Dulles, bank president and chairman of the board of the bank Samuel C. Waugh stated that the bank would only consider granting the loan if the department insisted on the grounds of 'overriding political factors'.[35] This reluctance from the bank, although technical in nature, provided the department with the opportunity that Secretary Dulles had been looking for.[36] The department therefore told the bank that there was no pressing (political) reason why the bank should go the extra mile for the Israelis in this case. In fact, the department told the bank that it would be better if the Israelis were told that the final decision on the loan request was being further deferred.[37]

But more than that, the US State Department asked Waugh to be very specific in his communication with the Israelis. Waugh was to tell Israel that the deferral was first and foremost prompted by worries of the United States regarding Israel's immigration policies and the Palestinian refugee problem.[38] Much of the immigration to Israel came from Eastern European countries, and the American administration had some concern regarding what this meant in terms of Israel's potential to develop more Communist leanings.

So, on 6 January 1958, Waugh had the thankless task of telling Israel's ambassador Abba Eban that the bank for the moment had decided against the granting of the loan. He told Eban that the decision was political and that it was the US State Department that held the final authority in the matter, though he also emphasized that the decision itself was *not* final.[39] Eban's reacted to this with both disappointment and anger. He immediately called a meeting with the US State Department exclusively dedicated to this particular issue, in which he lectured the American officials on the history of the situation, stretching back to the spring of 1956.[40] For Eban, it was not only about politics and economics but also a personal blow. Eban had promised the Israeli government that he could deliver the Export–Import Bank money. If he were forced to return to the Knesset, amid its annual budget discussions, to tell his colleagues that the deal was off, his personal credibility would be 'irrevocably shaken'.[41] He asked Herter and Dulles to consider the matter in this light also.[42]

Herter tried to reassure Eban that the decision was not yet final. In diplomatic turns, he told Eban that he did not think it accurate to derive from this the conclusion that the department was 'opposed' to an Export–Import Bank loan to Israel.[43] Instead, Herter told Eban, this was in reality a delay prompted by a few regional matters that were of 'great concern' to the United States.[44] He reminded Eban that these had been the topic of previous bilateral consultations as well.[45] One was the regional impact of the large-scale Jewish immigration to Israel; the other was the Palestinian refugee problem. The United States was simply wondering, Herter told Eban, what Israel could do to contribute to a solution to the refugee problem. The projects Israel wanted to finance with the loan were related to large-scale water irrigation, apparently, to make more arable land in Israel – or, as Herter put it, to 'broaden the base for a larger population'.[46] Might there be any connection between these projects and a solution to the refugee problem? Herter then moved on to spelling it out: Would the planned projects mainly cater to Jewish immigrants, or would they also enable Israel to contribute to the solution of the refugee problem?

Eban repeated to Herter what he had told Waugh the week before: he strongly resented the fact that the United States was attaching 'political conditions' to its financial aid. The aid given to Israel from the Soviet Union, Eban continued, never came with strings attached. Eban told Herter that Israel had also discussed the current situation regarding the Israeli loan request with its allies in Africa and Asia, and they were all in agreement on this point. If it now turned out that the United States were indeed determined to attach political conditions to this particular aid request, Eban warned Herter of the 'adverse psychological repercussions' that would follow.

In the Cold War game, this was the smaller state's trump card, and Eban knew how to play it. He also knew that the Americans were concerned about Israel's immigration policies not only because the Arab states claimed that the consequences would involve further Israeli expansionism but also because many of the Jewish immigrants to Israel were coming from Eastern Europe and, down the line, possibly from the Soviet Union itself.[47] This scenario sounded the alarm in Washington, D.C., where the spread of communism in the Middle East was as frightful as anything else. In addition, the United States cited the fragile Israeli economy as one reason for the bank's reluctance to grant the loan, but by granting the loan, Eban argued, the United States would be directly contributing to the health of that economy. So, was it not in the Americans direct interest to do so and thus create a situation in which Israel would not be so dependent on outside aid?[48]

Having made his principal objections, Eban moved on to the concrete issues brought up by Herter. Eban could not see how they were at all relevant to the application. The projects would mainly focus on strengthening existing agriculture and thus only serve to benefit people already living in Israel (that the projects aimed to establish 10,000 new homesteads for immigrants was dismissed by Eban as 'less important').[49] Regarding the Americans' interest in the issue of the Palestinian refugees, Eban's message remained the same: Israel would not solve this problem by itself, but it would contribute to the only viable solution that there ever could be – namely the economic development of the area. Israel could not do this unilaterally, nor could it begin to do it in isolation. Eban then added that he had discussed the question of economic development matter with Hammarskjöld the day before, and that the secretary general had agreed with this analysis. Israel would await the development of a general agreed-upon solution to the refugee problem and make its particular contribution to it only at that point.[50]

Nevertheless, Herter still wanted Eban to provide the US State Department with formal explanations concerning these two matters. He also told Eban that he hoped the ensuing memorandum would be able to confirm that the development projects to be financed by the loan would 'assist in Israel's capacity to make a contribution to the refugee problem'.[51]

Eban and Herter met again a fortnight later, at the end of January. And according to the American records, Herter's tone was completely different after this meeting. He told Dulles that Eban had been more forthcoming on the refugee issue than ever before and had even made 'the flat statement … that the granting of this loan would assist Israel's capacity to help out in the refugee problem', in accordance to the department's request.[52] Herter even reported to a colleague that Eban had told him that Israel would take back 'thousands' of refugees and be willing to pay generous compensation to the ones who were not repatriating.[53]

Herter could therefore only recommend that Dulles tell the US Export–Import Bank that the State Department had reversed its position and was now in favour of granting Israel a loan for 24 million US dollars (half of what Israel sought) for these two water projects.[54] Knowing the Israeli position on the refugee issue and the attitude taken by Eban in the 14 January meeting, however, it seems rather fantastic that he would make such concessions just two weeks later. That he could do so with the blessing of the Israeli government seems even more unlikely. The Israeli records shed a different light on this episode, offering some alternative explanations.

First, the Israeli records do not suggest that Eban was mandated to give any such concession. Yes, Eban had recommended to Meir that the formal memorandum requested by Herter should incorporate a sentence stating, 'Israel's capacity to help solve the refugee problem would be enhanced if the loan strengthened its economy.'[55] Eban, true to character, sought to balance between enough ambiguity to avoid committing Israel to anything it did not like and enough of Herter's language to satisfy the Americans. Even so, it was too much for Golda Meir, an Israeli hardliner who loathed compromising on what she saw as an Israeli security issue. For Meir, 'the Arabs' were something to fear – 'the adversary, the foe, the architect of our [Israel's] destruction'.[56] She rejected Eban's arrangement, instructing him that while he was authorized to reiterate Israel's stated position on the refugee problem in oral exchanges with the Americans, nothing was to go on the record as linking the refugee issue in any way to the loan.[57]

The main reason why Herter accepted the Israeli statement as enough was therefore not to find in a changed Israeli position. Rather, the Israeli records suggest that it was Herter who ended up changing his position.

According to Eban's account of the meeting between Herter and himself on 14 January, there was still firm opposition to the granting of the loan from the State Department and the president of the bank. Herter, on the other hand, had according to Eban reconsidered the matter and was 'looking for a practical way out' of the situation.[58] Eban attributed this sudden shift in Herter's position to the 'pressure' applied to the undersecretary by 'Israel's friends'.[59] In this internal report to Golda Meir, Eban does not offer any more details about who these 'friends' were or how they worked with Herter. As earlier, 'friends' is used as a catchall term only discreetly implying that Israel had channels of influence to the White House and the general political environment in Washington, D.C.

At this particular moment, pro-Israel gestures seem to have come from the very highest level of the US government, as Eisenhower's name is included as 'among those who exerted pressure'. Eban wrote this in a report to the Israeli Ministry of Foreign Affairs. Though it can't be confirmed by other sources, it seems unlikely that a seasoned diplomat like Abba Eban would fabricate such a story. From the previous episode with the US Export–Import Bank in 1949, we also know that Truman played a similar role in ushering through the loan. Although Truman was a president who was much more openly supportive of Israel, this nevertheless indicates that intervention from the top in matters such as this had a historic precedence.[60] While it is no proof of 'pressure', it is worth nothing that Herter also had met with the two US congressmen, Kenneth B. Keating (38th District New York) and Hugh Scott (6th District Pennsylvania), who came to him to 'inquire' regarding the administration's decision to postpone the loan. The memorandum of this conversation clearly states that the congressmen's inquiry was at least partly prompted by Isaiah 'Si' Kenen of the American Zionist Committee for Public Affairs, who had been contacted by Eban.[61] Herter's own moves in Washington also seem to confirm that Eban was right to understand him as a man looking for a way out.

After the initial conversation with the very disappointed Eban, Herter had turned to Waugh at the Export–Import Bank. He asked Waugh whether the bank would be able to break down the Israeli loan request into separate parts.[62] Waugh had gone back to study the matter and concluded that it would indeed be possible to view the application as relevant to two distinct initiatives, one of which was directly connected to two water development projects in the north of Israel and in Tel Aviv, respectively.[63] The total cost of the stipulated projects amounted to about 24 million US dollars.[64] Waugh added to this that he saw great potential in these projects, both in terms of a general decrease in the need for foreign imports to Israel in the future and in terms of the positive growth in the country's agricultural sector, which again would help increase Israel's holding of foreign exchange. In other words, Waugh signalled that the bank was supportive of granting Israel a limited loan of this size, unless the State Department still desired otherwise.[65]

Before arguing his newfound position to Secretary Dulles, Herter had also taken it upon himself to locate previous loan applications regarding other water projects that were comparable to these two. This record showed that traditionally, if the bank had no economic or technical reason to reject them, the US State Department had a history of backing such projects.[66] Noteworthy, these were all steps that Herter and the US State Department could have done from the beginning, if their initial inclination had been to find justifications for the bank's granting of the loan. The point remained, however, that the whole idea of not granting the loan was that Dulles had been looking for opportunities to increase the US leverage with the Israelis. The fact that Herter repositioned himself with such great speed on the matter has to be understood as related to the pressure that Eban referred to in the internal Israeli communication with Meir.

Finally, Eban had made a genuine effort to address the American worry on the issue of Jewish immigration from Communist countries. He had stated not only that the stipulated immigration numbers were drastically reduced from the previous year but also that there was no indication that any of the immigrants would be coming from the Soviet Union.[67] On this point, then, Eban's remarks were probably genuinely reassuring to Herter. Despite this breakthrough, though, and despite the fact that the granted loan constituted of only about half the original sum applied for by Israel, the fact remains that the Americans allowed Israel to once more dodge the main issue – that is, the effort to tie the loan to progress on the Palestinian refugee issue.

In the end, then, the US Export–Import Bank episode of 1957–8 therefore bore some resemblance to the first time American diplomats tried to use Israel's need for financial aid as a means of obtaining Israeli concessions on the refugee issue. In 1958, as in 1949, getting the Israelis to budge on the refugees was the main motivation for the American tactical considerations use of the loan application as leverage. And in both episodes the idea fell to pieces before it could be tested in any significant way. In 1949, the man behind the strategy, George McGhee, found himself backed against the wall without the support of the White House within hours of informing the Israelis that the Americans wanted something in return for the granting of the loan. And, in 1958, Undersecretary Herter ended up in much the same position. Common to both episodes was also the fact that they were more a matter of immediate tactics than the result of a longer-term strategy towards the region and the conflict. When things got complicated, there was no willingness at the State Department or at the White House to withstand the pressure from Israel and its supporters – or 'friends' – in the United States. The US influence over its small power ally in the Middle East was very limited. In this respect, the episode also represents another illustration of an effort to utilize economic power as leverage in international bargaining, but their domestic political considerations ended up trumping strategic foreign policy calculations. The inability of the United States to apply efficient pressure towards Israel, even in cases where it clearly had substantial leverage, must also be seen as a consequence of the domination of short-term tactics over longer-term strategy in US Middle East policy.

Regional shake-up and the revival of the PCC

Despite these two episodes' striking similarities, a few substantial contextual differences are worth noting as well. Notably, Herter's decision to suddenly grant the loan in early 1958 must be considered in light of the major regional developments that same year. Supported by the Soviet Union and under the banner of Arab nationalism, Nasser was touring the region, campaigning for the overthrow of pro-Western regimes in the Middle East. Nasser's behaviour, coupled with an increasingly Soviet-dominated stronghold in Syria, created a new situation in which Israeli and American interests converged more than ever before. Israel was not the only state that worried about Nasser and his regional ambitions, and it understood that it had to manoeuvre skilfully to make the most out of this changed environment. The result was the emergence of a so-called 'alliance of the periphery'.[68]

Those non-Arab states on the edges of the Middle East – Turkey and Iran to the north and Ethiopia to the south – became Israel's strategic partners under the guiding principle that 'my enemy's enemy is my friend'.[69] Throughout the spring of 1958 and beyond, this development would only be further hastened in an atmosphere of increasing volatility in the Middle East.

When Syria and Egypt proclaimed the union of their two states as the new United Arab Republic (UAR) in February 1958, it only served to reinforce to Washington that the Cold War was stepping up a notch in the Middle East.[70] Soon afterwards, civil war erupted in Lebanon and on 22 May 1958, Lebanon brought a complaint against the UAR to the UN Security Council.[71] And then, in June, pro-Soviet officers in the Iraqi army, led by General Abdul Karim Kassem, revolted against the pro-Western government of Nuri al-Said, taking power and killing King Faisal and al-Said at the same time.[72] Next in line was the pro-Western Lebanese government of Maronite Christian president Camille Chamou, who had won election with direct financial aid from the CIA against the opposition known as the National Front in the summer of 1957. His victory unleashed months of bombings and political assassinations the following winter, and by May 1958, Lebanon was a country in all-out civil war. This prompted the United States to activate the Eisenhower doctrine and send 15,000 US Marines to Beirut in support of Chamoun in July 1958.[73] All in all, the tumultuous events of the spring and summer of 1958 guaranteed that when it came to the Middle East, Israel was in the end the least of the Western powers' worries. Taking a strong position against a development loan request in this atmosphere probably seemed like the wrong place to spend any political capital. So, the problem endured, no closer to a breakthrough than at the start of Villard's initial study group. It was back to the drawing table at the State Department.

One of the main motivations in the early stages of the Villard study and the State Department's effort to create progress on the refugee issue had been the US Congress' demands for positive development on the issue, as expressed through the amended Mutual Security Act. In 1957, Dulles had to tell Congress that it would still be in the best interests of the United States to continue its financial assistance to UNRWA, despite the lack of progress on the refugee problem.[74] Congress approved this assistance for the fiscal year 1958, but with the problem no closer to resolution, its members were still left largely unsatisfied. If the State Department wanted to secure Congress's further financial support, it would need to provide proof that reasonable steps were being taken to address the refugee problem.

Against this background, the natural place to start for the American diplomats was trying to look for opportunities to phase out UNRWA or to get rid of the whole structure. To Hammarskjöld at the UN, Herter made it clear that he believed that UNRWA, in its present condition, no longer constituted the 'proper way' to handle the refugee problem.[75] The State Department thought that to continue UNRWA in its current form would send a message to Israel and the Arab states that they did not have to solve the refugee problem, and that the United States was willing to continue to pay for the status quo.[76]

Hammarskjöld's perspective, as the head of the United Nations, was of course different from that of the Americans. While he well understood that the Americans would like to pay less for the welfare of the Palestinian refugees, he also understood that this would amount to a disastrous situation for UNRWA and thus for the UN in general. Diminished support to the refugees could potentially lead to a further destabilization of the region, a problem that again would have direct impact on the UN. Under Hammarskjöld, as well, the UN was facing huge financial challenges: the United Nations Emergency Force (UNEF), the peacekeeping force established and stationed in Sinai after the Suez Crisis in 1956, threatened on its own to wreck the whole UN budget. This pressure made Hammarskjöld especially inclined to worry about the consequences of phasing out UNRWA.[77]

Hammarskjöld presented a report about the future of UNRWA to the UN member states on 13 June 1959.[78] The Americans disliked the report, since it to them did not go far enough. The Arab states disliked it because it suggested that most of the refugee problem would have to be solved via resettlement.[79] The Arab states were united in their condemnation of the UN's thinking but remained as uncoordinated as ever in terms of their overall Palestine policy. The Arab heads of states failed to produce a larger strategy, let alone agreement, on how the refugee issue would be best approached at the General Assembly debate. Although the Arab states were thought of and referred to as a bloc in the UN, the fact remained that the Arab world was torn by its internal rivalries.[80]

The Israelis, in contrast, could be more content with Hammarskjöld's recommendations. They found the report well in line with Israel's position.[81] 'Apart from a quite moderately phrased reference to the 1948 resolution [Resolution 194], there is practically no mention of repatriation as a solution for the future', Israeli diplomats noted. They could also find reason to applaud in the fact that there was only marginal mention of Israel's conditional agreement regarding the payment of compensation and overall a general 'retreat from the principle of the freedom of choice'.

The 1959 Hammarskjöld report had not produced any suggestions as to what might succeed UNWRA but instead recommended an open-ended continuation of the agency. It therefore had not managed to move the refugee discussion any further along – in fact, it was back to where it started in 1957, before both the Villard study and Hammarskjöld's proposals. And with a mere six months to go before UNWRA's mandate expired, it could not be overlooked that even if progress on the political process seemed impossible, the future care for the refugees had to be guaranteed. But the US delegation remained wary of simply embracing a position that called for the indefinite perpetuation of UNRWA. This would be a risky arrangement to bring back to the US Congress, which remained critical of US spending for UNRWA efforts. The United States paid 70 per cent of UNRWA's annual budget, and Congress was worried that relief to the Palestinian refugees had become a 'treadmill-type operation'.[82] While criticism about excessive foreign-aid spending did not exclusively target aid to this region, the fact was that, among all of the international organizations for which Congress appropriated funds, UNRWA was the only one that encountered 'real trouble'. In the late 1950s, members of Congress realized that they had untapped potential to influence US policy on international questions through, among other things, their 'appropriations power'. Its actions in the case of UNRWA would be one example of how this materialized in practice.[83] According to Senator Albert Gore, he and many others were facing mounting criticism from their constituencies because of the stream of money Congress continued to send without obtaining any kind of progress regarding a solution to the Palestinian refugee issue.[84]

The department therefore concluded that it still needed to show Congress 'tangible evidence' of some progress on the refugee question.[85] So, by the autumn of 1959, the department resumed looking for alternative ways to revive a process aimed at the resolution of the refugee issue. It was in this context that the American UN delegation in November argued that the time had come to shake the dust off the dormant PCC.

The PCC that was about to be revived was not the same as the one established more than a decade earlier. After its early years of negotiation efforts, the PCC had gradually lost belief in the wisdom and realism of aiming for a full-fledged Arab–Israeli peace agreement.[86] Pablo de Azcárate, who was the commission's first secretary, had already in 1950 expressed that in his opinion the refugee issue was destined for a 'natural death'. It would be up to the Israelis to find the 'proper channels in which to direct this decline'.[87] And while the PCC's original mandate had been to actively facilitate a solution for the refugees – be it repatriation, resettlement and/or compensation – De Azcárate seemed to have believed, or at least hoped, that the whole question would simply wither away in time. He expected that the discussion about compensation would drag on for 'years and years', during which time the refugee problem would find its 'natural solution'.[88]

De Azcárate's comment reflected the commission's downcast perspective on its own potential. The lost faith in its ability to solve the problem of the Palestinian refugees was behind the commission's altered tactics from the early 1950s. It shifted its focus to more tangible, 'technical' efforts regarding the refugees' property, like the negotiations to release the Palestinian refugees' frozen assets in banks on Israeli-held territory.[89]

So, when the PCC in December 1959 was requested 'to make further efforts to secure implementation of paragraph 11 of resolution 194 (III) of 1948', it was in other words a commission much different in outlook and in composition from the one originally established by that resolution. As would soon become evident, the 1959 revival of the PCC was not a revival of the international and multilateral track that had been the commission's original set-up. Though it would keep a façade as a UN effort, the revived PCC was merely a vessel for the next American-orchestrated attempt to solve the refugee problem, the so-called Johnson plan.

The Johnson mission:
A real college try?

With the election of John F. Kennedy for president, optimism on behalf of what the United States could do, both at home and abroad, soared. His campaign slogan sold him as the candidate for change and big new ideas. He was also a foreign policy-oriented president. Kennedy was confident that he and his new frontiersmen had a better and sounder understating of both the Middle East and the current times than the previous administration. Would the new frontiersmen's promise of 'a time for greatness' ring true also for the US Middle East policy?[1]

Kennedy thought that Eisenhower's policy had left the United States isolated in its approach to the Middle East.[2] Kennedy's general approach to the Middle East was that he would offer US support and friendship to both Israel and the Arab world and thus repair the damages done by the Eisenhower administration. As a young senator, Kennedy allegedly had a 'strong conviction' that something had to be done for the 'impoverished and tragic existence' of the Palestinian refugees. To keep them lingering in makeshift camps along Israel's borders meant 'constant sources of national antagonism, economic chaos and communist exploitation of human misery'.[3] Later, as a (still young) senator campaigning for the presidency, Kennedy held one of his 'major' foreign policy speeches in front of the Zionists of America convention.[4] Here he pledged that upon his election, the United States (and the world) would fain a president who would use America's influence in the world to move the parties towards a peace settlement. 'All the authority and prestige' of the White House should be used 'to call into conference the leaders of Israel and the Arab states', Kennedy stated. As president, Kennedy promised, he would bring to the Oval Office a sense of leadership that was 'impartial but firm, deliberate but bold'. Aside from these statements, however, there were few direct signals regarding where Kennedy would take the US policy towards the Arab–Israeli conflict.[5]

A time for greatness?

The US State Department had used the last UN General Assembly of the 1950s to revive the Palestine Conciliation Commission (PCC). As expected, the PCC was unable to alter the situation. But with Kennedy in the Oval Office, the leading officers at the State Department's Middle East desk got renewed hope for an American-led effort to resolve the refugee problem. At the end of April 1961, Assistant Secretary of State George Ball approached President Kennedy with a memorandum reminding him of the campaign pledge he had made to the Zionist Convention of America the previous autumn.[6]

More specifically, Ball suggested that the time had come for the United States to make a 'serious attempt' to solve the refugee problem.[7] At the State Department, the career diplomats were back to favouring a 'piecemeal' approach to the Arab–Israeli conflict. Ball told Kennedy that the State Department feared that if the revival of the PCC failed, and no progress were to be obtained from this process, it could have potentially destructive repercussions throughout the region. He urged the president to push for a new initiative.[8] Concretely, the State Department advocated electing a special representative who would be sent to the region on a 'reconnaissance mission'.[9] Although the Americans themselves would handpick this special representative, Ball recommended that the mission be best kept under UN auspices.[10]

At no point was the principal dimension of the Palestinian refugee problem discussed or cited as a motivating factor for a new US effort. This was not an effort to try to make things right or to address deeply rooted political problems or grievances. It was, as Acting Secretary of State Chester Bowles admitted, an effort prompted by the 'tactical and rather negative factors' of avoiding a diplomatic showdown at the UN and encouraging Congress to continue to approve sufficient appropriations to the refugees. Still, the department declared that it was sincerely interested in doing something to make progress on the Arab–Israeli conflict – as Bowles put it, to give it 'a real college try'.[11]

Kennedy's first four months in the White House had given the young president a few harsh lessons in political realities. World events rarely conform to the pledges of US presidential candidates, and Kennedy's presidency was no exception, starting as it had with the disastrous events of the Cuban Bay of Pigs. And when it came to Middle East politics, the promised impartiality was also proving difficult to translate into actual policy. Indeed, after the most recent diplomatic battle at the United Nations General Assembly in the spring of 1961, the department's report was that the administration was viewed by the Arab states as more pro-Israeli than ever. This would be problematic enough in terms of the US Middle East policy specifically, but it had wider foreign policy implications as well: because of the Americans' behaviour at the UN, the Arabs had penalized Washington by voting against the US wishes on matters such as Cuba.[12]

If the US State Department's proposed new surge regarding the refugee problem were to have any chance of success, the administration needed to reach out to Arab leaders soon and preferably in advance of an upcoming (unofficial) visit to the United States from the Israeli prime minister David Ben-Gurion in May 1961. Ball was nervous that Ben-Gurion's visit would be inaccurately associated with the forthcoming US initiative on the refugee problem. If the Arab world were to conclude that the initiative had arisen directly from the meeting between Kennedy and Ben-Gurion, it would be doomed. So, to pre-empt this, it was decided that Kennedy would write a series of letters to the Arab leaders first.[13]

In these letters, Kennedy expressed the new administration's desire to help find a solution for the Arab–Israeli conflict. In particular, Kennedy stated that he wanted to help 'resolve the tragic Palestine refugee problem', on the basis of 'the principle of repatriation or compensation for properties', to assist in finding a solution to the development of the Jordan River and to look at 'other aspects' of the conflict as well.[14] Kennedy furthermore stated 'unequivocally' that his administration's position was 'anchored' in 'the firm bedrock of support for General Assembly recommendations concerning the refugees'.[15] This was, first and foremost, a reference to Resolution 194 and, more specifically, its paragraph 11.

The most noteworthy aspect of these letters is not what Kennedy wrote but what he left out. The term *resettlement* was not used once. This was unprecedented. While there could be little doubt that resettlement would be part of the solution – indeed, the concept of compensation implicitly referred to resettlement, as the two were intrinsically linked – this was the first time that the term was left out of a US president's correspondence. As the State Department's analysis put it, the letters positioned the United States '*far* more emphatically on the side of repatriation or compensation than ever before'.[16] Could this be taken as a sign that Kennedy's White House was pointing its Palestine policy in a new direction? Or was it first and foremost a result of the US State Department's eagerness and, perhaps impatience, to secure some long-lost Arab goodwill? It is difficult to determine whether sloppiness or deliberate vagueness best explains the exact formulation of the letters, but as things developed, it would at least become plain that Kennedy was not an unforeseen champion of Palestinian repatriation.

Initially, both President Kennedy and Secretary of State Dean Rusk had been reluctant to meet with Israeli prime minister Ben-Gurion so early into the presidency. Mostly, their concern centred on the negative effect this could have in the Arab world.[17] But for Kennedy there were also other considerations, rooted in national politics, that might help to explain why Kennedy, against Rusk's advice and his own initial trepidation, went ahead with the Ben-Gurion meeting at the Waldorf Astoria Hotel in New York City. At the US State Department, several people remained convinced that it was a bad idea for Kennedy to meet Ben-Gurion at this time. Feldman dismissed their objections on the grounds that the president had already agreed and the Israelis informed, so backing out was impossible.[18]

Kennedy had won the presidential election with a very slight margin over then vice president Richard Nixon. Kennedy owed this win to, among other things, the Jewish American community, which had come out in overwhelming numbers for the young senator. Kennedy won an unprecedented 83 per cent of the Jewish vote.[19] Yet this is not enough to explain his willingness to meet with Ben-Gurion: to properly understand Kennedy's politics on the Arab–Israeli conflict in general, one must also account for the role played by Myer (Mike) Feldman and Abraham (Abe) Feinberg. It was these two men who convinced Kennedy to go through with the Ben-Gurion meeting in the end. Feldman was Kennedy's deputy special assistant/counsel and the 'de facto ambassador' to American Jewry.[20] Although his position originated in the domestic policy sphere, he would become highly engaged in foreign policy matters.

Feinberg had been the main man behind financing President Harry Truman's famous whistle-stop tour in the presidential campaign of 1948. He had also played an important role as a top-tier fundraiser for the Kennedy campaign in 1960 and was Kennedy's other confidante on all issues Jewish and/ or Israeli. Feinberg was a staunch supporter of Israel and founder and president of Americans for the *Haganah* (the pre-state Israeli Defence Forces), as well as chairman of the Bonds for Israel Conference. Unlike Feldman, Feinberg did not hold an official position in the Kennedy administration, but he acted, on several occasions, as an unofficial diplomat between the administration and the Israeli government.[21]

In April 1961, Feinberg had recently returned from a trip to Israel. With him, he carried an unofficial message from Israeli leaders saying that it was 'extremely urgent' that they meet with President Kennedy. Knowing that Rusk and Kennedy were worried about the potential backlash in the region, Feldman (who promptly became involved) and Feinberg proposed that the latter would invite Ben-Gurion to New York at the end of May, when the president also 'happened to be there' (on personal matters) and in this way give the two leaders an opportunity to meet 'quietly', without any official acknowledgement of the event.[22] Kennedy accepted this proposal.

The main issues for the two leaders' discussion included regional disarmament; the US sale of arms to Israel (specifically, Hawk missiles); Israel's atomic energy activities at the new reactor in Dimona; the sharing and development of the Jordan River; the (Syrian-Egyptian) United Arab Republic's role in the region; and, finally, the Palestinian refugee problem.[23] In his briefing to Kennedy before the meeting, Rusk emphasized the great American desire for progress on the refugee issue that was seen as the 'central issue at the moment'.[24] What the United States wanted and needed from Israel was a gesture regarding repatriation.[25] The American decision to single out the refugee issue came out of a belief that an overall settlement seemed unlikely. Progress on the refugee issue could 'break [the] log-jam', the president's briefing papers stated.[26]

The State Department wanted Kennedy to tell Ben-Gurion that the United States had plans to tackle the refugee problem and that they envisioned a solution involving three different albeit intertwined aspects: (a) repatriation and refugees living in peace with their Jewish–Israeli neighbours; (b) resettlement in special work projects in Arab countries; and (c) resettlement in non-Arab countries. The Americans felt strongly that their approach had to encompass an Israeli acknowledgement of the principle of repatriation (important to the Arab side) as well as assurance from the Americans that most of the refugees would accede to resettlement, in keeping with Israel's wishes. While the State Department believed that progress, and hopefully a deal, could only follow from some intersection of these diametrically opposed positions, it was Israeli acknowledgement on the principle of repatriation that would kick off any substantial talks on the matter. Thus, a genuine Israeli move in this direction was thought to be essential to moving forward. If Israel cooperated on this, the Americans hoped it would break the 'psychological barrier' between the adversaries and lead to progress on other options, such as resettlement both within and outside of the region.[27] If the United States were able to obtain Israeli assurances regarding acceptance of the 'principle of choice' for the refugees, it would have to be considered a 'solid break-through toward peace' in the Middle East, Kennedy's briefing papers stated.[28] The concept of 'principle of choice' would later become a Johnson mission buzzword, although not exactly as the Americans hoped in the spring of 1961. The first sense of which way the wind was blowing came already on 30 May 1961, when the two leaders met in Ben-Gurion's suite at the legendary Waldorf Astoria Hotel.[29]

The meeting covered most of the topics for which the Americans had prepared but did not go into depth on any one issue. The ambition to secure Israeli compliance with the stated American effort to make progress on the refugee problem was nowhere close to being fulfilled, and the most noteworthy development occurred not in the meeting but after it. Ben-Gurion told the press that he and Kennedy had found a 'large measure of agreement' in the meeting and that Kennedy had offered 'a suggestion that might be a solution' to the refugee problem.[30] To the American diplomats who knew what had actually been said in the meeting, this was not only very surprising but also very unhelpful in terms of an overall strategy for pushing forward with a refugee initiative. After the letters to the Arab leaders and Ben-Gurion's comments, rumours started spreading in the region of a 'Kennedy Plan' or a 'formula' for repatriation and resettlement.[31]

Although the Americans managed to stymie the rumours about US–Israeli agreement on the refugee question, Ben-Gurion's statement and the lukewarm regional reception that Kennedy's letters to the Arab leaders had been given hobbled the American refugee initiative from the start. This annoyed the State Department officials who were working on it. They felt that Ben-Gurion and Israel were throwing away an effort that would ultimately also help Israel in the end. The Americans therefore put in a new attempt to rally some crucial support for the initiative in Israel and among 'Israel's friends' in the United States: Mike Feldman asked Armin Meyer, at the time the deputy assistant secretary at the Bureau of Near Eastern Affairs, to compile a list of reasons why Israel would benefit from its cooperation with the American initiative on the refugee issue.[32]

Meyer thus compiled a list of Israeli 'incentives for movement' on the Palestine refugee problem as follows: Israel could dispose of the issue to which Israel was the most vulnerable to criticism; the solution to the problem was the sine qua non for Israel's acceptance in the region; it would eliminate the 'annual hassle' at the General Assembly that was so detrimental to Israel (and to the United States); it would ward off a reconstitution of the PCC and forestall a series of increasingly anti-Israeli moves at future General Assembly debates, including the upcoming one in particular; it would 'dramatize Israel's peace protestations' and improve Israel's international image; it would take the 'edge off' the nuclear reactor in Dimona, the potential sale of US missiles to Israel and the Jordan water issue; it would reduce the tension in the region and hopefully also the arms burden; it would avoid area turmoil if UNRWA collapsed, and it would place the onus of failure on the Arabs; it would show the new US administration that Israel was cooperative; and, finally, it would take advantage of the current US willingness to finance a solution to the refugee issue.[33]

The list was meant to help prepare the ground for the sending of a special representative on a mission to the region.[34] As the current and subsequent chapters show, it had little to no effect on the Israeli leadership's positions.

For the United States, the main objective of this proposed mission was to be able to present arrangements for repatriation and resettlement of a significant number of refugees to the General Assembly, or, if this proved to be out of reach, to at least be in a position to document why it was not possible. This explanation had to be good enough to assure the other UN member states that the United States (and the PCC) had given the matter a 'real try'.[35] A secondary objective was to avoid jeopardizing the US relations with either Israel or the Arabs, and if the mission were unsuccessful, it was equally important that it be concluded in such a way that it did not become an obstacle to any future effort to solve the refugee problem or undermine the department's position vis-à-vis the US Congress, when UNRWA funds were up for discussion again.[36]

The Johnson mission

Originally, the department was looking to sign up a 'distinguished non-American official' to lead the mission.[37] This turned out to be more difficult than expected. After attempting to enlist the services of a Turk, a Canadian and then a Swiss diplomat, the Americans finally settled on an American.[38] In Joseph 'Joe' Esrey Johnson, the State Department felt confident that they had found someone of 'unimpeachable pedigree and antecedents'.[39] Johnson had several links in the American foreign policy establishment, having been previously employed at the US State Department, where he had served as chief of international security affairs.

At the time of the request, Johnson was president of the renowned Carnegie Endowment for International Peace. About a week after he was first presented with the idea, he accepted the position, on 17 August 1961.[40] The next week a UN press release was issued to announce the PCC's appointment of Johnson as its new special representative.[41] It is important to understand, however, that for the Johnson mission, the PCC was nothing but a name on the letterhead.

In the existing literature on efforts to solve the Arab–Israeli conflict in this time period, most studies mention the Johnson mission only in passing.[42] In a few of these works, one gets the impression that Johnson was a PCC man, handpicked by the commission itself.[43] The United States did its utmost to portray it as a PCC endeavour, yet it would be a mistake to take this at face value. It was the State Department's idea that they should approach the refugee problem through a UN framework. From the American records, it is clear that Johnson's position as the PCC's special representative had been tacked on to the existing PCC structure as a 'special device' to increase the commission's 'flexibility'.[44] While Johnson was not taking instructions from the US administration on all issues and at all times – and in this way had a role that in theory was independent from the US government – his mission still existed thanks to the will and indulgence of the US government upon the recommendation of the US State Department. Internally, the Americans referred to Johnson as a 'partially free-wheeling' agent, and as such, he was 'responsive to US G[overnment] influence'.[45] The point is important because the close coordination between Johnson and the department allowed the latter to keep close tabs on Johnson and made sure that he did not independently develop any plans that were 'politically or financially impractical for [the] US to implement or support'.[46]

Although he was determined to give the mission his best, Johnson harboured few illusions about his mission's potential for success. Or as Johnson himself put it to Rusk as he departed for the first regional tour, he was 'not at the time applying for the Nobel Peace Prize'.[47]

Between 14 April and 12 May 1961, Johnson and his 'alter ego', Sherwood Moe, toured the region.[48] They started with a stop in Israel and travelled on to Beirut, Damascus, Cairo and Amman, before returning once more to Israel.[49] After spending a month in the region, Johnson returned to the United States with a mixed impression. On the surface, there was no doubt that the parties' public attitudes remained as opposed to a deal as ever. Each side insisted that any action would depend on the behaviour of the other. The Arabs continued to insist that repatriation was their sine qua non, while Israel maintained that repatriation was out of the question as long there was no change in 'basic Arab attitudes' towards Israel.[50]

Yet it had also become clear to Johnson that there was some internal Arab disagreement as well. For example, Lebanon's position was that resettlement had to mean refugees settling within the borders of the former mandate of Palestine (the parts allotted to an independent Arab state in 1947).[51] This position did not sit well with the Jordanians, who had no desire for an independent Palestine. That did not mean that Jordan was any less interested in moving forward than Lebanon: in fact, Johnson returned from his first trip with the impression that Jordan was the one Arab country that was most anxious to solve the refugee problem. But Jordan worried, with good reason, that the US plan was to first reach a deal on the refugee problem with Egypt and Israel and only later to include the other Arab states.[52] This would leave Jordan with much less room to manoeuvre and would likely force it into accepting positions that it felt painful. Jordan's situation was different from Egypt's, and a deal established on the latter's positions would likely bad fit for the Jordanian regime.

Although Egypt was the dominant Arab nation and Nasser was the dominant Arab leader, his country had relatively few refugees within it. Egypt formally controlled the Gaza Strip but did little but administer the small piece of land. All in all, Nasser could likely endure the status quo longer than other Arab nations, and perhaps even benefit from it, from a domestic and regional perspective. Alternatively, he could conclude that Egypt could sign on to a refugee deal that would not entail any great economic development package for the Arab host nations that would resettle the refugees – because he would be resettling so few, if any, Palestinians in Egypt, his 'payment' would be minimal in such a deal – so why bother? Both of these scenarios worried Jordan, who sought the financial compensation and area development that many thought would be included in any refugee deal. Unlike Egypt, that is, Jordan had the largest portion of the refugee population within its borders, and its portion of a host-nation development package would be significant. Completely dependent on such external help, Jordan could not afford to let Nasser negotiate away its one chance of making this existing liability into an asset.

This aside, the most important consequence from Johnson's trip was that he returned from it convinced that the key to any solution, no matter what the numbers of the repatriation/resettlement ratio looked like, was to give a choice to the refugees. They had to be asked if they wanted repatriation or resettlement, and this had to be what Johnson called a 'meaningful choice'.[53] This had been the crux of the initial Villard study conclusion as well: In a meaningful choice it would not suffice, Johnson argued, to merely present the refugees with the option of either going to Israel or staying on in the camps. They had to be given a chance to learn what Israel had become – to fully grasp what they would be returning to – before they were represented with such an alternative.[54]

The refugees' opinion about their own future could be sought through a referendum, Johnson suggested.[55] Johnson decided he would propose to the parties that they start by asking a 'pilot group' of approximately 20,000 refugees, whether they would opt for return or resettlement.[56] There was some hope that by shifting the weight of responsibility regarding the refugees future from the Arab leaders to the refugees themselves – as the pilot project questionnaire was intended to do – the domestic factor would also be taken out of the Arab leaders' equation. If the refugees themselves made the call, the Arab leaders could not use the results to attack each other.[57]

In Israel, though, developments moved in a less, not more, compromising direction. In October 1961, just weeks after Johnson had toured the region for the first time, Ben-Gurion took to the podium of the Knesset to categorically reject the concept of 'free choice' as '"insidious" and "designed to destroy

Israel".[58] The State Department perceived it as a deliberate salvo in Johnson's direction.[59] Ben-Gurion's statement was followed by a speech that was similar in tone and content from Foreign Minister Golda Meir, and then, in a vote on 6 November 1961, the Knesset passed a resolution stating that 'the Arab refugees should not be returned to Israeli territory and that the sole solution to the problem is their settlement in the Arab countries'. The resolution was adapted by a vote of sixty-eight to seven. The Mapam party called for a resolution that allowed for the repatriation of a specific number of refugees in the context of future peace negotiations, but it was defeated with a vote of seven to sixty. It is worth mentioning in this context that this negative vote constituted an unprecedented cooperation across party lines in the Knesset, which illustrates the consensus across the Israeli political spectrum which existed on this issue.[60]

Therefore, the Israeli leadership's freedom of action in the matter was further limited, not extended. It would be harder for the Israeli government to deviate in any settlement from the public image that the government itself had created. From a negotiation perspective, it made sense to manoeuvre domestically in a way that ensured that the leadership's hands were 'tied' when it arrived at the international negotiating table.[61] Time was working *for* the Israelis: The unsolved refugee problem had become a 'useful bargaining point' for Israel and could be leveraged to improve Israel's position regarding other, thornier issues.[62]

Israel did not just position itself rhetorically against repatriation. It also worked continuously to capitalize upon its opportunities to populate the Central Galilee as well as the Negev desert. The physical presence of a large Jewish population in these areas, of course, further bolstered their arguments against repatriation.[63] Taking these developments into account, the US embassy in Tel Aviv concluded that Johnson's only means of getting the Israelis to budge was if he himself were prepared to play hardball.[64]

But if Johnson were to have a chance to play ball at all, let alone hardball, he would first of all need more time. By 15 October, the General Assembly was expecting its next update from the PCC. It was clear to Johnson that this was utterly unrealistic.[65] Before he could concentrate on any of the substantial matters, he had to make sure that formalities were in place and that entailed ensuring that his mission got prolonged support from the UN General Assembly. At the UN a small, but substantial, brouhaha occurred, when a draft resolution calling for direct negotiations between Israel and the Arab states was promoted by the so-called Brazzaville group, acting on Israel's wishes.[66] The Brazzaville resolution was a direct effort to undercut the Johnson mission, embarrass the Americans and put the onus for the lack of progress on the Arab states.[67] In the end, though, the American diplomats and Johnson got it their way, when the General Assembly on 20 December requested the PCC to 'intensify its efforts' at Arab–Israeli conflict resolution.[68]

Before going back to the region a second time, Johnson was determined to have developed a more concrete idea of how he could approach the question of resettlement and repatriation. He therefore initiated a series of studies on ways to determine the wishes of the refugees and regarding the arrangements of repatriation and resettlement.[69] Throughout January and February 1962, several 'working papers' were developed and presented in meetings with the State Department. After consultations in the United States and in Europe, Johnson travelled to Jerusalem in the second week of April 1962, the first stop on his second regional trip. His arrival came at a tense moment. Fighting had once again erupted at the Israeli–Syrian border, prompting a Security Council resolution addressing the situation just days before Johnsons first meeting with Golda Meir.[70]

Getting to concretes: Johnson's second trip to the region

While the first trip was exploratory in nature, this second trip was an opportunity for Johnson to test a few concrete ideas. In the first meeting, he presented to Meir some of the ideas from his so-called 'working paper five'.[71] He focused on the issue of refugee choice and told her about his idea of surveying a pilot group of 10,000 to 20,000 people as to whether they preferred repatriation or resettlement. Johnson asked Meir under what conditions Israel would agree to repatriate a share of these 20,000 people as the beginning of a solution to the refugee problem? He also made it clear that Israel would not have to accept all of those who possibly requested repatriation, only some of them.[72]

Meir objected that even a hypothetical share of those people would represent a 'security risk' for Israel. She would not, however, admit that Israel's position therefore amounted to 'not one refugee', claiming instead that Israel simply 'had no place for them'.[73] Of course, this claim did not jibe the fact that Israel was then accepting thousands of Jewish immigrants, but Meir went ahead and argued at length along these lines, adding that she could not comprehend why they would 'wish to come' in the first place.[74] If there were to be any chance of Israel agreeing to Johnson's idea of a pilot group, Israel would require, as a precondition, that the Arabs make it clear in public that they were ready to live at peace with Israel. Evidence of such intention, Meir continued, would be a 'six months moratorium' on 'anti-Israel propaganda'.[75]

In the second meeting with Meir, Johnson suggested that the movement of 20,000 refugees – some repatriated to Israel, most resettled in other places – would initiate momentum that could push them towards a comprehensive solution to the problem. Meir was unimpressed. Israel believed that if they allowed for the return of some of the refugees, they would never hear the end of it, and new claims would surely follow. A disappointed Johnson could only conclude that Meir and her team were 'manifestly determined' to frame his ideas as a threat to Israel's security, despite repeated assurances that this was not the case.[76]

The stop in Jerusalem gave the second phase of the mission a rough start. Instead of obtaining Israel's consent to move forward with the pilot project, or indeed obtaining Israel's acceptance of any of his proposals, Johnson had been presented with additional Israeli conditions for its cooperation to his efforts. This inclination to put further conditions on acceptance worried both the US UN delegation in New York and Secretary Rusk in Washington.[77] Nor would it be the last time American diplomats would lament this tendency.

Just prior to Johnson's arrival in the region, the Arab League held a meeting in Riyadh on 4 April, where it was decided that no Arab leader could agree to anything but 'substantial' repatriation.[78] In many ways, this was the regional equivalent of the Israeli leadership 'tying' its hands at the domestic level. By whipping up regional sentiment against any deal that fell short of repatriation, the Arab leaders were also doing what they could to ensure that their room to manoeuvre was severely limited. They further decided that the various Arab delegations' main talking point in the conversations with Johnson should continue to be insistence on Israeli acknowledgement of the principle of repatriation.[79] No Arab government could afford to absorb the political costs of appearing to give up on their common Palestine cause.[80] But in the subsequent off-the-record talks with Johnson, the Arab story became a little more nuanced – both Beirut and Damascus indicated that they were in fact willing to cooperate to solve the problem.[81]

In Damascus, Johnson found some ambiguity to the Syrian position. Though they were unwilling to discuss the details of a refugee scheme, they were still prepared to cooperate in some fashion. The Syrians also indicated to Johnson that the Arab League's insistence on the Israeli acknowledgement of paragraph 11 was mostly for domestic purposes.[82] In Beirut, likewise, Lebanese foreign minister Philippe Takla admitted to Johnson that one of the biggest obstacles to progress on the refugee issue was intra-Arab politics. In Lebanon's case, Takla continued, its position was fully dictated by its adherence to any united Arab view that existed. 'As long as [the] refugees remain refugees', Takla explained to Johnson, they were welcome in Lebanon. But if a solution were to be adopted that changed the refugees' status, 'they would have to leave'. They would have to either repatriate or go someplace else and resettle.[83]

In talks with American diplomats prior to Johnson's arrival, Takla had made statements along similar lines but also made it clear that Lebanon was specifically saying that the *Muslim* Palestinians had to be moved and resettled outside Lebanon. If Johnson would register this detail, Lebanese cooperation would come much more easily.[84] The precarious demographic balance of Lebanon would be substantially tilted if the hundreds and thousands of Palestinian refugees, who were predominantly Sunni Muslim, were to become Lebanese citizens, and this was something that both Christian and Shia Muslim elements in Lebanon feared. Lebanon was made up of many different sectarian groups, the political influence of which the so-called National Pact, established in 1943, had aimed to balance, based on the 1932 census. It was a delicate arrangement at best, however, as had been recently violently demonstrated by the outbreak of civil war in 1958. The Lebanese Muslims (Sunnis, Shiites and Druze) felt underrepresented in the Lebanese system and already suspected that the Christians were refusing to authorize a new census because they were afraid of the new demographic reality it would reflect.[85] A substantial influx of Palestinian Sunni Muslims into this mix could mean a potential disaster for Lebanon, the government feared.

The reactions from Amman were ambiguous as well and again confirmed to Johnson and the US State Department that the Arab opposition to the mission was multifaceted. Here, in a meeting in May 1962 King Hussein told American ambassador William B. Macomber, Jr, that the solution to the refugee problem should be found in the economic development of the Arab countries, not along the lines that Johnson was proposing.[86] Macomber could not hide his astonishment. For years, the Arabs had touted paragraph 11 of Resolution 194 at the UN, and when a mission based on this premise had finally materialized – and one that proposed a solution along the lines of compensation and repatriation – they shunned it altogether and refused to cooperate. The Arabs should not be expecting to find much sympathy for their position at the coming fall's UNGA session, Ambassador Macomber warned the Jordanians.[87] Had this insight into the Jordanian mindset arrived at a different time – for example, during the negotiations of Eric Johnston over the water sharing agreements, the Clapp mission or even the Alpha Plan – Macomber's reaction might have been less agitated. By the spring of 1962, though, it was not regional development that was in vogue at the US State Department, it was the Johnson plan. And the Johnson mission's mandate was rooted in paragraph 11 of Resolution 194 – the holy grail of the Arab states' Palestine policy. But now, the Jordanians were retreating from this position before a completely dumbfounded ambassador Macomber. Jordanian prime minister al-Tel acknowledged to Macomber that he had 'never been so embarrassed in his life' as when he had to tell Johnson upon the latter's visit that his proposals were unacceptable.[88]

Both the prime minister and the king admitted that they were conducting a 'double-faced' policy. The Arabs had insisted on the principles manifested in paragraph 11 at the UN 'on the assumption that no one would really try to make good on it', the prime minster told the US ambassador. 'Now that somebody was', however, 'the Arabs would have to back off'.[89] Macomber fully well understood the magnitude of what the Jordanians were telling him. This was a clear break with the official 'Arab line' and would 'constitute heresy in [the] eyes of many Arabs', Macomber wrote. For the Jordanian leadership, the self-proclaimed true champions of the Palestinian cause, leaks from this conversation could be potentially disastrous, and in Macomber's opinion it would be unsafe for them if word got out that these were their genuine opinions.[90] To understand why Jordan opposed the first diplomatic effort since the Lausanne talks in 1949 that invoked Resolution 194, one must consider at least two things: Jordan's need for external developmental aid and the Jordanian king's desire to keep the Palestinians under his control.

In Project Alpha, the Johnston water scheme and Hammarskjöld's plan of the late 1950s, economic development had been the main carrot in getting the Arab states to cooperate. The more refugees that could be resettled, the more economic developmental aid the various Arab countries could expect. Since

Jordan was hosting the biggest group of refugees, its leadership anticipated a substantial economic package if they cooperated with resettlement schemes. For the Jordanians, then, this was a way of turning a regime liability into an asset. The Johnson mission, in contrast, was focused on the *refugees'* preferences and on slowly but surely working towards a solution. There were no grand schemes regarding aid incentives and development projects. Amman might have feared that if Johnson succeeded and was actually able to remove the refugee dimension from the conflict, this would also signal the end of Jordan's claims and of all international attention and financial support in general.

The second thing was what could be called the Palestinian factor. Johnson was the first involved actor to have stated so explicitly that the refugees' voices needed to be heard, and he was the first Western envoy to talk about the refugees' preferences. For the Jordanians any effort that promoted a stronger *Palestinian* identity was unwelcome, given the internal Arab rivalry and especially King Hussein's desire to challenge Nasser as the leader of the Arab world. In this regional bid for primacy, an increased population – especially if it could be linked to economic aid – had to be considered an asset rather than a drawback – for a poor and resourceless desert kingdom.

In addition to the Johnson mission, there was another, simultaneous, development occurring that might have exacerbated the Jordanian leadership's fear of the Palestinian factor: In April 1962, there were rumours in the diplomatic community in Beirut that parts of the Palestinian refugee community was organizing a 'Palestine provisional committee' or 'government' of sorts.[91] This particular concern was one that the Jordanians and the Americans shared.[92] In Washington, D.C., the Palestinian dimension of the Arab–Israeli conflict was mostly overlooked or ignored. Palestinian aspirations of any kind had little room within this framework of understanding.

Again, then, Johnson left the region with mixed feelings, though his general impression was that the Arab side was less rigid compared to what he had experienced during his trip the summer before. None of the Arab leaders with whom Johnson had met had challenged him when he stated that Israel was here to stay, and he saw this as a step in the right direction. He was resigned, however, to the fact that any new or revised proposal had to abandon his initial idea regarding the pilot project of 20,000 refugees. That said, though, Johnson was still committed to the idea that any sustainable solution depended upon giving the refugees an opportunity to state their own preferences.[93] In Johnson's mind, the sense of injustice among the refugees – the need to 'put matters right' or 'at least as right as possible' – was at the heart of the matter.[94] This conviction continued to guide Johnson, as his mission continued on its bumpy ride. Johnson's approach moved from asking the parties to openly support his efforts to creating a situation where they didn't have to agree or disagree with what he did. He wanted to create a situation where Israeli and Arab leaderships just needed to agree to look the other way and approve him a 'tacit acquiescence' as he began to work on the task that he felt was an important premise for any resolution to the refugee problem – figuring out what the Palestinian opinion on repatriation and resettlement really was.[95]

Up to this point, there had been no major disagreement between Johnson and the State Department about the direction of the mission. Foggy Bottom had neither objected to Johnson's insistence on privileging the refugees' preference. But when the time came for Johnson to produce a questionnaire, meant to provide each individual refugee with an opportunity to express his or her preference, the special representative and the State Department got into their first substantial disagreement.

Kennedy and the Arab–Israeli conflict

Joseph Johnson was resolute that for his mission to move forward, he needed a better overview of the refugees' own preference. If they were deciding themselves, would they choose return to what was now a new country, the state of Israel? Or would they prefer resettlement?

To enlighten himself and the mission, Johnson therefore developed a questionnaire. It was short, not more than one page, and was supposed to be voluntary. The questionnaire's main objective was to help the Johnson team determine whether the refugees preferred return or to be resettled in an Arab country or elsewhere, with compensation. If the latter, the questionnaire next asked for a prioritized list of four possible countries that the refugee 'would like to live in'.[1] What, then, about the question of compensation? Since 1948, compensation had become a concept inseparable from the concept of resettlement. It habitually followed as one part of the same category: 'resettlement and compensation'.

For Johnson, however, compensation was a matter that belonged in both categories – with resettlement *and* with repatriation. All those who had fled had left something behind. All had material losses. For Johnson, it was essential that the questionnaire framed the choice as one between 'repatriation with compensation for loss or damage to property' or 'compensation and resettlement'.[2] He was not prepared, in other words, to accept the previously held US position – that compensation should be paid only to those who resettled in countries other than Israel.

Johnson's position recalled that of the British diplomats who had worked on the Alpha Plan six years previous. If a refugee had lost his or her property and was unable to return to reclaim it for whatever reason, it should not matter, Johnson argued, whether that person was technically in the repatriation category: he or she was entitled to compensation. Johnson's position on compensation reflects his strong emphasis on justice as a necessary part of a solution to the refugee problem. 'I cannot agree', Johnson wrote to his counterparts at the State Department, 'that ... a refugee who is repatriated but who has lost his property should not be compensated for that loss in the same manner as the refugee who has decided not to return is compensated'.[3]

The State Department's position, on the other hand, was that the refugees' choice was either repatriation *or* compensation. If for no other reason, the department argued, compensation for the repatriates had to be dropped as a nod to the 'political realism' of the situation.[4] Israel would never accept a proposal that allowed for compensation either way. In addition, such a principle would undermine the effort to make sure that repatriation would appear to be the lesser option. As Francis Russell put it during the internal Anglo-American deliberations on Alpha early in 1955, removing compensation from the equation was the best way to 'deliberately ... discourage repatriation'.[5] Just as the British had protested this logic in 1955, however, Johnson did so in 1962 as well. He thought that the reality of living in Israel at this time would provide the refugees with so many disincentives that the whole aspect of compensation would become minor in comparison. He flipped the State Department's argument on its head: if Israeli obduracy was the main reason for not allowing repatriation and compensation, then the same would certainly be true for the other side of the table. If it did *not* state that all who had lost property would be eligible for compensation, the plan would be politically unpalatable for the Arab leaders and for the Palestinian refugees in particular.[6]

To try to bridge the gap between the department's position and Johnson's, some State Department officials suggested that the repatriates could be given the opportunity to present a claim for compensation to Israeli authorities after their return and resettlement in Israeli society. Israel would serve as administrator, but the money would still come from a UN fund for compensation. Johnson had serious reservations about the wisdom of this suggestion. To him it seemed fantastic to believe that Israeli authorities would treat such claims in a fair manner.[7] 'Anyone who is slightly familiar with the laws and practices of the Israeli government', Johnson argued, 'must conclude that to leave the returning refugee no recourse but to the Israeli authorities is effectively to deny him substantial justice'.[8]

Not ready to give up on his position, Johnson also pleaded his case in legal terms. The matter's legislative history should be interpreted as support for his position, Johnson claimed. In 1948, when UNGA Resolution 194 was discussed and passed by the UN General Assembly in the first place, the British delegation had expressed their belief that compensation was due to whomever had lost property, no matter whether the person returned or was resettled. As long as the property was out of reach for the refugee, compensation was due. Johnson's argument now was that since the United States had worked with the UK to draft the parts of the resolution that dealt with the compensation question (the US delegate had even stated as much to the General Assembly), this had to be interpreted as US concurrence with the principle.[9]

The US State Department would not relent. In their reply to Johnson, they countered by stating that Johnson's was not the only possible interpretation of the matter's legislative history. Their argument remained grounded in the belief that the Johnson plan was already so 'distasteful' to Israel that if the plan were to incorporate his position on compensation as well, Israel was sure to immediately bring down the curtain.[10]

The department knew fully well, of course, that Johnson's work ahead was completely dependent on its support. If Johnson accepted the department's view, Rusk promised him the president's endorsement, as well as the department's general pledge of active support and assistance in securing a relatively prompt implementation of his plan.[11] This was what the Johnson mission needed to stay alive. It was clear to most of the actors that the mission was on its last legs unless Kennedy came out in support of it in some way. Johnson was experienced enough to understand that he could not resist the department in the end, and in a memorandum on 7 August 1962, he formally, if reluctantly, acceded to the department's view. To the formal letter, he added a note stating, for the record, that he did not personally agree with the department's reasoning or with the final position taken.[12]

So, by dangling the carrot of presidential endorsement before Johnson's nose, Rusk and the department managed to get him to change his position on this particular issue. Keeping the department's end of the deal, Rusk then brought the matter before the president in early August, asking him for his 'general approval and support' of the plan.[13] But to promise that Johnson would get time with the president or promise to bring the plan to the president was one thing. To secure presidential endorsement and get Kennedy to agree to use his own personal prestige and political capital on behalf of the plan was quite another.

Domestic dimensions: Ensuring presidential support

Before examining Kennedy's deliberations over whether to give the Johnson mission the clout of the Oval Office, the complex realities behind the US State Department's actions must be considered. The Johnson plan was one part of a much larger regional puzzle, as is demonstrated by the often-clashing advice that would arrive from the various US embassies in the region. A typical trait of US foreign policy, especially in terms of the Arab–Israeli conflict, is the perennial disagreement among the diplomatic corps at the region's respective embassies about the facts on the ground in the Middle East. This was evident throughout the Johnson plan, with, for example, the ambassadors in Beirut and Tel Aviv taking very different positions on the best course of action. The view from Beirut was that the Johnson plan was a very positive development that deserved more than the department's half-hearted attention, while Tel Aviv argued the opposite. The department had to balance and triangulate all of these views in order to maintain its overarching foreign policy perspective.[14] Indeed, in terms of US–Israel relations alone, the Johnson mission was but one of several aspects confronting the department – others included Israel's security concerns and its repeated requests for US support in the military domain, as well as certain other 'frictions' in the relationship between the two countries. These frictions stemmed from Israel's policy of retaliatory raids; its uncooperative attitude with the UN and the peacekeeping machinery in the region; sovereignty claims regarding Lake Tiberias; the objection by the United States to the establishment of foreign diplomatic missions to Israel in Jerusalem; the Brazzaville resolution; the Americans' restrain in training so-called third country nationals in Israel (military training); and, finally, Israel's general distrust of the Johnson mission.[15] Added to all of this was the nuclear issue, which was emerging as one of, if not *the*, most 'delicate' matters by the spring of 1961. Since 1958, Israel, with French support, had developed a nuclear reactor in the Israeli city of Dimona, in the Negev desert, and this had been on Kennedy's agenda since before his inauguration.[16]

Of course, stepping back yet again, the Middle East was also just one part of a much larger global puzzle. Kennedy's foreign policy challenges were numerous. The new frontiersmen's first months in office had entailed more than a handful of potentially devastating situations, all with potentially catastrophic global ramifications. First off was the disastrous Bay of Pigs invasion in January 1961, followed by communist uprisings in Laos and South Vietnam, the May 1961 Vienna summit with Kennedy's archnemesis, the Soviet premier Nikita Khrushchev, and the Berlin Crisis. All of these had demanded Kennedy's attention and would indeed continue to do so throughout the autumn of 1962, with the Cuba Crisis in as the most dramatic episode by far.[17] Much attention had to be given to Berlin, Congo and Vietnam. In this volatile global situation, the Middle East was 'kind of simmered in the background' for Kennedy and his men.[18]

Still, it would be inaccurate to conclude that Kennedy's safe distance to the Arab–Israeli conflict was only a cause of international events. These foreign policy challenges might have taken most of the president's attention, but when Johnson had finalized his plan in the early summer of 1962, and sought the president's support, it was mostly domestic concerns that caused Kennedy's reluctance: political America was gearing up for the midterm elections in November, and the emerging question involved whether Kennedy possessed enough domestic political capital to push ahead with a major foreign policy initiative in the Middle East – while knowing that Israel deeply mistrusted the whole enterprise – in the midst of a congressional election campaign.

Kennedy was a president who remained sensitive to the voice and opinions of Jewish America. His appointment of Myer Feldman as his special counsel was perhaps the strongest testament to this fact. In Feldman's own words, the two were a duo of a 'liberal Catholic' and a 'conservative Jew'.[19] Initially, Feldman functioned as Kennedy's de facto 'ambassador to American Jewry'.[20] By the summer of 1962, however, Feldman's mandate moved beyond the domestic arena and into the foreign policy sphere.

When Kennedy first approached Feldman to advise him on Middle East matters, Feldman had, according to his own recollection, challenged the president on the wisdom of the move. 'I said quite frankly that I had an emotional sympathy with Israel', Feldman recalled in one of several oral history interviews conducted with him after Kennedy's assassination.[21] Feldman told Kennedy that he was 'sure' this emotional connection would 'color his advice' and asked the president if he were sure that there was no one else for the job.[22] Kennedy insisted and allegedly told Feldman that he both anticipated and appreciated his sympathies for Israel, and that he wanted Feldman to 'go into' the issues and 'keep him advised' on anything that was happening that 'he ought to know about'.[23] This produced a White House instruction to the State Department to clear all cables and actions that had a potential 'domestic political impact' with Feldman during the course of the congressional election campaign.[24]

Feldman's role in the Kennedy administration would cause much irritation at the State Department and at times provoke internal friction within the president's group of foreign policy advisors.[25] Aside from Secretary of State Dean Rusk, others involved with the Johnson mission and plan included George Talbot, Robert Strong, James Ludlow, William Crawford and James Grant from the State Department. In addition to these men, two men of the National Security Council (led by the influential national security advisor Mac Bundy), Robert (Bob) Komer and Carl Kaysen, were the administration's most central figures in this particular matter.

Reportedly, Kennedy, like several other presidents before him, was weary of what he thought was a slow and inefficient State Department.[26] This apparent animosity towards Foggy Bottom helps to further explain why a domestic policy advisor like Myer Feldman could have such substantial influence in the foreign policy realm.[27]

Presenting the Johnson plan to the parties

Throughout the summer of 1962, the department and Johnson wanted to present the Johnson plan to the parties and notably Israel and Egypt. Before the parties were physically handed the text of the plan, however, the diplomats at the State Department agreed that it would be wise to send a special emissary on a pre-emptive trip to see Ben-Gurion. The Israeli leader had to be prepared for what was coming. They acknowledged that this would mean that the Israelis got a 'secret shot' at the Johnson plan, before it was formally put to paper and then became public.[28]

The State Department knew that Ben-Gurion favoured this kind of 'ultra-secret personal diplomacy'.[29] For this reason, the group working on the Johnson plan was sure that a message from a presidential special emissary would pack more punch than any UN special representative, or even US secretary of state, could hope to do. Who, then, would be better suited for such a mission than Mike Feldman? Here was a man who was trusted by the Israelis and who also was close enough to Kennedy to carry his message with the requisite clout.[30] But what exactly would the message to Ben-Gurion be? On this point, the jury was still out, and to properly understand the coming twists and turns of the Johnson mission, one must connect it to another central aspect of US–Israel relations – Israel's requests for expanded US military support. In particular, Israel was seeking a US commitment to deliver to Israel its state-of-the-art surface-to-air missile, popularly known as the Hawk.

In the summer of 1962, the relationship between Israel and the United States was complicated by friction. Among other things, Israel had for some time sought to establish a close military relationship with the United States, to the latter's sometime discomfort. Israel was also pushing for US support for its plans to divert the water of the Jordan River, and it wanted access to a wider range of US military equipment. Specifically, ever since the new frontiersmen had taken office, Israel had sought the Hawk, a surface-to-air missile that would reduce Israel's vulnerability to surprise air attacks by low-flying Egyptian aircraft.[31] The US to this point had been unwilling to provide Israel with anything that was not for purely defensive purposes, and the Hawk, although technically speaking a defensive weapon, was a step up in this regard. It was an advanced weapons system, and it would signal the de facto entry of the United States to the major arms race in the region. Israel would also be the first country outside the North Atlantic Treaty Organization (NATO) to receive it. In terms of US–Israeli strategic cooperation, the Hawk sale would indeed have represented 'the crossing of the Rubicon'.[32]

While Israel's relatively extensive list of demands certainly made for challenging bilateral consultations between the two countries, it also provided the United States with some leverage. This was especially true of the pending decision to sell Israel the Hawk missile, which was championed by the unlikely alliance of a domestic-oriented Myer Feldman and the US Department of Defence.[33] In turn, Secretary Rusk and Assistant Secretary Talbot sought to readjust their course and argue that the sale of the Hawk missile, even as an internally forgone conclusion, should, at the very least, be linked to Israeli cooperation on the Johnson plan.[34]

'Our resolve on the quid pro quo is firm and remains firm', Talbot wrote to Feldman before the latter was sent to meet with Ben-Gurion. In exchange for the missiles, the United States would ask for Israel's cooperation on the Johnson plan. The United States would also ask the Israelis to scrap any plans they might have to reintroduce the so-called Brazzaville resolution at the upcoming UN General Assembly session. This resolution had meant much embarrassment and wasted energy for the United States the year before, and the State Department did not want to see that situation repeated. Even if the United States were not in principle opposed to the idea of direct negotiations, a new resolution calling for that at this point would be directly interfering with what the State Department was trying to accomplish though the Johnson mission. So, if the US government were to genuinely commit to the Johnson mission soon, avoiding the resolution at the coming General Assembly was even more important.

In return, Israel would be given US assurances on the delivery of the Hawk missile, a security guarantee and a guarantee of US financial help on the implementation of the compensation question. In addition, but only if 'absolutely necessary', Feldman could discuss with Ben-Gurion a secret agreement between the United States and Israel on the numerical 'ceiling' of refugee repatriation. At the State Department, George Talbot knew that any promises about a repatriation ceiling would be an outright gift to Ben-Gurion, thus they would have to be discreet and never written down. 'It will put us in his [Ben-Gurion's] hands', Talbot cautioned Feldman. By leaking such an understanding, Ben-Gurion could kill the Johnson plan in an instant.

For the department, it was vital that Feldman succeed in communicating to the Israelis that the Americans were ready to support them but only conditionally. 'I hardly need stress', Rusk wrote in his last instructions before Feldman met with Ben-Gurion and Meir, 'that it would be most unfortunate if [the] Israelis were to end up with the Hawks and strengthened security assurances while being responsible for derailing the Johnson Plan before it could even be given a good try'.[35]

But the department and Secretary Rusk were not the only ones weighing in on what the presidential special emissary should communicate to the Israeli leadership. A typical trait of Kennedy's presidential management style was that he often asked people that he knew held different opinions on a topic to make their case before him, before he himself decided what he thought was the most convincing alternative.[36] And the second presidential briefing on the Johnson plan came from Feldman, who was no fan of the Johnson plan in the first place. His view differed substantially from the department's perspective. Feldman warned the president that the plan's chances of success were 'slim'.[37] Its only chance of success was if it were to be coupled with a security guarantee and the promise of provision of the Hawks, he continued. The department had made the case that this arrangement had to be presented to the Israelis as a quid pro quo. But Kennedy's emissary Feldman was probably the least resolved of anyone as to holding firm on this point.[38] In fact, Feldman himself wanted the president to authorize him to tell Ben-Gurion that the Hawks were a done deal and that it was only a question of when they would be ready for Israel's use.[39] Feldman told Kennedy that he could not go to Israel and begin to 'bargain' with them: 'Any self-respecting government' was going to 'resent' doing this, Feldman stated.[40] Over the next couple of weeks, Feldman continued to make his case to the president in a 'series of private meetings', where he pushed 'relentlessly' for his own strategy.[41]

Abe Feinberg seconded Feldman's advice. Together the two stressed to Kennedy that the Hawk sale would gain 'widespread approval' among supporters of Israel in the United States, which would constitute a most welcome endorsement during an election campaign.[42] This would have mattered to Kennedy, who himself was concerned that the Johnson plan would spur rumours of 'big repatriation', despite the fact that the State Department told him that it leaned heavily towards resettlement. Rumours of repatriation, Kennedy argued, would stir people up before the upcoming election and he did not want 'to get into a costly fight without getting something' in return. Kennedy felt that he was 'still living with [the] residue of [the] December vote', a reference to the US vote in the General Assembly the year before, which apparently caused 'serious dissatisfactions' within the American Jewish community'.[43] Kennedy did not want 'to live with residue of another fight for years and years'.[44]

The details of the decision-making process regarding whether or not to actively tie the Hawk sale to the refugee issue have been difficult to pin down. The only direct reference to it seems to be Feldman's own recollection of what happened. According to him, the president's initial inclination had been to do as Talbot and the State Department recommended: to try to use the Hawk deal to get something back from Israel. When Feldman protested that this would hurt the pride of the Israelis, however, Kennedy allegedly reversed his position and said that Feldman should present the Hawks to the Israelis for simply a little cooperation in return.[45] One must consider here the possibility of Feldman inflating the image of his own influence on the president's actions, and that, consequently, there could be other, alternative explanations as to why Kennedy decided against the advice of the State Department. This does not change the fact, however, that Kennedy did just so, because within the first few minutes of their three-and-a-half-hour meeting on 19 August, Feldman had told Prime Minister David Ben-Gurion and Foreign Minister Golda Meir that, if Israel still wanted the Hawk, 'we shall let you have it'.[46]

With that out of the way, Feldman could move on to discuss the Johnson plan. Talbot, as mentioned, had cautioned against entering a numbers game with the Israelis – only if Feldman felt it was absolutely necessary was a repatriation ceiling to be discussed with Ben-Gurion. As in the case of the Hawks, however, Feldman felt otherwise and promptly told the Israelis that under no circumstances would the Americans pressure them to allow more than one-tenth of the refugees to return to Israel.[47] If the first trial run of asking 1,000 refugees what they would prefer showed that 'more than a small proportion' sought repatriation, the Americans would say, 'let's drop the plan since the security of Israel will be jeopardized'.[48] In any case, the United States would make sure that 'everything would be done' to encourage compensation and resettlement instead of repatriation, and that Israel 'at all times' would be in control of the processing of the refugees' wishes.[49] In agreeing to allow the Johnson plan to move forward Israel thus had 'nothing to lose', Feldman argued.[50]

What, then, did the American administration want from Israel? They were merely asking Israel 'not to stand in the way', Feldman told Meir and Ben-Gurion. This was Johnson's principle of tacit acquiescence in practice. If the Israelis could just 'wait and see', Feldman promised that the Americans would keep them closely advised on anything that came out of their consultations with the Arabs; all Israel really needed to do was make sure that they were not 'the first to reject' the plan.[51] Feldman then went on to reassure them that what they were facing was really a watered-down Johnson plan in any case: 'There were things there [in the original plan] that the President and I felt were not consistent with Israel's interest', he told them. These points, he continued, had all been 'modified'. 'Please remember that you have a good friend in the White House, a better one than you ever had', Feldman reminded the Israelis: 'Consult with him and try to see his problem, and get his support', he further urged Meir. For good measure, Feldman added that he had 'never taken anything' to Kennedy in a matter concerning Israel where Kennedy did not end up deciding 'for Israel'.

After Feldman had concluded his talks in Israel, it was time to seek out Nasser's preliminary reaction to the Johnson plan. For this mission, the US State Department dispatched Robert Strong, the director of the Office of Near Eastern Affairs, and John Badeau, the ambassador to Egypt. Badeau tried to impress upon Nasser what a great proposal this was for the Arab states: because it did not exclude the possibility of some repatriation, it was much nearer to the Arab position than any plan had been before. In communications back to the State Department, Badeau characterized Nasser's response as 'moderate' and 'slightly encouraging'. In general, the Americans found Nasser to be less negative than expected. He did not reject the plan outright and even admitted that it had some merit.[52]

Nasser told the Americans that if Johnson would only agree to stay away from the numbers game regarding the repatriation/resettlement ratio, there was a genuine chance that the refugees would accept his plan. Strong and Badeau, two seasoned diplomats, viewed this as noteworthy and even the 'most optimistic statement' of the whole conversation.[53] In other words, Nasser's response was comparable to the response Feldman had received in Israel: not an endorsement but not a firm rejection either. The State Department interpreted the outcomes of these consultations as justification for taking the mission to the next level. But did they also have the president's green light to proceed in this regard?[54]

Kennedy and the question of Palestine

Back in Washington, D.C., President Kennedy and his team assembled to assess their options. They discussed how to get UN secretary general U Thant to endorse the Johnson plan; when to bring it to the parties; how to move forward with its arrangements; and how to get the two other PCC members, France and Turkey, to agree to it. Getting U Thant to endorse the plan was becoming a major issue. Thant was sceptical about devoting such large amounts of UN money and resources to the establishment of the administrator at the Government House and the compensation funds, when the plan was not even endorsed by the parties it addressed. Without even a UN resolution to back it up, the arrangement would put Thant and the UN in a very vulnerable position.[55] But the crux of the issue remained whether the United States would put its weight behind the plan or not.

In a telling moment, the president himself marvelled at how the Israelis could possibly believe that more than one in ten of the Palestinians would want to return: 'It's like a Negro wanting to go back to Mississippi, isn't it?', Kennedy wondered out loud, to the amusement of the others.[56] In fact, the quip reflects fairly well what by 1962 had become a truism among those American officials and diplomats who worked on Middle East issues: that the Palestinian refugees' stated desire to return was nothing but empty rhetoric. There was no genuine consideration as to whether this was an accurate reading of the Palestinian predicament. Even when these officials were faced with the direct efforts of the refugees to organize themselves to improve their conditions, or to have their voices heard, there is little evidence of any willingness and/or ability to frame any of it in relation to a claim for return. Up until 1962, no decision maker in Washington had even tried to connect these dots.

The American record of the discussion on 27 August is inconclusive. It is therefore difficult to say decidedly what position President Kennedy decided on by the end of the meeting. Fortunately, the Israeli records help shed more light on further developments and from this one can infer that Kennedy's final decision was to continue to be uncommitted to the plan, to stay low and to keep withholding the approval seal of the Oval Office.

On 28 August, the day after the White House meeting, the Israeli embassy sent a report back to Meir at the Foreign Ministry. It reported that 'F' (likely Feldman) had brought Meir's 'request' that the United States should 'not take any action' on the Johnson plan directly to the president, and, importantly, that that the latter had thus decided that the United States was 'not behind the report'.[57] The American administration would instead adopt a 'wait and see' attitude, like Meir had asked them to.[58] For the Israelis, the Johnson plan was a no go: 'Golda believes even more strongly than ever that the Johnson plan is dead and that it is only a question of arranging a suitable burial', an internal Israeli briefing memorandum stated on 30 August.[59] A month later, Meir told

Rusk that not only did Israel oppose the Johnson plan but also found the entire 'concept of repatriation' to be 'unacceptable'.[60]

The Israelis' adamant refusal to allow the Johnson mission any leeway put the United States in a bind. It also reinforced the already existing tensions within the Kennedy administration, between his foreign and his domestic policy advisors. On the one side stood Myer Feldman and on the other, a collection of his foreign policy men, which included Secretary Rusk, Assistant Secretary Talbot, and Robert Komer and Carl Kaysen of the National Security Council (NSC).[61]

Feldman continued to make the case that the president was better off immediately disengaging from the whole plan.[62] Feldman did what he could to promote his view to the president and did not seem to care much about what the president's other advisors thought about it. Feldman's arguments carried weight with Kennedy. Talbot and the State Department was instructed by the White House to lie low on the Johnson plan, since the president did not want 'trouble with American Jewry at this time'.[63] It was especially important that this admittedly general directive was heeded 'between now and the election', the message from the Oval Office concluded.[64]

Feldman's reading of the domestic situation was challenged by Komer and Kaysen at the NSC. 'I don't see how we lose, even domestically, by holding firm a little longer', Komer wrote to Kaysen after the president's instruction to back off the Johnson plan had been issued.[65] Komer also made his case to Kennedy directly: 'For once, [the] Israelis will have a hard time worrying us over domestic repercussions because of [the] Hawk deal', he maintained.[66] If the administration leaked the news of the sale, Israel would have a hard time convincing American Jewish leaders that the US government was not acting in Israel's best interest.

In fact, the Hawk deal was already somewhat out in the open. In an effort to milk the Hawk sale as much as possible in the domestic context, Feldman had advised Kennedy to spread the news to a handful of Jewish American leaders on 13 September to capitalize upon the situation. This way these leaders could include the joyous news in their sermons in the upcoming Jewish High Holidays, starting with Rosh Hashanah on 29 September. According to Feldman and Feinberg, these sermons were instrumental in shaping the Jewish American vote.[67] For Feldman and the president, this was a purely positive outcome. For Komer and Kaysen at the NSC, however, it was a more complex dilemma: If the United States, on top of the news of the Hawk deal, disavowed of the Johnson plan, what consequences would this have for the administration's relationship with the Arab world?[68]

The two did not only worry about the larger regional consequences but reacted strongly also to the very premise of the president's decision and, implicitly, to Feldman's behaviour.[69] That Feldman had the ear of the president in matters concerning Israel was old news by this point, but Kaysen and Komer had never been as frustrated by this as they were by late September. It had reached the point where they were no longer inclined to hold back their opinions about Feldman in front of the president. Feldman shouldn't be the 'sole intermediary' between the president and Washington on something that is 'at least partly foreign policy in nature', Komer quipped bitterly to Kaysen.[70] Next, Kaysen sent a memo to Kennedy spelling out their growing irritation with Feldman's role: 'Part of the problem', he wrote Kennedy, 'is Mike Feldman's tendency to take only the Israeli side of the problem into account'.[71]

The NSC and State Department officers not only found Feldman's domestic analysis to be misguided but also strongly believed that the Israelis were making a huge mistake by refusing to cooperate. Their frustration with Israel was multilayered. On a general level, they still believed that a resolution to the refugee problem was in Israel's genuine best interest: it would improve the atmosphere surrounding the negotiation of an overall settlement of the conflict; it would enhance Israel's security; it would improve Israel's international standing; and it would advance Israel's broader interests. Moreover, UN could move on to tackle other elements of the Arab–Israeli conflict, and one of the Arab states' main complaints against Israel would be neutralized.[72]

In addition, these American officials also thought that the negative consequences that would follow upon an Israeli rejection of the Johnson plan should likewise motivate Israel to acquiesce to it: At the UN, Israel's image would take a beating, making it harder for Israel to gain international support for its causes in the future. And if the Arabs learned that the Israelis were blocking the plan, they would most likely decide to endorse it, thereby gaining the moral high ground. The Arabs could then use this advantageous position to reintroduce their resolution calling for a custodian of the refugees' property in Israel and the issue of the sharing of the Jordan River. The latter was a question of major importance for Israel, and if things played out in this manner, the Americans would have a hard time supporting Israel's position over the Arabs.[73]

Furthermore, the State Department thought Israel should reconsider the consequences of its non-compliance for the Palestinian factor – or the concept of a Palestine entity. The department's fear was that if Israel caused the Johnson plan to fail, it would breathe new life into this already budding movement. Even though they had managed to stymie efforts in this direction so far, the potential 'Algerianization' of the Palestine problem was still viewed by the department as a potentially very harmful. This possibility should worry Israel too, the department argued.[74] The Americans were right to worry about this, of course. The Algerian movement became a model for all national liberation movements in this period, and the Palestinians were no exception.[75]

On a secondary level, the Americans also feared that the Israelis' uncooperative attitude would reflect badly on the United States. Indeed, an 'open rejection' (unilaterally) by Israel in and of itself would be embarrassing, because the United States had done a lot to support Israel: the Americans had come through for Israeli on the issue of withdrawal from Tiberias at the UN, and they had decided to shift their arms policy and sell Israel the Hawk missiles (without any concessions in return).[76] Although few people were aware of it at the time, the United States had even acquiesced to Israel's desire to continue development of the nuclear reactor in Dimona. If it got out that the Israelis had enjoyed support on all these issues and *still* brought down the Johnson plan, the Arabs states would have a 'field day in the UN'.[77]

The problem with the internal American deliberations, however, was that they were based on the idea that the Israeli leadership, at the end of the day, was interested in reaching a deal on the refugee problem. But in Israel, the Johnson plan remained a no go. In fact, Israel had only hardened its position since Johnson took on the mission.[78] The Americans were also wrong to assume that the Israelis did not understand that it was crucial it avoided the blame for the plan's failure. Ever since late August, the Israelis had worked to make sure that Johnson plan was dead, while escaping the responsibility of killing it.[79]

7

The end of the road for the Johnson mission

The American dilemma was by now familiar to the officials working on the Johnson mission: Should the administration come out in support of Johnson and risk the anger of Israel and a potential confrontation with an antagonistic Jewish American community, or should they remain non-committal and evasive and possibly raise the Arab states' suspicion that the United States was caving to Israel's pressure?

At the State Department, the diplomats worried that allowing Israel to publicly sink the Johnson plan would put the Americans' overall Middle East policy in jeopardy.[1] In Secretary Rusk's view, Johnson's proposals and the work put into them had too much value to simply be thrown away.[2] Johnson's proposals were seen as the (potential) 'thin edge of the wedge' that was necessary to split open the whole Arab–Israeli conflict.[3] And although Rusk thought the plan was a 'long shot', he had warned President Kennedy that the alternative – to do nothing – had 'many risks too'.[4]

Kennedy's concerns over potential risks were different though. He was not interested in a fight with American Jewry right before the midterm elections, and so far the administration had been able to help in this regard simply by not saying much at all. But when news of the Johnson plan leaked to the domestic press in early October, it forced upon the Kennedy administration a reassessment of strategy.[5] They could no longer evade taking a clear stand on the plan, but at the same time they needed to take care that their wording doing so did not prompt an abrupt Israeli rejection: 'If it is to be rejected,' Rusk noted in a briefing to the president, 'it must be rejected either by the Arabs and Israel or by the Arabs alone.'[6]

The Arab response to the Johnson plan, however, consisted of a set of objections rather than an outright rejection. After debating different alternatives, the American officials returned to the idea that their best way out of the situation was to 'bargain the Israelis into acceptance'.[7] This would turn out to be an extremely tough sell.

Through a process of negotiations with both Israelis and Arabs, the Americans would work out a set of 'amplifications' or 'clarifications' that would accompany Johnson's ideas.[8] The negotiations would be conducted between Assistant Secretary of Near Eastern Affairs Phil Talbot (with assistance from Assistant Secretary of International Organizations Affairs at the State Department Harlan Cleveland) and Israeli ambassador Avraham Harman.

Since the words 'Johnson plan' were enough to bring down the curtain for the Israeli leadership, Rusk thought it would be more constructive to move beyond the details of the actual plan but to keep its essence:[9] 'I suspect we will end up with something very much like the Johnson Plan', Rusk briefed his State Department officials, but it would need a 'different label'.[10] The actual Johnson plan was gradually pushed to the background, while Feldman's talks with Meir and Ben-Gurion in Jerusalem became the new starting point for this last effort to save the scraps of the Johnson plan.

This, it should be noted, was in great contrast to the approach that the United States took with the Arab states at this time. On 15 October 1962, Syria, Jordan and Lebanon delivered to Johnson a *note verbale*. In it the Arabs stated their scepticism but did not outright reject the plan. Rather, the Arabs told Johnson that they wanted to engage in further explorations of the issues. The reason for this, they stated, was to safeguard Arab interests in general and the principle of paragraph 11 of UNGA Resolution 194 in particular.[11] Rusk instructed the UN delegation to let the Arab foreign ministers know that the United States greatly regretted this development and the fact that the Arabs were insisting on prior assurances in relation to the plan. Internally, however, the American diplomats' analysis of the Arab position was more nuanced: 'We have made more progress with the Arabs in terms of accepting realities than at any time in the past fourteen years', Talbot wrote to Rusk.[12] Nevertheless, while Talbot and his team began engaging the Israeli diplomats in a discussion, trying to bridge their differences on the Johnson plan, the Arab leaders' request for further clarifications was dismissed as 'unreasonable'.[13] In conversations the next day, the Arabs claimed that they had not initially wanted to take such a critical line in their *note verbale*, but that their hand had been forced by the news of the US–Israel Hawks deal.[14]

But why would the Israelis, who had so clearly signalled that the Johnson plan was a no go, agree to further talks on the same basis? First, Israel could ill afford to dismiss the idea out of hand. The diplomatic consequences could be painful. Second, agreeing to engage in quiet talks with the Americans also presented the Israelis with an opportunity to escape the burden of being framed as the obstructing party. Moreover, such talks could do little harm to the Israeli position.[15] In short, Israel had more to lose by declining the Americans' invitation than accepting it.

US–Israel bilateral negotiations: The Harman–Talbot talks

The date 12 October 1962 marked the first of a series of meetings between Israel and the United States, referred to as the Harman–Talbot talks.[16]

One of the main issues the Israelis wanted Harman to address in his talks with Talbot was the Israeli resentment to the concept of 'freedom of choice' for the refugees. 'There can be no such thing as freedom of choice except within an agreed context of 90–10 [per cent]', Harman stated in the first meeting with Talbot.[17] The message was reiterated by Golda Meir. Meir stated that Israel would 'not cooperate in any operation involving expression of refugee preference'.[18] If pressed on this, or on the 90-10 ratio, Israel would, Meir threatened, 'return to its position of pre-1951'.[19]

A second assurance the Israelis wanted from the American diplomats was for the latter to commit to using their power and influence within the PCC to ensure that it did not in any way endorse Johnson's ideas or include them in its annual report. Harman also wanted Talbot to promise that the United States would refrain from endorsing or mentioning the Johnson proposal in any way, if the American delegation were to present a draft resolution to the UN General Assembly that autumn. Moreover, Harman wanted the United States to leave the Johnson plan out of all its speeches to the assembly. Israeli and American interests converged somewhat on this point. Because the plan, and indeed Johnson's very name, had become so unpalatable to Israel (and Kennedy thus far remained uncommitted), the American diplomats realized that if they really were intent upon keeping certain elements of the plan alive for future talks, they had to relabel the whole initiative. Internally, Secretary Rusk referred to this as the 'metamorphosis' of the Johnson mission.[20]

Finally, Israel wanted the Americans to agree to make sure that any potential Arab UN draft resolutions were kept from being tabled at the assembly. Failing that, the Americans needed to promise that they would vote no on any tabled resolutions and furthermore use their influence at the UN to get others to do the same.[21]

By the end of November and after several bilateral meetings, the American diplomats presented to the Israelis a so-called 'package' deal. As indicated, the deal promised that the United States would heed Israel's request and not endorse or refer to the Johnson plan in any way at the UN General Assembly. The Americans could not promise, however, to eliminate all references to Resolution 194. Indeed, because it was unavoidable that a potential new UNGA resolution called for the continuation of the PCC, it was impossible to omit reference to paragraph 11 as well – since it after all was the very basis of the establishment of the commission.[22] Additionally, constructing a resolution without the customary reference to Resolution 194 would cause an extended debate at the UN Special Committee, which was exactly what the Americans were hoping to avoid. That would in turn provide the Arab states with the opportunity to suggest amendments that would certainly include the reference to paragraph 11 but in a likely more aggressive way. It was better to keep a lid on all this and simply refer to the resolution in the first place, the Americans argued. After further Israeli protestation, the Americans assured Israel that the reference to the resolution would be kept descriptive only. The Americans reassured the Israelis that it was neither in their interest to add 'a gram of anything' to the legislative history of the refugee resolution.[23]

In all, though, the American diplomats felt that the deal they had offered Israel was giving Israel 'practically everything' that it wanted. It was an 'excellent package' that Israel should appreciate. In fact, the American diplomats expected the Israeli government to be 'ecstatic' about it.[24] Far from it, the Israeli response would be better described as evasive. Disgruntled American diplomats laconically summarized the Israeli policy: 'We'll talk but don't expect any give or flexibility in our stand.'[25]

Despite their own perception of having presented the Israelis with a generous deal, the State Department officials understood that if they were to stand a chance getting Israel to agree to their proposal, they would need President Kennedy's personal involvement.[26] After the Middle East meeting at the White House in late August, the president and his administration had been busied with other, more pressing matters. The autumn of 1962 had been dominated by the Cuba Crisis, and it was therefore not surprising that Kennedy thus far had been otherwise occupied. Now that that the crisis was resolved, however, the State Department needed clarifications regarding which direction Kennedy wanted to take US Palestine policy. Could the department officers convince the president that it was time for him to step up to the plate? Once again, the department officers feared interference from Feldman. Having recently returned from another new trip to Israel, Feldman was known to be as 'anti-Johnson Plan as ever' and liable to 'stick in a few more knives' into the plan.[27]

A tug of war in Washington, D.C.

Komer, Kaysen and the State Department officials' chase for the president's attention was further complicated by the Kennedy White House's general discontent with the department. Kennedy had come to the presidency with mixed feelings about the foreign policy establishment based at Foggy Bottom, which he saw as full of 'career boys'. The notion was that the department commanded loyalty and adherence to established policy, while people with strong views of their own tended to be divested from the service after a while. To be a 'career boy', then, implied that one understood and accepted the internal rules of the game and seldom, if ever, questioned the policy or the opinion of higher-ranking officers.[28] This must have been a particularly fatal flaw in the context of the new frontiersmen's ambitions for a dynamic and Socratic policymaking administration. Although perhaps not on par with Truman's level of animosity towards the 'striped-pants boys', Kennedy's impression of Foreign Service officers was that they generally knew too little about the nations to which they had been assigned, were indifferent to the language and customs of other places and 'spent too much time at tennis and cocktails'.[29]

On a systemic level, those in the Kennedy White House also had a severe antipathy towards the bureaucratic 'layering' of the department, which they thought slowed down the process of policymaking considerably.[30] This tension had only been exacerbated over the course of Kennedy's first few months in office, where he felt let down by the department in its treatment in the Bay of Pigs Crisis, the situation in Laos and what Kennedy's biographer and fellow new frontiersman, Schlesinger, called the 'maddening delay' in answering Nikita Khrushchev's *aide memoire* before the Berlin Crisis erupted fully.[31]

The dislike and the disdain for the career diplomats were evident in both the rhetoric and practice of the Kennedy administration. According to Arthur M. Schlesinger, Jr, a senior aide and close friend of Kennedy, the president dreamed of establishing 'a secret office of thirty people to run foreign policy while maintaining the State Department as a façade in which people might contentedly carry papers from bureau to bureau'.[32] Kennedy's dream was never realized of course, but he did boost the NSC's role at the expense of the State Department and the NSC staff became 'indispensable' to him. The NSC staff was streamlined from seventy-one to forty-eight people, who were instructed to replace what traditionally had been long and detailed policy papers with 'crisp and timely' National Security Action Memoranda (NSAMs). The name of the game was 'action' over 'planning'.[33] Under the leadership of the influential and powerful McGeorge (Mac) Bundy – one of 'the best and the brightest' – these men played a central part in the shaping of the Kennedy administration's foreign policy.[34]

Komer and Kaysen, as part of the trusted NSC staff, knew and understood their president's antipathy towards the State Department. They figured that if the department's view, which in this particular case they actually agreed with, were to stand a chance of getting through to the president, it needed to be stripped of what they referred to as 'state prose'.[35] Reportedly, this type of prose 'just kind of slid along' and was not 'crisp' and 'well reasoned', like the advice Kennedy received from his team of advisors inside the White House.[36]

For Komer and Kaysen, though, this was about something more than the White House versus the State Department. For them, it was really a question of what factors in US political life should drive Kennedy's Middle East policy. Should Kennedy be guided by the advice of his team of foreign policy experts, or should he listen to dictates derived from the 'the political behavior of the Jewish American community'?[37] The two advisors were done hiding their opposition to Myer Feldman and what deemed to be his outsized influence on the president's policy.

Feldman had 'shortcomings as both reporter and intermediary' in his consultations with the Israelis, Komer wrote. Feldman's domestic political calculations could therefore very well be wrong.[38] If the Johnson plan worked, Komer argued, it would be so beneficial to Israel that it would give the administration a chance to 'reap major domestic gains'.[39] Moreover, if Kennedy continued to follow Feldman's advice and do nothing, the refugee problem would likely become an 'increasing irritant' in the US–Israel relationship. This would be a negative development in and of itself, but it had potentially larger implications as well: increased animosity between the United States and Israel would potentially boost the Arab states' position at the UN, which might incline the Arab delegations to solicit US action on various issues, not all of which the administration would be able to avoid or reject. If this happened, Kennedy would again face disappointed voters from the ranks of those who always expected the United States to be as pro-Israel as possible. In other words, Kaysen painted an alternative picture for Kennedy where *not* supporting Johnson's efforts would instigate a domino-like process with consequences both domestic *and* international.[40]

Kaysen and Komer directly urged Kennedy to look past Feldman and exploit the freedom to manoeuvre that successful midterm elections had given him, by moving 'swiftly' to implement Johnson's proposals.[41] 'We all know the real reason why we hesitate to push the Johnson Plan', Komer wrote Bundy. 'But now, just after the elections, is the time when we can exert the maximum leverage on Israel at minimum political cost.'[42] To move ahead, Komer told the president, 'We have to do something we have never done before … we have to pressure Israel to come around.'[43] His advice went unheeded.

The two State Department officials failed swaying their president's mind on the matter. On 9 December 1962, four days after Komer wrote to Kennedy, the United States and Israel reached a final seven-point agreement referred to as the 'presidential package deal'.[44] In it, the United States agreed to keep the Johnson plan out of the main body of the annual PCC report, to guarantee that the PCC would not refer to or endorse Johnson's proposals (or any of their elements) and to only allow Johnson to attach his proposals to the PCC report if they were formulated them in a 'non-substantive' way.[45]

The United States would further work to discourage everyone from raising Johnson's proposals in the general debate in the assembly, and if someone else did, the United States would not support these statements, no matter what. (Israel, for its part, would refrain from criticizing Johnson personally in this context.) And if the United States felt it necessary to introduce a draft resolution of its own (which, as discussed, was their default way out of the vice-like grip of the General Assembly debate), this too would refrain from referring to any of the elements in the Johnson plan. In addition, the United

States committed to only referring to paragraph 11 in a passive manner – for example, in the context of past activities of the PCC. Paragraph 11 was not to be part of any description of future activity or of the continuation of any discussions between the parties. This 'doctrine of non-reference' applied both to any related America statement and to the text of any related American draft resolution. If any amendment proposed for the US resolution text *did* include an active reference to paragraph 11, the United States would vote against it or 'do its best to defeat it'.[46] The United States also committed to voting against any Arab resolution proposals suggesting the establishment of a UN custodian for the refugees' property in Israel as well as any suggestion for reconfiguring the PCC.[47] In return, Israel would make sure that the Brazzaville resolution calling for direct negotiations was not pushed to a vote that year and promised to discuss it with the United States before taking any action to promote it again in the following spring's assembly. Last, Israel pledged to continue bilateral talks with the United States on the 'substance of the refugee problem'.[48] To this latter point, however, Israel had attached the sweeping conditions that these talks would not be based on paragraph 11 or the terms of reference of the PCC or any of the 'Johnsonian devices' – in particular, the use of a questionnaire or a poll to ask the refugees about their preferences.[49]

In the end, the presidential package worked in favour of both the United States and Israel, neither of which suffered directly from events in the 1962 General Assembly debate on the Palestine problem. The Americans avoided the Arab states' call for a custodian for property rights and the Brazzaville resolution's call for direct negotiations. They also avoided having a big debate in the General Assembly about the Johnson plan. This was an important step towards diffusing responsibility for the mission's failure. Technically, this was an Israeli concession from the Harman–Talbot talks, but in reality, it had no particular cost to the Israelis. Indeed, the opposite was true. Israel understood that it would not be good to be left with all the blame, while the Arab side emerged as the more flexible party. For the Israelis to withhold their public criticism of the plan was, strictly speaking, as much in their interest as in the American diplomats'.

The United States under the leadership of John F. Kennedy had been a generous and supportive friend to Israel – in the words of Komer, this ministration had 'done more to satisfy Israeli security preoccupations than any of its predecessors'.[50] Komer's point is well illustrated by the list of what Israel had obtained from the administration over the course of its first two years. Even before the Harman–Talbot talks, Israel had been promised the Hawks they had sought for so long.[51] They had also been assured of the US support on the Jordan River issue which was due to appear on the 1963 fall agenda of the General Assembly. Finally, Israel had been given increased economic aid and various other security assurances. According to himself, Feldman was instrumental also in respect to increased aid. He apparently single-handedly convinced the president to up the annual aid from 10 million dollars – the State Department's highest bid – to 45 million dollars. Feldman brought before the president the reasoning of the Israeli ambassador and added a few of his own thoughts, admittedly 'more emotional, perhaps'. At the end of Feldman's briefing, which went on for ten minutes, Kennedy allegedly told Feldman, 'Okay, forty-five million dollars. You tell them.'[52] What had the United States gotten in return for all of this? Virtually nothing: 'The score is 4-0' in Israel's favour, Komer summed up.[53] Indeed, it was a 'grand slam' for Israel, Governor Adlai Stevenson noted from his position on the UN delegation in New York.[54]

To this list of political goals achieved by Israel, one could also add the establishment and development of the nuclear reactor in the Israeli city of Dimona, in the Negev desert.[55] This is a clear indication of how unwilling Kennedy was to challenge Israel about anything once he was in office. As a campaigning senator and as president, Kennedy had talked at length about the need to strengthen non-proliferation efforts in general and to secure a Nuclear Test Ban Treaty (NTBT) in particular. In August 1963, Secretary of State Rusk signed the limited test ban treaty on behalf of the United States, together with Andrei Gromyko of the Soviet Union and Alec Douglas-Home of the UK – the treaty had been a priority ever since Kennedy met with Khrushchev in Vienna in June 1961. Reaching such an agreement with the Soviet premier was high on Kennedy's foreign policy agenda, among other things because it would reduce the risk of new countries going nuclear.[56] 'I am haunted', the president said in March 1962, 'by the feeling that by 1970, unless we are successful [in the Nuclear Test Ban Treaty negotiations], there may be ten nuclear powers instead of four ... I regard that as the greatest possible danger'.[57]

While Kennedy preached non-proliferation, however, Israel was busy completing its new nuclear reactor in Dimona. With French support, it had been building the nuclear centre since 1958 – a fact that had escaped the Americans for about two years. Only on December 21 did the story finally break in a *New York Times* article. When the Americans first realized that the reactor in Dimona was real, it appeared perfectly clear that a nuclear Israel collided head on with US wider Middle East policy and its global non-proliferation policy. When the Kennedy administration expressed its concern to the Israelis, though, there was little sympathy. According to then US ambassador to Israel Walworth Barbour, the Israelis simply shrugged and told the Americans, 'Well, this isn't your business. You don't have anything to do with it. The French gave it to us, so whoa.'[58]

The Israelis maintained that the plant was for strictly peaceful purposes, just like the smaller one in Soreq. The Americans, unwilling to take their word for it, started to press the Israelis to allow inspection trips, which they did in the end, albeit after much hesitation and diversions. Significantly, the agreement to allow annual inspections did not arrive until the summer of 1963, when Kennedy took Israel to task for the first time for its evasiveness on the nuclear issue.[59] In the period leading up to this point, and even after the agreement was in place, Israel granted only limited access to the inspectors and concealed key parts of the program as well.[60] Knowing that Israel despite this was allowed to continue its program, without any significant protest from the Americans (until 1963), it is certainly not unreasonable to assume that the Israelis were not too worried about the US pressure for Israel to comply with the refugee initiative. The Israelis clearly felt that they could do more or less what they wanted when it came to the Johnson plan. Kennedy's White House would be spending no political capital on the Johnson mission's fate.

A bitter representative and a special relationship

With the development in the General Assembly debate throughout the late autumn and winter of 1962, it was evident to all that the Johnson mission had reached its final stage. And on 1 February 1963, Johnson formally resigned as the PCC's special representative.[61] Five days later Kennedy commended him for his efforts.[62] It was not enough for Johnson. He remained disappointed at the lack of support his mission had received from Washington D.C. In his resignation letter to the UN, Johnson laconically stated that although he felt he had made some real progress in terms of thinking about how UNGA Resolution 194's key paragraph, number 11, should and could be implemented some twelve years after it was first passed, there was a limit to what he could practically do as a single individual representing the commission. He felt that he had taken the problem 'as far as is practicable'. He concluded his letter by stating that in his mind, paragraph 11 remained the 'proper basis for an equitable resolution of the tragic human problem of the Arab refugee'.[63]

Off the record, Johnson was less diplomatic. He was bitter at the administration for not having backed him up more when the Israelis refused to talk directly with him in the autumn of 1962. It was not the first time that a US envoy was let down in this way, of course. Mark Etheridge came to pretty much the same conclusion as Johnson following the process he led in 1949. But the disappointment Johnson felt towards his government was nothing compared to the bitterness he harboured towards the Jewish American leaders, who he claimed had been misled about the details of his proposals by Israel. These leaders had then 'continued [to] successfully frustrate attempts [to] reach [a] compromise solution', Johnson complained to the department upon resigning from his position.[64] This was the prevailing perspective at Foggy Bottom too. In a briefing memorandum to Rusk, Talbot and Cleveland both lamented the 'strong campaign' that the Jewish community had conducted against Johnson's proposals, 'severely distorting the true nature of the Plan'.[65] Johnson felt that, as a PCC member, the United States 'owed it to him' to step up and work at putting the record straight whenever they could.[66]

At the State Department, some officials tried to boost Johnson's morale. His plan and the proposals, they said, had 'a great deal of value'. Even the problem of the misinformed Jewish leadership would be possible to overcome, they thought, and to this end the officials suggested that Johnson might consider writing about his mission in a public high-profile magazine, for example *Foreign Affairs*, once he had officially resigned from the PCC. On a more general level, Johnson and the department officers wondered how long these Jewish Americans could keep up their support for the 'present intransigent Israel[i] position on the refugees'. It did not seem, to them, to be consistent 'with the best traditions of Jewish humanitarianism'.[67]

Several years after the plan was buried, in 1966, Johnson did in fact write an article on his mission and its basic recommendations and proposals. In addition to describing his lessons learned and thoughts about a solution, the article, published in the *Middle East Journal*, voiced some of his bitterness. He slammed the 'inaccurate, misleading, even untrue reports' that had circulated in Jewish American circles in the summer and autumn of 1962 and made no secret about how detrimental they had been for his mission.[68]

On 27 December 1962, with the General Assembly session behind them and the presidential package agreement to continue bilateral talks on the refugee issue in place, Foreign Minister Meir and President Kennedy met in Florida to talk about US–Israel relations and regional and global challenges. The record of this conversation continues to demonstrate Kennedy's clear reluctance to put pressure on Israel for it to make a concession on the refugee question. Instead, Kennedy told Meir that he 'fully realized' that Israel could not accept a 'flood of embittered refugees'.[69] According to Meir's account of this meeting, Kennedy leaned over to her, took her hand and told her: 'Don't worry. *Nothing* will happen to Israel.'[70] In fact, Kennedy 'did not expect' that Israel 'could be more forthcoming on the refugees' than what it had indicated to this point.[71] Gathering from all of this that Israel's position was safe, Meir seems to have concluded that she could afford to portray herself and Israel as at least open to discussion. Recalling Ben-Gurion's pledge to Kennedy at the Waldorf–Astoria meeting back in May 1961, she noted that although Israel did not expect the Arab countries to cooperate, Israel's position was 'by all means try'.[72]

If Kennedy had asked Johnson, or Talbot and Komer (who both sat in on the meeting with Meir), what this really meant, the experience of these men over the last eighteen months would likely have led them to translate Meir's message for him as follows: By all means *you* try, but we will not budge an inch. It is easy to see why Israel maintained this posturing, of course, because to this point it had cost nothing to do so. And for a country that seemingly had no desire – or need – to move past the status quo, it was a rational position as well.

The next reminder that Israel intended to give nary and inch came about a month later, in late January 1963. The US ambassador to Israel William Barbour had just met with Prime Minster Ben-Gurion to follow-up on the Florida meeting between Kennedy and Meir. After the meeting, Ben-Gurion sent a message to clarify Israel's position to Barbour. 'My dear ambassador', he began, 'I forgot to mention yesterday one point which perhaps goes without saying: namely, that [it] is the withdrawal of the Johnson plan – and that alone – which makes talks between us possible on tackling and solving the refugee problem.'[73] Barbour and the department were dumbfounded. Was it not part of the president's package deal that Israel had agreed to enter bilateral talks *without* any further preconditions? Yes, the Americans had agreed that the

Johnson plan as such was dead, but this did not mean that its proposals were *automatically* off the table.[74] Ben-Gurion's letter appeared to 'lay down rules so restrictive as to preclude any progress', Talbot and Cleveland despaired.[75] This time, the State Department received the White House's blessing to charge the Israelis with this inconsistency in the form of a letter from Kennedy to Ben-Gurion.[76]

But the White House was not prepared to do much more than this. According to Feldman, Kennedy had by 1963 'given up' on his hope to 'use the refugees as the key to peace in the Middle East'.[77] The failure of the Johnson mission marked the last US effort to resolve the Palestinian refugee problem separately from an overall Arab–Israeli settlement.

The 1967 War:
Changed parameters of the
Arab–Israeli conflict

With the assassination of John F. Kennedy and Lyndon B. Johnson's entry into the White House, US attention to solving the refugee problem came to an end. The Johnson administration took the developing 'special relationship' between the United States and Israel to new lengths. Johnson, a Texas Democrat, was well known for his strong sympathies towards Israel, and he surrounded himself with like advisors. Johnson was fundamentally uninterested in the fate of the Palestinian refugees and of the politics of the Palestinian struggle, and his 1964 re-election was based on a Democratic Party platform that officially pledged to 'encourage the resettlement of Arab refugees in lands where there is room and opportunity'.[1] Johnson spent little time and political capital on Middle East peacemaking. Indeed, it was not until events in the region forced his administration's hand that President Johnson in any substantial way approached the Arab–Israeli conflict.

While Johnson and the Democratic Party looked the other way, the Palestinians, for the first time since the 1948 War and their displacement, managed to shift some of the momentum and power from the Arab states and back to themselves. Both the Kennedy and the Eisenhower administrations had feared the establishment of a Palestinian 'entity' and done their utmost to quell this movement whenever it appeared on their radars. By 1964, however, and on President Johnson's watch, the Palestinian entity was no longer just a concept but an evolving reality.[2]

In 1964, the Palestine Liberation Organization (PLO) was established at the Arab summit in Cairo in 1964, and Ahmed Shuqayri became its first chairman.[3] Though by word and declaration this move might have seemed like an Arab act of strengthening Palestinians self-determination, the reality was that it was just another move to try to 'co-opt and restrain' the Palestinian resistance movement.[4] The Arab leaders were terrified that Palestinian guerrilla organizations, among which Fatah was the most important, would end up pulling them into an unwanted war with Israel. Here again, though, the Arab states were not united, and in the end Syria broke with Egypt and Jordan and actively supported Fatah's commando operations into Israel. Throughout 1966 and the spring of 1967, Fatah mounted numerous operations along Israel's borders both to the east towards Jordan and to the north towards Syria.[5]

This development reflected a new dynamic in intra-Arab politics. For years following the events of 1948, the Arab regimes had exploited the Palestinian issue in their regional rivalries. This changed as the Palestinian national movement began to gain momentum, forcing the Arab states to see the Palestinians as an independent actor on the regional stage.[6] The Palestinian guerrillas, or *fedayeen*, were largely successful in their tactic of egging the Israelis on.[7] In the summer and autumn of 1967, then, a pattern of Palestinian commando raids and Israeli retaliations emerged. Fatah launched attacks from Jordan, and armed clashes took place on the Israeli–Syrian border as well. This volatile situation, coupled with Nasser's decision to expel the UNEF force from Sinai in May 1967 and the closing of the Tiran Strait about a week later, made it clear that the region was yet again plunging into war.[8]

The 1967 War did not result from any deliberate planning on the part of its participants.[9] None of the actors had generated grand schemes or war plans, and no one was able to fully control the conflict's progress or outcome.[10] The 1967 War became yet another illustration of the fact that the Arab states could not act either separately or collectively – instead, they kept 'getting in one another's way'.[11] None of the two superpowers intervened to halt the escalation. Neither the United States nor the Soviet Union acted to stop the war from erupting. The Soviet Union's contribution was to leak an erroneous intelligence brief to Egypt, stating that Israeli troops were mobilizing in the Sinai desert. The Johnson administration, after much back and forth, ended up giving Israel the infamous 'yellow light' for its pre-emptive strike on Egypt.[12]

On 5 June 1967, Israeli jets set course for Egypt. Their orders were to 'fly, soar at the enemy, destroy him and scatter him throughout the desert so that Israel may live, secure in its land, for generations'.[13] At least the first half of these orders was accomplished: within three hours most of the Egyptian

Air Force was wiped out. For the next five days, the Israeli Defence Forces continued to press ahead, and by the end of the sixth day, they had won the 'most spectacular military victory' in the history of the state.[14]

When the guns fell silent on 10 June 1967, the frontiers of the Middle East were redrawn in more ways than one. In the most literal sense, the war undid the armistice lines of 1949: Israel now occupied the Sinai Peninsula, the Golan Heights, Gaza Strip and the West Bank, including East Jerusalem – a territorial expansion that more than doubled the original Israeli territory of the November 1947 Partition Plan. Sinai and the Golan Heights, neither of which was part of Palestine, were important mainly for military strategic purposes. The Gaza Strip, the West Bank and East Jerusalem, on the other hand, were all parts of the original mandate of Palestine and were all of significant emotional, symbolic and religious significance.[15]

Israel moved quickly to annex and make East Jerusalem a permanent part of the state. Only a few weeks after the war was over, on 27 June, the Israeli Knesset passed legislation that gave the city a legal status that was different from the West Bank. Before the 1967 War, East Jerusalem had been an integral part of the West Bank and under Jordanian control. By decreeing its separateness, Israel could place the entire city of Jerusalem under Israeli law and administration – a move that caused international protest at the time, and that remains deeply contested to this day.[16] For Israel, the West Bank and the Gaza Strip were a welcome territorial addition. They faced a problem, though, with the large Palestinian population that lived on these lands.[17] In this lay the dual ambition of the post-1967 War Israel: the desire to keep as much of the newly acquired territories as possible while minimizing the number of Palestinians living in them.[18]

In terms of the Palestinian refugee problem, it only enlarged during the 1967 War. For the Palestinians, the war represented a second catastrophe or 'setback' – *al Naksa* in Arabic.[19] In total, over 320,000 additional Palestinians fled or were expelled from the West Bank and Gaza.[20] The international diplomatic focus would be on territories, however, not people.

Land for peace and the Palestinian national movement

Among the many folders of papers from Joseph Johnson, President Kennedy's special representative, that has been deposited at the Herbert Hoover

Presidential Library lies an editorial from the *Richmond Times-Dispatch* dated 11 June 1967, the day the 1967 War ended. Its headline reads, 'Begin with the Refugees' and goes on to state that if peace were ever to come to the Middle East, a start had to be made towards a solution for this 'festering problem'.[21] Though Johnson had ended his mission in 1962, the saved news clipping suggests that he still followed the matter and the regional developments.

Perhaps he also saved this particular editorial because it was speaking to what in essence had been his guiding analysis during the months that he was tasked with Arab–Israeli peacemaking. His opinion had been that the refugee issue should be addressed and prioritized in Arab–Israeli peacemaking efforts. This could not, though, be further from the approach that the international community took in the aftermath of the 1967 War. There was some initial hope in London and Washington, D.C., that the new circumstances created by the war – more than 50 per cent of the 1948 refugees were now living in territories occupied by Israel – could be leveraged in the interest of a solution to the problem. But it soon became clear that territories, not people, would take centre stage in the post-war peacemaking efforts. Arieh Kochavi writes, however, that during the first weeks after the war, both Britain and the United States considered a solution to the refugee problem as the main goal. One of the possibilities mentioned in this regard was even the revival of the Johnson plan.[22] In the ensuing summer months and throughout the autumn of 1967, the UN took to trying to find a way to stabilize the situation. The result of that diplomatic activity arrived on 22 November, when the UN Security Council passed Resolution 242.[23]

In the words of historian Avi Shlaim, UNSC Resolution 242 was a 'masterpiece of deliberate British ambiguity' that in this way secured the necessary support of all of the relevant countries, including both superpowers, Israel, Jordan and Egypt (though not Syria).[24] The very heart of that ambiguity, and the reason why the resolution could be carried by the Security Council, was a pointed omission of the definite article – 'the' – in the text. Rather than asking Israel to withdraw 'from *the* territories occupied in the recent conflict', which would refer to all of the territories taken from the Arab states during the war, Resolution 242 called for Israel to merely withdraw 'from territories occupied'.

Resolution 242 also requested the UN to designate a special representative to promote a peaceful settlement to the conflict, in keeping with the 'provisions and principles' of the resolution. The very next day, on 23 November 1967, UN secretary general U Thant announced that the man chosen for this mission was Swedish diplomat Gunnar Jarring. Jarring's mission would end in April 1969, and it produced no real progress.[25] Because the most important issues of the larger Middle East negotiations were territorial, Resolution 242 was insufficient to propel Jarring's mission. It merely called for a 'just settlement' to the refugee problem.[26] There was no part of the settlement machinery under Resolution 242 that dealt with the Palestinians as other than refugees.[27]

If the Palestinian refugee issue had been the main topic for the UN in the aftermath of the war in 1948, the Israeli occupation was what dominated after 1967. The fate of the Arab territory captured by Israel in the 1948 War and the fate of the refugees from that same war were reduced to 'secondary' status.[28] Under the new formula – 'land-for-peace' – there was no space left for the Palestinian refugee problem. Indeed, as historian Mark Tessler notes, even if Jarring had been successful in his endeavours, the Palestinian dimension of the conflict would not have risen to the surface, because his mission was based on the assumption that peace could be achieved only if the parties agreed to return to the situation before the June War.[29] Yet the issues and political grievances from 1948 had not vanished, and indeed, opaque as this might have been at the time, Palestinians political aspirations were still at the core of the Arab–Israeli conflict, as was increasingly apparent also from the general upswing in the prominence of the Palestinian nationalist movement.[30]

In the 1950s and early 1960s, the Palestinians had not sought national liberation outside the system of their Arab host states. Mostly, they had joined Arab opposition groups and nursed the hope that new Arab leaders would come to power and seek the liberation of Palestine. Historian Yezid Sayigh notes that this is in large part was explained by the enduring strength of the Palestinian support for Nasser and his pan-Arab ideology.[31] But by the mid-1960s, this was all starting to change. Palestinians in exile were fed up with subordinating their needs and rights to those of the Arab regimes.[32] And with the humiliating Arab defeat of June 1967, the Palestinian guerrillas' suspicions, ever since the UAR fell to pieces in the summer of 1961, were finally confirmed: the Arab states would never be united or able enough to fight for the Palestinians' cause. The Palestinians needed to take matters into their own hands and become 'masters of their own fate'.[33]

The PLO, which the Arab states had established in 1964 to try keep the Palestinian national movement under their continued control, had not turned out as expected. Its appointed chairman, Ahmad Shuqayri, had 'substantially exceeded' the mandate given to him by the Arab leaders and moved swiftly to establish a more autonomous structure.[34] Shuqayri had created a 'statelike body' that boasted a constitution, an executive, a legislative assembly, a set of government departments, an army (the Palestine Liberation Army), an audited budget and internal charter statutes.[35] And while all of this might have been more than what the Arab regimes wanted, it was still not enough for Shuqauri's fellow Palestinians. Within the PLO, *Fatah* emerged as the most dominant Palestinian political party in the aftermath of the 1967 War. With the Battle of Karameh in Jordan in 1968, among the most important battles in the folklore of the Palestinian resistance, the Palestinian guerrilla movement claimed its place as the number one actor in the Palestinian struggle.

In the winter and spring of 1968, the IDF moved to attack Palestinian guerrilla positions east of the Jordan River. On 21 March, they faced in the Jordanian village of Karameh. The heavily outnumbered Fatah men managed to inflict substantial damage and casualties on the stronger Israeli forces. To this day, this fight remains surrounded by myths about the scale of Fatah's win over the Israeli forces. And even though many more Palestinians were killed at Karameh, the battle propelled Fatah – and its founder Yasser Arafat – to the front of the Palestinian nationalist movement.[36]

The most remarkable fact about the Johnson administration's Middle East policy was its 'almost complete blindness' to the rise of this Palestinian national movement and the PLO right under its nose.[37] Having said that, Johnson's administration was not alone in this. All of the previous administrations since 1948 – Democratic or Republican – had failed to fully grasp the essence of the Palestinian grievances and struggle. Within the American foreign policy establishment, there was a common belief that the Palestinians could not possibly *want* to return. The cry for repatriation was seen as nothing more than an empty slogan, and default US policy had been to regard the Palestinian problem as a 'refugee and a Jordanian problem'.[38] One notable exception to this general dismissal of the Palestinians was National Security Council official Harold (Hal) Saunders, who in 1968 voiced a critical questioning of the whole US approach. Saunders argued that the United States might be better off mounting a 'major campaign' in favour of a refugee settlement, removing the issue from the post-1967 War negotiations led by Jarring. Saunders thought this action had the great benefit of removing the most symbolic Arab grievance from the overall conflict. But Sauder's thinking was atypical. The general thinking in the American foreign policy establishment was better reflected in the so-called '90 days action paper' that was written in late November 1968 as a brief for the incoming secretary of state, William P. Rogers. The paper set out the US position on the Arab–Israeli problem and the search for a peace settlement, and it did not mention the Palestinian dimension at all.[39]

US Palestine policy readjusted?

Only by the end of 1970, the Americans seemed to be coming to grips with the inadequacy of this analysis. There was a growing recognition among members of the American public, including their politicians in the US Congress, of the Palestinians as more than just refugees.[40] The *fedayeen* movement despite its small size had placed the Palestinian struggle on the front pages and had made it a political force to be reckoned with in the Arab world.[41]

The Jordanian Black September – King Hussein's violent crackdown on the flourishing Palestinian guerrilla movement – made the US State Department seriously question whether leaders of established Arab states, particularly King Hussein, could 'commit themselves to a peace agreement with Israel without the assent of the organized Palestinians'.[42] 'Since the Palestinians have become more able to influence events and are asserting their right to determine their own future', a State Department briefing paper stated, 'We have become increasingly aware of a possible imbalance in our approach to the problem.'[43] This 'imbalance' was manifesting itself on several levels, but the most important was that the United States still did not have any established channels to the Palestinians – no means of tapping into the mood and aspirations of the Palestinian nationalist movement. While Israel's interests were 'fully reflected in intergovernmental negotiations', the paper went on to admit, a 'significant element on the Arab side – the Palestinians – is not'.[44]

Reasons for and against readjusting the Americans' Palestine policy were listed. In the 'pro' column, the fundamental point touched on the fact that the very premise of the American reading of the conflict should change:

> The problem of the Palestinians is no longer just a problem of refugee resettlement ... it now has a political dimension that must be dealt with if there is to be a viable settlement. This is the reasoning for a move at the present time to involve the Palestinians in the political process of negotiating a settlement.[45]

What had been almost unspeakable some eight years before – the establishment of a 'Palestine entity' – during Johnson's mission was suddenly being seriously discussed as an alternative option for a refocused US policy.[46]

After two decades locked in the humanitarian box, the Palestine refugee problem was, for the first time, being understood as part of a larger *political* context.[47] Gradually taking hold at the US State Department was the idea that the Palestine problem might in fact be the 'missing link of the Arab-Israeli puzzle'.[48] New tendencies in American strategic thinking began to arise:

> A real Arab-Israeli settlement would be an agreement on the final disposition of the Palestine mandate and of the persons displaced in the process of its partition. The issue is whether, after 20 years, the final partition of Palestine is to be accepted.[49]

These proposals arguing for a new US Palestine policy were never adopted by the Nixon administration, and the United States eventually decided to rather renew their strong support for King Hussein and Jordan. Nonetheless, the arguments made *for* the US support of the formal establishment of such a Palestine entity did signal a significant shift from the line that had dominated since 1948.[50]

Still, the diplomatic process continued to lead nowhere, and Israel was not about to give up its newly acquired territorial control. In the period after the 1967 War, the US consulate in Jerusalem reported that they kept hearing talk about the Israeli government's tactic of 'creating facts' on the ground.[51] At its core, the tactic aimed to 'sculpt' the reality on the ground, before serious negotiations about that reality even begin.[52] Though the consulate at the time thought it unreasonable to assume that this constituted a 'leitmotif in Israeli thinking', it would soon become clear that this tactic was precisely what has allowed Israel to refuse to withdraw from the occupied Palestinian territories and instead gradually consolidate its control there.[53] In fact, this has remained a main pillar of Israel's settlement project and its policy towards the occupied territories to this day.[54] By massive settlement expansion and the gradual introduction of Israeli administration, jurisdiction and law in the territories, this 'creeping annexation' of the land has long added significant obstacles to the national aspirations of the Palestinian people.[55] More than 70 years after the creation of the Palestinian refugee problem, this lack of Palestinian statehood is ultimately also closely connected to the lack of a solution to the fate of the refugees.

Conclusion

There is no one single explanation as to why international diplomacy failed to find a solution to the Palestinian refugee issue in the first two decades of the Arab–Israeli conflict. The diplomatic efforts and initiatives documented throughout this book show how the international community thought about the refugee problem from its origin and until after the 1967 War and shed light on how this thinking developed.

In the post-war world order of bipolarity, it was decidedly the Western superpower that was most involved. Both within the UN system and outside it, the United States was the most important and most involved actor in the international community. That the United States was a superpower had scant effect, however, on the parties relevant to the solution of the Palestinian refugee problem. In fact, one factor that stands out as particularly significant in explaining the failure of international diplomacy to solve the refugee problem is the very limited influence that the United States had on the Lilliput state of Israel. For observers of the today's political climate, this observation comes perhaps as no surprise, but it's important to recall that the events and episodes discussed herein took place in the formative years of the state of Israel. At war with all its neighbours and facing huge financial, political and military challenges, Israel was a truly vulnerable nation state in its youth. Despite this, the United States – with all its potential cultural, military and economic leverage – seemed to be unable to influence this young state's decisions and foreign-policy behaviour in any substantial way. What explains this remarkable state of affairs?

In analysing the dynamic in US–Israel relations, one cannot get around the domestic US dimensions of the relationship.[1] The mid-1970s has been defined as the benchmark for the entry of a 'uniquely disciplined and tactically superb actor' onto the US domestic scene in the pro-Israeli 'lobby'.[2] But as this book has shown, the weight of such domestic factors in US politics was substantial even during the early years of Israel's existence. While most of the story told here comes before the emergence of the American Israel Public Affairs Committee (AIPAC), it is beyond any doubt that the active involvement of the Jewish American community played a role in shaping US policies towards the region and the Palestinian question also before that time.

On occasion, especially when there were issues of major contention, Israel benefited greatly from its powerful supporters, both in the UN and in Washington, people who are loosely referred to as 'friends' in the Israeli records. In 1949, at Lake Success, UN secretary general Trygve Lie and his executive assistant, Andrew Cordier, were already practically the best friends that Israel could have asked for. Within and around the Truman administration, as well, there were a number of influential people who were highly supportive of the Zionist cause and who had the president's ear, including David Niles, Max Lowenthal, Clark Clifford, Abraham Feinberg and, last but not least, Truman's close personal friend, Eddy Jacobson. These men had both formal and informal access to the White House and could be tapped by the Israeli leadership to support Israel's cause in conversations with the president.

Many of the same mechanisms were present under Kennedy's years in the Oval Office. John F. Kennedy, too, feared the consequences of losing support among American Jews in the congressional elections of 1962. According to Joseph Johnson, Kennedy's fear was based not on losing the Jewish voters directly but on losing the support of the 'fat cats' of the Democratic Party.[3] Just as the Republican Party's biggest financial supporters were largely 'WASPs or Catholic', the Democrats' donors, Johnson noted, were 'heavily Jewish'.[4] An example of this alignment was the pivotal pre-election meeting between Kennedy and about thirty top Jewish American leaders (of which 90 per cent were considered Zionists) in Abe Feinberg's apartment at the Pierre Hotel in New York. The meeting, suggested by Feldman, Feinberg and Abraham A. Ribicoff, was meant to introduce Kennedy to these men and to get the men to contribute financially to the campaign. Feldman himself thought the 'enormous support' Kennedy received from the Jewish electorate in November 1960 was at least partly due to this meeting.[5]

While it can't be said to be the only reasoning behind his policy towards Israel, it remains a fact that Kennedy decided to move swiftly on the decision to sell Israel the Hawk missiles, against other advice given to him. Domestic political pressure must also be counted among the reasons why Kennedy decided against lending the Johnson mission the presidential support that it needed. Kennedy did nothing to halt the anti-Johnson plan campaign that Israel undertook both at home in Israel and in the Jewish community in the United States. For Kennedy, the domestically derived advice of Myer Feldman weighed more heavily than that of his foreign policy advisors, including his secretary of state, Dean Rusk, as well as members of the NSC (Robert Komer and Carl Kaysen, in particular).

The notable exception to this rule in US politics seems to be President Eisenhower. During the 1956 Suez Crisis, Eisenhower was determined to ensure that Israel's Jewish American 'friends' could not influence his administration's policies towards Israel.[6] Yet, Eisenhower's years were not as free of these constraints as one might imagine and concerns about the impact of electoral politics surfaced also in this administration. Eisenhower's secretary of state, John Foster Dulles, tried to strike a bipartisan agreement about keeping the Arab–Israeli conflict clear of US domestic politics and election campaigns. He did so to no avail. Governor Adelai Stevenson (D), who would eventually become Kennedy's UN ambassador, not only turned Dulles down but also rushed to tell the Israelis that he had done as much. In a similar vein, the Eisenhower administration's decision for Dulles to give a formal speech in August 1955 was as a direct effort to anchor US policy regarding the conflict and commit the administration to the presented positions before the White House would be swept up into the congressional election campaign.

There can be no doubt, thus, that these 'friends' of Israel had influence on US policy towards the Arab–Israeli conflict and towards the Palestinian refugee problem more specifically. At no point were the swiftness and effectiveness of these actors more evident than in the two episodes that most clearly represented US economic leverage over Israel, involving the US Export–Import Bank.

In 1949, George McGhee at the State Department suggested that the United States should hold up the payment of part of an already granted Israeli loan, to get the Israelis to repatriate what he referred to as a 'considerable' number of refugees (at least 200,000). After having enlisted the support of both then secretary of state Dean Acheson and President Truman, McGhee proceeded to tell the Israelis about the holdup. Within twenty-four hours, however, the plan had backfired: McGhee was informed that Truman wished to 'disassociate' himself from the whole initiative, and that the money to Israel would be released. The episode left McGhee stunned at the speed and effectiveness of Israel's supporters in the United States.

The Eisenhower years provide another somewhat similar experience. As detailed above, in January 1958, then undersecretary of state Christian Herter had taken an initiative to delay an Israeli loan application to the US Export–Import Bank which came from the State Department. The idea had backing from Secretary Dulles. The plan was to use the loan application as leverage to secure a commitment from Israel on moving forward on the refugee issue. Israel would have to state that the projects that it planned to develop with the help of the money would also improve its ability to accept the repatriation of a (unspecified) number of refugees. Before it could be put to the test, however, this initiative, too, came to an abrupt halt. According to the Israeli records, American Zionists with influence were once more put to good use. Herter, due to 'pressure by Israel's friends', decided to back away from the idea. He started looking for a way out, and within a month, Israel was granted the loan, albeit for only half of the requested amount.

Exactly *how* Israel's 'friends' applied the pressure they did is not so easily determined from the archival records. Joseph Johnson saw in these 'friends' a Zionist 'machine' which again relied upon the 'Jewish press' – by which he meant American Jewish newspapers such as the *Jewish Weekly Observer* and other small, largely unknown news outlets – which he felt played a key role in applying public pressure to his own mission and plan.[7] These newspapers were 'largely Zionist' and aimed to reach 'small town Jews' and businessmen; thus they served as a 'consistent communications mechanism' for the Zionist organizations.[8]

One has to keep in mind, though, that Johnson personally felt extremely embittered towards the process, his mission's failure and the criticism that he and his plan had faced. More solid research remains to be conducted, regarding the ways and methods of the helpers whom Israel inspired in the American Jewish community.[9] In general, though, these episodes also serve as effective illustrations of the internal institutional differences that exist when it comes to the making of US foreign policy. 1600 Pennsylvania Avenue is a short stroll from the State Department at Foggy Bottom, but at times like these, the two institutions were miles apart. Domestic political considerations, often short-term and sometimes misguided, trumped the longer-term international strategic calculations. At times of competing interests, politics not policy drove US (in)action in Arab–Israeli peacemaking. This systemic challenge is of course not one reserved solely for this question, nor is it one that the United States is alone in facing.

Another domestic dimension worth mentioning in this respect is the role of the US Congress. US aid designated for the Palestinian refugee problem was appropriated through the Mutual Security Act. In 1954, the Senate Committee on Foreign Relations had voted to amend this act by including a paragraph stating that before new allocations would be designated, the president should determine whether Israel and the Arab host states were taking steps towards the resettlement and repatriation of the refugees. This would have a profound influence on the State Department's Palestine policy and was among the chief reasons why the department decided it was time to revive the PCC in 1959 and further initiate the Johnson mission. The problem with allowing Congress's demands for progress to motivate US policy was that it represented a hollow pretence for the requisite determination and willingness to lean on the actors involved. Since the main motivation was to show Congress that the State Department was trying, it did not really matter whether the given effort was a failure or a success. In terms of Johnson, of course it would have been better, overall, if he had succeeded. When his mission stumbled and met with opposition, however, there was no real sense of urgency to back him in Washington. The point to Congress had already been made.

This point about Congress's role in the development of US foreign policy is also closely tied to a more general observation regarding the problem of timing in international diplomacy. Trying to find a good or 'ripe' time for negotiation efforts that is clear of US presidential elections, midterm congressional elections, Israeli elections, UN General Assembly sessions, Arab League meetings or summits of the Non-Aligned Movement (NAM) was, and still is, a very complex task. Such events impact the pace and dynamic of the various diplomatic efforts. These meetings, summits and electoral politics bring about domestic regional and international posturing, often played out in the press. The noise, attention and contested nature of these events are more or less the polar opposite to the quiet, discreet and conducive environment that international negotiations tend to need, in order to be successful.

For example, the PCC's attempt to facilitate the second release of the Palestinian refugees' blocked accounts was motivated in part by the commission's scheduled annual report, due to be presented at the General

Assembly; the first effort to bring Alpha to Nasser collided with the latter's participation at the 1955 NAM summit, which represented a genuine restriction on Nasser's room to manoeuvre; Dulles's decision to take Alpha public in the summer of 1955, against the wishes of his British counterpart, was heavily influenced by the administration's domestic considerations connected to the midterm election season; though Johnson throughout his mission heard more nuanced views from individual Arab leaders, the 1964 Arab League Summit in Cairo produced yet another round of non-pragmatic and dogmatic slogans and complicated the regional and intra-Arab dynamics further. Also, as discussed, the upcoming midterm elections represented the main reason why Kennedy decided not to officially endorse the Johnson mission, and, once those elections were over in early November, there was not enough time for the United States to put any heat on the parties before the General Assembly debate started again. If each respective US effort to solve the Arab–Israeli conflict can be described as searching for a window of opportunity, the constantly shifting winds that these kinds of outside events produced were usually brisk enough to blow that window shut.

Finally, one must consider another explanatory factor regarding why the United States had such limited leverage over Israel, and, ultimately, why none of the efforts detailed here succeeded in moving towards a solution for the refugee problem: the international community, led here by the United States, never managed to increase the cost of 'no-agreement' for the concerned parties.[10] Israel could uphold its hard-line policy on the refugee issue because the cost of doing so was so small. Paradoxically, one of the main reasons for this was the success of the UN track at the Island of Rhodes in 1949 and specifically the 'negative peace' that the armistice agreements produced there. These agreements cemented a situation in which Israel felt that it was in no hurry to make peace with the Arabs, let alone give any major concessions on the refugee issue.

As has been pointed out elsewhere, the result was that Israel did not feel that it 'needed' peace as badly as the Arabs did. Powerful Israeli figures such as Abba Eban and David Ben-Gurion were two proponents of this view. Ben-Gurion, explaining Eban's thinking, said,

> He sees no need to run after peace. An armistice is sufficient for us; if we run after peace – the Arabs will demand of us a price – borders [i.e. border rectification] or refugees or both. We will wait a few years.[11]

For the Arab states, too, the Rhodes armistice agreements had produced relative security, meaning that the most dramatic cost of no agreement – war – was, if not eliminated, then drastically reduced. While casting themselves as protectors and champions of the Palestinian refugees' rights, the Arab regimes displayed none of the creativity, compromise, pragmatism or political willingness that would have been necessary to secure a sustainable solution.

The Arab states' initial goal had been full refugee repatriation, in accordance with UN General Assembly Resolution 194 of 1948. The main motivation behind this unanimous demand was that the Arab leaders were sensitive towards the fact that the plight of the Palestinian refugees generated great sympathy among the Arab public in general. But there can be no doubt that for the Arab states that had lost both honour and land during the 1948 War; the refugee issue also represented a valuable bargaining chip in the later negotiations with Israel. In certain ways, the Arab regimes had benefited from the 'disappearance' of the Palestinians – both Jordan and Egypt had increased their territories, and in Lebanon, Beirut replaced Haifa as the uncontested transit port of the Eastern Mediterranean. Therefore, though they could never admit to it in public, several Arab states too had a 'vested interest in Palestinian failure'.[12]

Arab governments did nothing to support Palestinian statehood. Instead, they made sure that the potential Palestinian elite was deprived of a territorial and institutional basis to exercise social and political control and influence over their co-Palestinians in the diaspora. Paradoxically, it was therefore only for the Palestinian refugees that the costs of no agreement with Israel had catastrophic consequences. Because of the Palestinians denied access in most negotiations and their general marginalization as political actors in this period, however, there was little that the refugees themselves could do to alter this situation.

Notes

Chapter 1

1   The author, Frank Jarvis, was a land expert in United Nations Palestine Conciliation Commission (PCC). He sent the limerick in a letter to Joseph Esrey Johnson, President John F. Kennedy's special representative tasked with solving the refugee issue, on 14 November 1962, as Johnson's mission was on its last legs.

2   Avi Shlaim, 'The Debate about 1948', *International Journal of Middle East Studies* 27, no. 03 (1995): 287. Other main issues of contention in the 1948 debate are British mandate policy; the military balance during the 1948 War; the nature of the relationship between Israel and Transjordan; the Arabs aims for the 1948 War; and, finally, why peace was never obtained between Israel and the Arab states in the immediate aftermath of the war.

3   Shlaim, 'The Debate about 1948', 288; Avi Shlaim, 'The War of Israeli Historians', *Annales* 59, no. 1 (2004): 161–7; Kenneth W. Stein, 'A Historiographic Review of Literature on the Origins of the Arab-Israeli Conflict', *American Historical Review* 96, no. 5 (1991): 1457.

4   Other important scholars in the group of new historians include Avi Shlaim, Ilan Pappé, Tom Segev and Simha Flaphan. Shlaim, 'The Debate about 1948'; Nur Masalha, *The Palestine Nakba: Decolonizing History, Narrating the Subaltern, Reclaiming Memory* (London: Zed Books, 2012), 152–3.

5   Benny Morris, *The Birth of the Palestinian Refugee Problem Revisited*, 2nd edn (Cambridge: Cambridge University Press, 2004). The work referred to here is the revised 2004 version, *The Birth of the Palestinian Refugee Problem: Revisited. The Birth* was originally published in 1988. In the second edition of the book, the number of regional expulsions and the extent of these were greater than what had been indicated in the original publication.

6   Morris, *The Birth*.

7   Ibid.

8   Avi Shlaim, *The Iron Wall: Israel and the Arab World* (New York: W. W. Norton, 2001), 27. Rashid Khalidi writes about what he calls the 'failure' of the Palestinians and their leadership in the fateful years 1947–9 in Rashid Khalidi, 'The Palestinians and 1948: The Underlying Causes of Failure', in *The War for*

Palestine: Rewriting the History of 1948, ed. Eugene L. Rogan and Avi Shlaim (Cambridge: Cambridge University Press, 2007), 12–36; Khalidi gives an even more detailed account of this era in Rashid Khalidi, *The Iron Cage: The Story of the Palestinian Struggle for Statehood* (Boston: Beacon Press, 2006).

9   Khalidi, 'The Palestinians and 1948', 14.

10   Ibid., 164.

11   Ilan Pappé, *The Making of the Arab-Israeli Conflict, 1947-1951*, 4th edn (London: I.B. Tauris, 2006), 99.

12   Ibid., 99.

13   Morris, *The Birth*, 588.

14   It should be noted that the discussion of the actual number of refugees is a contentious one. While traditional Zionist narratives hold it to be 600,000 or less, the Arab narrative claims that as many as 800,000 to 900,000 people fled. Morris's estimate is 700,000, but he too admits that it is difficult to establish a precise number. Historians like Nur Masalha and Ilan Pappé both refer to 750,000. This is also the number with which UNRWA operated, although it should be noted that its estimates were undertaken in 1950, as the agency first became operational. The original number of refugees might therefore have been somewhat lower. Because of the lack of a precise and authoritative number, I have chosen to adopt Morris's relatively wide-ranging estimates. Other estimates, though, are wider still. Simon Waldman, in his *Anglo-American Diplomacy and the Palestinian Refugee Problem, 1948–51*, has a longer discussion about this. See Waldman, *Anglo-American Diplomacy and the Palestinian Refugee Problem, 1948–51* (London: Palgrave Macmillan, 2015), 12–13.

15   Ilan Pappé, 'The History, Historiography and Relevance of the Palestinian Refugee Problem', *Journal of Philosophy of International Law and Global Politics* 1, no. 1 (2005): 1–13.

16   The public debate between Teveth and Morris took place mostly in the Israeli magazine *Tikkun* and one of the major liberal Israeli newspapers, *Haaretz*. Teveth's original four-article attack on the 'new' historians was published by *Haaretz*. Shlaim, 'The Debate about 1948'. For other criticisms, see, for example, Efraim Karsh, 'Benny Morris and the Reign of Error', *Middle East Quarterly*, 1 March 1999, http://www.meforum.org/466/benny-morris-and-the-reign-o f-error; Efraim Karsh, 'The Unbearable Lightness of My Critics', *Middle East Quarterly*, 1 June 2002, http://www.meforum.org/207/the-unbearable-lightnes s-of-my-critics; Efraim Karsh, 'Benny Morris's Reign of Error, Revisited', *Middle East Quarterly*, 1 March 2005, http://www.meforum.org/711/benny-morriss-reig n-of-error-revisited.

17 Nur Masalha, 'A Critique of Benny Morris', *Journal of Palestine Studies* 21, no. 1 (October 1991): 90–7; Morris, *The Birth*, 550.

18 Masalha, 'A Critique of Benny Morris'; Masalha, *The Palestine Nakba*, 170–2; Joel Beinin, 'No More Tears: Benny Morris and the Road Back from Liberal Zionism', *Middle East Report*, 2004, http://www.merip.org/mer/mer230/no-more-tears.

19 Masalha, *The Palestine Nakba*, 173.

20 Masalha, *Catastrophe Remembered: Palestine, Israel and the Internal Refugees* (London: Zed Books, 2005); Nur Masalha, *Expulsion of the Palestinians: The Concept of 'Transfer' in Zionist Political Thought, 1882–1948*, 5th edn (Washington, D.C.: Institute for Palestine Studies, 2009); Nur Masalha, 'The Historical Roots of the Palestinian Refugee Question', in *The Palestinian Refugees and the Right of Return*, ed. Naseer Aruri (London: Pluto Press, 2001); Masalha, *The Palestine Nakba*; Masalha, *The Politics of Denial: Israel and the Palestinian Refugee Problem* (London: Pluto Press, 2003).

21 Masalha, *The Palestine Nakba*, 175.

22 Benny Morris, 'Response to Finkelstein and Masalha', *Journal of Palestine Studies* 21, no. 1 (1991): 98–114; Pappé, *The Making*, 89–91.

23 Walid Khalidi, 'Why Did the Palestinians Leave?', *Middle East Forum*, 1959; Walid Khalidi, 'Plan Dalet: Master Plan for the Conquest of Palestine', *Middle East Forum*, 1961; See also these revised articles: W. Khalidi, 'Why Did the Palestinians Leave, Revisited', *Journal of Palestine Studies* 34, no. 2 (2005): 42–54; Walid Khalidi, 'Plan Dalet Revisited', *Journal of Palestine Studies*, n.d.; Pappé, 'The History, Historiography and Relevance of the Palestinian Refugee Problem'; Pappé, *The Making*.

24 Ilan Pappé, *The Ethnic Cleansing of Palestine* (Oxford: Oneworld Publications, 2007), 47. The standard work on this is Masalha, *Expulsion*.

25 Shlaim, *The Iron Wall*, 31.

26 Ibid.

27 Avi Shlaim, *Israel and Palestine: Reappraisals, Revisions, Refutations* (London: Verso, 2009), 56–9; Masalha, *The Palestine Nakba*, 173–5.

28 For Morris rebuttal to Finkelstein and Masalha, see Morris, 'Response to Finkelstein and Masalha'.

29 Shlaim, 'The Debate about 1948'; Stein, 'A Historiographic Review', 1462–3; Mordechai Bar-On, 'Conflicting Narratives or Narratives of Conflict: Can the Zionist and Palestinian Narratives of the 1948 War Be Bridged?', in *Israeli and Palestinian Narratives of Conflict: History's Double Helix*, ed. Robert I. Rothberg (Bloomington: Indiana University Press, 2006), 154–6.

30   Morris, *The Birth*, 2004; Rafi Nets-Zehngut, 'Palestinian Autobiographical
     Memory Regarding the 1948 Palestinian Exodus', *Political Psychology* 32, no. 2
     (2011): 271–95.

31   Anne O'Hare McCormick, 'Israel Speeds Resettlement of Areas Left by the
     Arabs', *New York Times*, 18 January 1949.

32   Morris, *The Birth*, chap. 6; Benny Morris, *Israel's Border Wars, 1949–1956: Arab
     Infiltration, Israeli Retaliation, and the Countdown to the Suez War*, 2nd edn
     (Oxford: Oxford University Press, 1997).

33   McCormick, 'Israel Speeds Resettlement'.

34   Facts and Figures about Refugees, *UN High Commissioner for Refugees*
     (UNHCR), http://www.unhcr.org.uk/about-us/key-facts-and-figures.html.

35   Daniel Bar-Tal and Gavriel Salomon, 'Israeli-Jewish Narratives of the Israeli-
     Palestinian Conflict: Evolution, Contents, Functions and Consequences', in
     Israeli and Palestinian Narratives of Conflict: History's Double Helix, ed. Robert
     I. Rothberg, Indiana Series in Middle East Studies (Bloomington: Indiana
     University Press, 2006), 19–22.

36   'Palestinian Refugees, ICG', 7, 10.

37   Abbas Shiblak, '*The Palestinian Refugee Issue: A Palestinian Perspective*', Briefing
     Paper (Chatham House, February 2009), 2; Masalha, *The Palestine Nakba*,
     10–11.

38   *Palestinian Refugees and the Politics of Peacemaking*, Middle East Report
     (International Crisis Group, February 2004), 6; Masalha, *The Palestine Nakba*,
     11–12.

39   Rashid Khalidi, *Palestinian Identity: The Construction of Modern National
     Consciousness* (New York: Columbia University Press, 1998), 194.

40   Ibid., 145–208, 193–4; Masalha, *The Palestine Nakba*, 12; See also: A. Hovdenak,
     'Trading Refugees for Land and Symbols: The Palestinian Negotiation Strategy in
     the Oslo Process', *Journal of Refugee Studies* 22, no. 1 (2008): 4.

41   Masalha, *The Palestine Nakba*; Ahmad H. Sa'di, 'Catastrophe, Memory and
     Identity: Al-Nakbah as a Component of Palestinian Identity', *Israel Studies* 7, no.
     2 (2002): 175–98.

42   Robert I. Rothberg, ed., *Israeli and Palestinian Narratives of Conflict: History's
     Double Helix* (Bloomington: Indiana University Press, 2006); Rafi Nets-Zehngut,
     'Origins of the Palestinian Refugee Problem: Changes in the Historical Memory
     of Israelis/Jews 1949–2004', *Journal of Peace Research* 48, no. 2 (2011): 235. See
     also Shlaim, 'The Debate about 1948', 287–304.

43   Rothberg, *History's Double Helix*; Nets-Zehngut, 'Changes in Historical Memory',
     235. See also Shlaim, 'The Debate about 1948'.

44 Shlaim, 'The Debate about 1948'. The man who has done perhaps most scholarly work that refutes this traditional Zionist claim is Israeli historian Benny Morris.

45 Bar-Tal and Salomon, 'Israeli-Jewish Narratives', 27.

46 Sharett as quoted by Varda Shiffer, 'The 1949 Israeli Offer to Repatriate 100.000 Palestinian Refugees', *Middle East Focus*, no. Fall (1986): 15. See also: Jacob Tovy, *Israel and the Palestinian Refugee Issue: The Formulation of Policy, 1948–1956* (New York: Routledge, 2014), 19; Don Peretz, *Israel and the Palestine Arabs* (Washington, D.C.: Middle East Institute, 1958), 50.

47 Morris, *The Birth*, 2.

48 Ibid., 2; See also, for example; Agha Hussein and Robert Malley, 'The Last Negotiation: How to End the Middle East Peace Process', *Foreign Affairs*, June 2002, 4; Donna E. Artz, 'Negotiating The Last Taboo: Palestinian Refugees', January 1996, http://prrn.mcgill.ca/prrn/papers/arzt1.html; Ilan Pappé, 'Visible and Invisible in the Israeli-Palestinian Conflict', in *Exile and Return: Predicaments of Palestinians and Jews*, ed. Ann M. Lesch and Ian S. Lustick (Philadelphia: University of Pennsylvania Press, 2005), 279; Peretz, *Israel*, 3; Simon A. Waldman, *Anglo-American Diplomacy and the Palestinian Refugee Problem, 1948-51* (London: Palgrave Macmillan, 2015), 17, 190.

49 Morris, *The Birth*, 194; Tovy, *Israel and the Palestinian Refugee Issue*, 14; Peretz, *Israel*, 11; Folke Bernadotte, *To Jerusalem*, trans. Joan Bulman (London: Hodder and Stoughton, 1951), 200.

50 Thomas J. Hamilton, 'Arab Refugee Case Placed before UN', *New York Times*, 6 August 1948.

51 'Progress Report of the Acting Mediator for Palestine/Supplement', 18 October 1948, UNISPAL.

52 'Progress Report of the United Nations Mediator on Palestine' (United Nations, 16 September 1948), UNISPAL, 'First Progress Report (supplement)'; For a discussion on Bernadotte's mission see Joseph Heller, 'Failure of a Mission: Bernadotte and Palestine, 1948', *Journal of Contemporary History* 14, no. 3 (July 1979): 515–34.

53 Bernadotte, *To Jerusalem*, 241.

54 Morris, *The Birth*, 594; Pappé, *The Making*, 148; 'UN A/RES/194 (III)', 11 December 1948, UNISPAL.

55 UN GA Res. 194 (III), para. 11. The resolution has been reaffirmed in each General Assembly session except 1951. By 2001 there had been approximately 49 UN General Assembly resolutions that in one form or another, have referred to Resolution 194. Jaber Suleiman, 'The Palestinian Liberation Organization: From the Right of Return to Bantustan', in *The Palestinian Refugees and the Right of Return*, ed. Naseer Aruri (London: Pluto Press, 2001), 89.

56 UN GA Res. 194 (III).

57 Matthew F. Jacobs, *Imagining the Middle East: The Building of an American Foreign Policy, 1918-1967* (Chapel Hill: University of North Carolina Press, 2011), 212–13, 220.

58 Tovy, *Israel and the Palestinian Refugee Issue*, 41. See also: George McGhee, *Envoy to the Middle World: Adventures in Diplomacy* (New York: Harper and Row, 1983), 28–9; Rusk to Webb, 3 March 1949, *Foreign Relations of the United States, 1949, The Near East, South Asia and Africa*, vol. 6 (US Government Printing Office, 1977), 788.

59 As quoted in Candace Karp, *Missed Opportunities: US Diplomatic Failures and the Arab-Israeli Conflict 1947-1967* (Claremont, CA: Regina Books, 2005), 65. See also: Waldman, *Anglo-American Diplomacy and the Palestinian Refugee Problem, 1948–51*, 3.

60 Two more recent publications share this volume's emphasis on the refugee problem, albeit with a considerably narrower gallery of actors and substantially shorter time frame. Jacob Tovy, 'Negotiating the Palestinian Refugees', *Middle East Quarterly*, Spring 2003; Waldman, *Anglo-American Diplomacy and the Palestinian Refugee Problem, 1948–51*.

61 Michael Dumper, *The Future for Palestinian Refugees: Toward Equity and Peace* (Boulder, CO: Lynne Rienner Publishers, 2007), 15.

62 See Eugene L. Rogan, *The Arabs: A History*, 2nd edn (New York: Basic Books, 2011); Avi Shlaim, *The Politics of Partition: King Abdullah, the Zionists, and Palestine 1921–1951*, abridged (Oxford: Oxford University Press, 1999); Avi Shlaim, *Lion of Jordan: The Life of King Hussein in War and Peace* (London: Penguin Books, 2009); Nigel Ashton, *King Hussein of Jordan: A Political Life* (New Haven: Yale University Press, 2008); Jørgen Jensehaugen and Hilde Henriksen Waage, 'Coercive Diplomacy: Israel, Transjordan and the UN – a Triangular Drama Revisited', *British Journal of Middle Eastern Studies* 39, no. 1 (2012): 79–100.

Chapter 2

1 Interview with Mark F. Etheridge, interview by Richard D. McKinzie, 4 June 1974, http://www.trumanlibrary.org/oralhist/ethridge.htm.

2 See Brian Urquhart, *Ralph Bunche: An American Odyssey* (W. W. Norton, 1998), 204–5; Pablo de Azcárate, *Mission in Palestine 1948-1952* (Washington, D.C.: The Middle East Institute, 1966), 146; David P. Forsythe, *United Nations Peacemaking:*

The Conciliation Commission for Palestine (Baltimore: Johns Hopkins University Press, 1972), 44. See also diary entry, 8 February 1949, Ralph Bunche, Ralph Bunche Diary, n.d., Ralph Bunche archives, collection 2051/Box 127/11, UCLA.

3   The negotiations between Israel and Syria were being conducted in Galilee, and Jordan and Israel also met for (secret) talks at King Abdullah's winter palace, Shuneh. The Rhodes negotiations arose from UN Security Council Resolution 62 of 16 November 1948. See Hilde Henriksen Waage, 'The Winner Takes All: The 1949 Island of Rhodes Armistice Negotiations Revisited', *Middle East Journal* 65 (2011): 279–304; Stian Johansen Tiller and Hilde Henriksen Waage, 'Powerful State, Powerless Mediator: The United States and the Peace Efforts of the Palestine Conciliation Commission, 1949–51', *International History Review* 33 (2011): 501–24; Jensehaugen and Waage, 'Coercive Diplomacy'; Hilde Henriksen Waage and Petter Stenberg, 'Cementing a State of Belligerency: The 1949 Armistice Negotiations Between Israel and Syria', *Middle East Journal*, forthcoming.

4   The negotiations and agreements took place in the following order: 24 February 1949: Israel-Egypt; 23 March 1949: Israel and Lebanon; 3 April 1949: Israel and Jordan; and 20 July 1949: Israel and Syria. Shlaim, *The Iron Wall*, 41; Waage, 'The Winner Takes All'.

5   Forsythe, *United Nations Peacemaking*, 40, 41.

6   Bunche to Eytan, 7 January 1949, *Documents on the Foreign Policy of Israel, December 1948–July 1949*, vol. 3 (Jerusalem: Israel State Archives Hamakor Press, 1983), 211.

7   Urquhart, *Ralph Bunche*, 201. This does not mean that Bunche never talked or consulted with the PCC about the refugee problem. From Bunche's own diary, we can see that he talked to both George McGhee of the US State Department and PCC chairman Mark Etheridge about the refugee problem. See diary entries for 25 March; 26 March; 6 April (all 1949) in Bunche, Ralph Bunche Diary, n.d., Ralph Bunche archives, collection 2051/Box 127/11. UCLA, Folder 11.

8   Interview with Mark F. Etheridge, para. 1–53.

9   Forsythe, *United Nations Peacemaking*, 29.

10   De Azcárate, *Mission in Palestine 1948-1952*, 135; Eytan to Sharett, 3 May 1949, Yehoshua, ed., *Documents on the Foreign Policy of Israel, May-December 1949*, vol. 4 (Jerusalem: Israeli Government Printer, 1986), 13.

11   Forsythe, *United Nations Peacemaking*, 38, 39; de Azcárate, *Mission in Palestine 1948-1952*, 138–9.

12   Forsythe, *United Nations Peacemaking*, 37.

13   'UNCCP Summary Record of Meeting, A/AC.25/SR/G/1', 9 February 1949, 11, http://unispal.un.org/UNISPAL.NSF/0/4D90CB23CEA544898525750F007A3

7B5.UN A/AC.25/SR/G/1, 7 February 1949, Summary Record of Meeting: 11. See also: Burdett to Secretary of State, 8 February 1949, *FRUS*, 6:738; Burdett to Secretary of State, 28 February 1949, ibid., 6:778; Neil Caplan, *The Lausanne Conference, 1949: A Case Study in Middle East Peacemaking* (Tel Aviv: Tel Aviv University, Moshe Dayan Center for Middle Eastern and African Studies, 1993), 21.

14   Patterson to Acheson, 15 February 1949, *FRUS*, VI:750–2; UN A/AC.25/SR/G/4, Summary Record of Meeting between PCC and Government of Egypt, 13 February 1949; UN A/AC.25/SR/G/5, Summary Record of Meeting between PCC and Government of Egypt, 15 February 1949; Dorze to Acheson, 19 February 1949, *FRUS*, VI:756–7; Dorze to Acheson, 20 February 1949, *FRUS*, VI:757; There is no printed version in vol. 6 of *FRUS* regarding the meeting with the Lebanese officials. It is written, however, that the opinions of Lebanon were parallel to the Syrian views. Pinkerton to Acheson, 24 February 1949, *FRUS*, VI:766–7.

15   Burdett to Secretary of State, 28 February 1949, *FRUS*, 6:777; Saadia Touval, *The Peace Brokers: Mediators in the Arab-Israeli Conflict, 1948-1979* (Princeton University Press, 1982), 81; Stian Johansen Tiller, 'Defending the UN Agenda: The Peace Efforts of the Palestine Conciliation Commission 1949-1951' (MA thesis, University of Oslo, 2009), 40; Professor Forsythe, *United Nations Peacemaking*, 42.

16   De Azcárate, *Mission in Palestine 1948-1952*, 145. See Burdett to Secretary of State, 28 February 1949, *FRUS*, 6:777; Burdett to Secretary of State, 26 February 1949, ibid., 6:772; Caplan, *The Lausanne Conference, 1949*, 23; Forsythe, *United Nations Peacemaking*, 42.

17   UNCCP Summary Record of Twenty Seventh Meeting, A/AC.25/SR.27, 21 March 1949, UNISPAL.

18   Burdett to Secretary of State, 26 February 1949, *FRUS*, 6:773; Caplan, *The Lausanne Conference, 1949*, 23; Forsythe, *United Nations Peacemaking*, 42.

19   Memorandum of Conversation, Rockwell, 22 March 1949, *FRUS*, 6:856.

20   'UNCCP SRM 7 February 1949', 11; Entry date of 6 April 1949, Ralph Bunche Diary, n.d., Ralph Bunche archives, collection 2051/Box 127/11, UCLA; Pinkerton to Secretary of State, 28 March 1949, *FRUS*, 6:877.

21   Burdett to Secretary of State, 14 March 1949; Memorandum of Conversation, 22 March 1949; Memorandum of Conversation, 24 March 1949; Pinkerton to Secretary of State, 28 March 1949; Memorandum of Conversation, 5 April 1949, *FRUS*, 6:825, 855, 878, 890. See also: Caplan, *The Lausanne Conference, 1949*, 29–30.

22 Pinkerton to Secretary of State, 28 March 1949, *FRUS*, 6:877.

23 Burdett to Secretary of State, 20 April 1949, *FRUS*, 6:925; Caplan, *The Lausanne Conference, 1949*, 35; Forsythe, *United Nations Peacemaking*, 1972, 47; Neil Caplan, *Futile Diplomacy: The United Nations, the Great Powers and Middle East Peacemaking 1948-1954*, vol. 3 (New York: Routledge, 1997), 71.

24 Pinkerton to Secretary of State, 28 March 1949, *FRUS*, 6:877.

25 Pinkerton to Secretary of State, 5 April 1949, *FRUS*, 6:894–5; Forsythe, *United Nations Peacemaking*, 46; Azcárate, *Mission in Palestine 1948-1952*, 149. Iraq broke ranks with the other Arab states on this particular point.

26 The following account is based on: Marte Heian-Engdal, Jørgen Jensehaugen and Hilde Henriksen Waage, '"Finishing the Enterprise": Israel's Admission to the UN', *International History Review* 35, no. 3 (2013): 465–85.

27 Waage, 'The Winner Takes All'.

28 Entry of 6 April 1949, Ralph Bunche Diary, Ralph Bunche archives, collection 2051/Box 127/11. UCLA.

29 Burdett to Secretary of State, 19 April 1949, *FRUS*, 6:923 (see footnote 1); Vincent to Secretary of State, 9 May 1949, *FRUS*, 6:989; Burdett to Secretary of State, 19 April 1949, *FRUS*, 6:923; Elath and Eban to Sharett, Washington, 26 April 1949, *DFPI*, 2: 593–4; Forsythe, *United Nations Peacemaking*, 48.

30 Etheridge to Secretary of State, 28 April 1949, *FRUS*, 6:955.

31 Sharett to Eytan, 2 April 1949, *Documents on the Foreign Policy of Israel, October 1948-April 1949*, vol. 2 (Jerusalem: Israel State Archives Keter Press, 1984), 541.

32 Peter L. Hahn, 'Alignment by Coincidence: Israel, the United States, and the Partition of Jerusalem, 1949–1953', *The International History Review* 21, no. 3 (1999): 669.

33 Sharett to Eytan, 2 April 1949, *DFPI*, 2:541; Hahn, 'Alignment by Coincidence', 670–1.

34 Waage, 'The Winner Takes All'; Jensehaugen and Waage, 'Coercive Diplomacy'.

35 Austin to Secretary of State, 20 April 1949, *FRUS*, 6:931; The PCC were informed by the latest development in the admissions question by Andrew Cordier. Cordier to Azcarate, 25 April 1949, AG20/S0161/0004/3, UN ARMS.

36 Waage, 'The Winner Takes All'; Jensehaugen and Waage, 'Coercive Diplomacy'.

37 Austin to Secretary of State, 20 April 1949, *FRUS*, 4:931–2.

38 Eban to Sharett, 29 April 1949, *DFPI*, 2:604. For Acheson's various appeals, see Elath and Eban to Sharett, 26 April 1949; Elath to Sharett, 29 April 1949, *DFPI*, 2:593, 605; Memo of Conversation, 26 April, *FRUS*, 4:944–5.

39 Abba Solomon Eban, *Abba Eban: An Autobiography* (New York: Random House, 1977), 141.

40 Ibid; Vincent to Secretary of State, 3 May 1949; Satterthwaite to Secretary of State, 4 May 1949, *FRUS*, 6:968, 973–4.

41 Eban to Eytan, 13 April 1949, *DFPI*, 2:573–4.

42 Sharett to Eytan, 16 April 1949, *DFPI*, 2:578.

43 Eban to Eytan, 15 April 1949, *DFPI*, 2:574.

44 Hahn, 'Alignment by Coincidence', 665–6.

45 See for example: Jørgen Jensehaugen, Marte Heian-Engdal and Hilde Henriksen Waage, 'Securing the State: From Zionist Ideology to Israeli Statehood', *Diplomacy and Statecraft* 23, no. 2 (June 2012): 280–303; Weizmann to Truman, 25 November 1947; Weizmann to Truman, 28 November 1947, *Political Documents of the Jewish Agency*, vol. ii (Jerusalem: Publishing House of the World Zionist Organization, 1998), 879–80, 889–90; Michael Joseph Cohen, *Truman and Israel* (University of California Press, 1990), 196–7; Peter Grose, *Israel in the Mind of America* (Schocken, 1984), 273, 277–8; Eban to Sharett, 16 June 1949, *DFPI*, 4:138.

46 Elath to Sharett, 4 May 1948, *DFPI*, 4:19.

47 Elath to Sharett, 10 May 1949, *DFPI*, 4:39.

48 Elath to Sharett, 4 May 1949, *DFPI*, 4:19.

49 Shlaim, *The Politics of Partition*, 212; Morris, *The Birth*, 309–19.

50 UNGA Res. 273 (III), 11 May 1949; UN GASR, 207th Meeting, 11 May 1949, A/PV.207.

51 Diary entry of 2 February 1949, Ralph Bunche Diary, n.d., Ralph Bunche archives, collection 2051/Box 127/11. UCLA.

52 Original emphasis. Interview with Mark F. Etheridge (see paragraph no. 49).

53 Etheridge to Secretary of State, 18 May 1949, *FRUS*, 6:1028–9. Eytan to Eban, 8 June 1949, RG 130/MFA/2442/5, ISA.

54 Eytan to Eban, 11 June 1949, RG 130/MFA/2442/5, ISA; Eban to Eytan, 9 June 1949, RG 130/MFA/2442/7, ISA; Caplan, *Futile Diplomacy*, 3:82.

55 Sharett to Eytan, 14 May 1949, RG 130/MFA/2442/7, ISA; Eytan to Sharett, 14 May 1949, RG 130/MFA/2442/5, ISA.

56 Caplan, *The Lausanne Conference, 1949*, 44. Eytan informed the Israeli Ministry of Foreign Affairs about this Egyptian development and underlined to them that the Egyptians were only asking for acceptance of the *principle*, not an actual return. Eytan to Raday, 14 May 1949, RG 130/MFA/2442/5, ISA; Eytan to Sharett, 14 May 1949, RG 130/MFA/2442/5. ISA; The same is confirmed in the reports to the UN Secretariat in New York, see Azcarate to Cordier, 20 May 1949, AG20/S0161/0004/2, UN ARMS.

57 Caplan, *Futile Diplomacy*, 3:86.

58 Indeed, the PCC charged that one of the causes of the looming deadlock was precisely the 'failure of the Arab delegations to distinguish between "hierarchy" and "chronology"'. UNCCP, Summary Record of Meeting, A/AC.25/Com.Gen/SR.4, 18 May 1949, 6, UNISPAL.

59 As opposed to a settlement based on the borders of 29 November 1947, a settlement based on the status quo, of course, would mean that the Jewish state could claim even more territory in Palestine than what had been allotted to her by the UN partition plan.

60 Eytan to Eban, 13 June 1949, *DFPI*, 4:128; Caplan, *Futile Diplomacy*, 3:87.

61 Sharett to Eytan, 29 May 1949, RG 130/MFA/2442/7, ISA. For a more detailed account of this point of tension in US–Israeli relations, see Caplan, *The Lausanne Conference, 1949*; Caplan, *Futile Diplomacy*, vol. 3; Morris, *The Birth*, 556–8, 570–4.

62 Morris, *The Birth*, 561.

63 Caplan, *The Lausanne Conference, 1949*, 62; Caplan, *Futile Diplomacy*, 3:89; Morris, *The Birth*, 565; Ilan Pappé, *Britain and the Arab-Israeli Conflict, 1948-51* (London: Macmillan Press, 1988), 135–6. Etheridge to Secretary of State, 2 June 1949, *FRUS*, 6:1085; Eytan to Sharett, 30 April 1949, *DFPI*, 2:615; Azcarate to Cordier, 20 May 1949, AG20/S0161/0004/2, UN ARMS.

64 Eytan to Sharett, Lausanne, 3 May 1949, *FRUS*, 6:11.

65 Eytan to Sharett, Lausanne, 3 May 1949, *DFPI*, 4:11; Jensehaugen and Waage, 'Coercive Diplomacy'.

66 Sharett to Elath, 18 January 1949, *DFPI*, 3:343.

67 Eytan to Sharett, 3 May 1949, *DFPI*, 4:11.

68 Eytan to Sharett, Lausanne, 3 May 1949, *DFPI*, 4:11.

69 Morris, *The Birth*, 564; Reports of the offer quickly reached the international press corps. See for example: Thomas Hamilton, 'Israel Assails U.S. on Arab Re-Entry', *New York Times*, 10 June 1949.

70 Sharett as quoted in Morris, *The Birth*, 562 (footnote 37).

71 Eytan to Sharett, 27 May 1949, RG 130/MFA/2442/5, ISA; Eytan to Sharett, 30 April 1949, *DFPI*, 2:615; Morris, *The Birth*, 563–4.

72 Eytan to Boisanger, Lausanne, 29 May 1949, *DFPI*, 4:74–5; Eytan to Etheridge, A/AC.25/IS.19, 29 May 1949, UNISPAL. See also: Eytan to Eban, Lausanne, 21 May 1949; Aide-Mémoire by the Government of the United States, 24 June 1949, *DFPI*, 4:58–9, 147.

73 Eytan to Sharett, 28 May 1949, RG 130/MFA/2442/5, ISA; UNCCP, Eytan to Etheridge, A/AC.25/IS.19, 29 May 1949; Azcarate to Secretary General Lie, 28 May 1949, AG20/S0161/0004/2, UN ARMS; See also: Morris, *The Birth*, 565–6.

74 Morris, *The Birth*, 564; Webb to US Del Lausanne, 4 June 1949, *DFPI*, 4:1090.

75 Pappé, *Britain and the Arab-Israeli Conflict, 1948-51*, 121–3; Morris, *The Birth*, 568.

76 Douglas of the British Foreign Office in a memorandum to Acheson, as quoted in Caplan, *The Lausanne Conference, 1949*, 66; Ilan Pappé, 'Britain and the Palestinian Refugees, 1948-1950', *Middle East Focus*, Fall 1986, 19.

77 Morris, *The Birth*, 567–9.

78 Gene Currivan, 'Egyptians Moving Refugees to Gaza', *New York Times*, 21 August 1949.

79 Morris, *The Birth*, 567–9.

80 Eytan to Sharett, 22 June 1949; Eban to Sharett, 17 June 1949, *DFPI*, 1986, 4:154, 139; Morris, *The Birth*, 570–1; Tovy, *Israel and the Palestinian Refugee Issue*, 57.

81 Eytan to Sharett, 28 May 1949, RG 130/MFA/2442/5, ISA.

82 Eban to McGhee, 8 July 1949, *DFPI*, 4:212–13.

83 Shlaim, *Israel and Palestine*, 70.

84 Ibid., 73.

85 Ibid.

86 Shlaim, *Israel and Palestine*, 62–76; Shlaim's account of Zaim's offer was first published in article form in 1986. See: Avi Shlaim, 'Huzni Zaim and the Plan to Resettle Palestinian Refugees in Syria', *Middle East Focus* (1986): 27–31; See also: Tovy, *Israel and the Palestinian Refugee Issue*, 175–6. According to Joshua Landis, Zaim's was not the last Syrian offer to resettle refugees. In 1952, Zaim's successor, Colonel Shishlaki, reached an agreement with UNRWA director Blandford, in the latter's effort to resettle 500,000 refugees in Syria. Landis notes that this policy initially received much support from the United States, but that it failed when US–Syrian relations faltered in the wake of the Egyptian revolution in July 1952. Blandford's efforts are treated in more detail in chapter 4:106–12. Also, See: Joshua Landis, 'Early US Policy toward Palestinian Refugees: The Syrian Option', in *The Palestinian Refugees: Old Problems – New Solutions*, ed. Joseph Ginat and Edward J. Perkins (Norman: University of Oklahoma Press, 2001), 84–5; Tovy, *Israel and the Palestinian Refugee Issue*, 176–7; Waage and Stenberg, 'Cementing a State of Belligerency: The 1949 Armistice Negotiations between Israel and Syria'.

87 Shlaim, *Israel and Palestine*, 64; Shlaim, 'Huzni Zaim and the Plan to Resettle Palestinian Refugees in Syria', 27.

88 Shlaim, *Israel and Palestine*, 70–1.

89 Landis, 'Early US Policies', 79; Shlaim, *Israel and Palestine*, 70–1.

90 Shlaim, *Israel and Palestine*, 68–9.

91 Schiffer, 'The 1949 Israeli Offer to Repatriate 100.000 Palestinian Refugees', 18.

92 See, for example, Pappé, *The Making*, 228–33; Morris, *The Birth*, 573–8; Tovy, *Israel and the Palestinian Refugee Issue*, 56–65; Peretz, *Israel*, 40–50; Masalha, *The Politics of Denial*, 67, 257.

93 Heyd to Herlitz, 1 July 1949, *DFPI*, 1986, 4:194; Pappé, *The Making*, 229–30; Tovy, *Israel and the Palestinian Refugee Issue*, 58.

94 Morris, *The Birth*, 573; Editorial note, *DFPI*, 4:206.

95 Gene Currivan, '100,000 Figure Given', *New York Times*, 2 August 1949.

96 Morris, *The Birth*, 573.

97 Sharett to Eban, 6 July 1949; Eban to Sharett, New York, 8 July 1949, *DFPI*, 4:207, 210; Cordier to Azcarate, 27 July 1949, AG20/S0161/0004/3, UN ARMS.

98 For more details on all of these figures and many more, see Cohen, *Truman and Israel*, 1990.

99 Sharett to Eban, 6 July 1949, *DFPI*, 4:207. See also: Tovy, *Israel and the Palestinian Refugee Issue*, 60.

100 Eban to Sharett, 8 July 1949, *DFPI*, 4:210.

101 Ibid.

102 Lourie and Rafael to Sharett, New York, 12 July 1949, *DFPI*, 4:218–19.

103 Elath to Sharett, Washington, 26 July 1949, *DFPI*, 4:250.

104 Lourie to Sharett, 19 July 1949, *DFPI*, 4:227.

105 Cohen, *Truman and Israel*, 92–3.

106 Lourie to Sharett, 19 July 1949, *DFPI*, 4:227.

107 To Acheson, Hilldring reported that upon receiving the 100,000 offer from the Israeli consul general in New York, he had promised only to pass the offer on to the president. 'I have not, of course, given Mr. Lourie any indication of the President's reaction to this proposal.' Hilldring to Secretary of State, 25 July 1949, *FRUS*, 6:1250–1.

108 Eban to Sharett, 27 July 1949; Eban to Shiloah, 28 July 1949, *DFPI*, 4:257, 259. See also Sharett to Elath, 21 July 1949 (237).

109 Azcarate to Cordier, 5 August 1949, AG20/S0161/0004/2, UN ARMS.

110 It appears as the news came to Acheson from Paul Porter, the new US delegate on the PCC, who had learned of the president's statement to Hilldring via Shiloah. See Elath to Sharett, 11 August 1949, *DFPI*, 4:320.

111 Secretary of State to US Del Lausanne, 9 August 1949, *FRUS*, 6:1291; McGhee expressed the same in a meeting with Elath, see: Elath to Sharett, 9 August 1949, *DFPI*, 4:309.

112 Ascheson to Porter, 9 August 1949, RG 130/MFA/2414/26, ISA; Shiloah to Sharett, 14 August 1949, RG 130/MFA/2442/6, ISA.

113 Elath to Sharett, 11 August 1949; Elath to Sharett, 18 August 1949, *DFPI*, 4:320, 368–9; Sharett to Shiloah, 13 August 1949, RG 130/MFA/2442/8, ISA.

114 Eytan to Shiloah, 11 August 1949, *DFPI*, 4:319.

115 Sharett to Shiloah, 10 August 1949, RG 130/MFA/2455/1, ISA.

116 Peretz, *Israel*, 72.

117 One of the methods employed by the Israelis was what Ilan Pappé calls 'rumor-mongering'. Pappé, *The Making*, 98.

118 Morris, *The Birth*, 505–48. For an overview of other steps Israel took to undermine the feasibility of repatriation, see Tovy, *Israel and the Palestinian Refugee Issue*, 26–31.

119 Peretz, *Israel*, 210. Before the Paris conference, there had been another effort, also unsuccessful, to negotiate in Geneva. For a detailed account of the Paris Conference (13 September to 17 November 1951), see Caplan, *Futile Diplomacy*, vol. 3.

120 A detailed account of these negotiations can be found in Marte Heian-Engdal, '"A Source of Considerable Annoyance": An Israeli–Palestinian Backchannel in the Efforts to Release the Blocked Palestinian Bank Accounts', *British Journal of Middle Eastern Studies* 43, no. 4, 644–60.

121 Caplan, *Futile Diplomacy*, 3:145.

122 For McGhee's own account of this process see George McGhee, *Envoy to the Middle World* (Harper Row, date unknown (page missing)), 28.

123 Albion Ross, 'U.N. Mid-East Unit Facing Hostility', *New York Times*, 3 September; Albion Ross, 'Boycott Move Reported', *New York Times*, 8 September 1949; Ross, 'U.N. Mid-East Unit Facing Hostility'; Albion Ross, 'Jordan and Israel in Refugee Plans', *New York Times*, n.d., 14 September 1949 edition. According to Pappé, the Clapp mission's final report was criticized by both Arabs and Israelis. Pappé, 'Britain and the Palestinian Refugees', 22. For the final report of the Mission, see Gordon R. Clapp, First Interim Report of the United Nations Economic Survey Mission for the Middle East, 16 November 1949, UNISPAL.

124 Karp, *Missed Opportunities*, 87; Tovy, *Israel and the Palestinian Refugee Issue*, 72–80; Peretz, *Israel*, 58–71.

125 For discussions on the establishment and role of UNRWA, see for example: McCann, 'The Role of UNRWA'; David P. Forsythe, 'UNRWA, the Palestine Refugees, and World Politics: 1949–1969', *International Organization* 25, no. 01 (1971): 26–45; Benjamin N. Schiff, *Refugees unto a Third Generation: UN Aid to Palestinians* (New York: Syracuse University Press, 1995).

Chapter 3

1 UN General Assembly Resolution/A/RES/302 (IV), 8 December 1949, UNISPAL.

2 Tovy, *Israel and the Palestinian Refugee Issue*, 81. For a discussion of the uniqueness of the Palestinian case, see Michael Kagan, 'The (Relative) Decline of Palestinian Exceptionalism and Its Consequences for Refugee Studies in the Middle East', *Journal of Refugee Studies* 22, no. 4 (2009): 417–38.

3 Wilcox to Herter, 10 May 1957, *Foreign Relations of the United States, 1955-1957, Near East*, vol. 17 (Washington, D.C.: United States Government Printing Office, 1990), 611.

4 Clapp, First Interim Report of the United Nations Economic Survey Mission for the Middle East; Mohammed K. Shadid, *United States Policy Towards Palestinian Refugees* (New York: St. Martin's Press, 1981), 58–9; Peter L. Hahn, *Caught in the Middle East: U.S. Policy toward the Arab-Israeli Conflict, 1945-1961* (Chapel Hill: University of North Carolina Press, 2006), 177.

5 Peretz, *Israel*, 20.

6 American Consul General, Jerusalem, to US State Department, 22 December 1952, NARA RG59/Lot55/D592/70.

7 On 25 January 1949, for example, then director of the Office of United Nations Affairs, Dean Rusk, gave a statement to this effect the US Senate's Foreign Relations Committee. Joseph C. Sattertwaite did the same as the director of the Office of Near Eastern and African Affairs at the US State Department on 23 February 1949. Both are quoted in Francis H. Russell, US Relations with the Arab States and Israel, 1918–52, October 1952, 59, RG59/A15632/1, NARA See also; McGhee to Wilcox, 26 July 1950, *Foreign Relations of the United States, 1950, The Near East, South Asia and Africa*, vol. 5 (Washington, D.C.: United States Government Printing Office, 1978), 958–9; American Consul General, Jerusalem, to US State Department, 22 December 1952, RG59/Lot55/D592/70. NARA; Mallory to Bergus, 13 December 1954, RG59/D518/28, NARA; Eban to Sharett, 25 October 1950 *DFPI*, 5:604. For a detailed scholarly analysis of the destabilizing effect that the refugee infiltration and subsequent Israeli response had in the early years of the conflict, see Morris, *Israel's Border Wars, 1949-1956*.

8 Bunche to Mrs George E. Hill, 25 May 1953, Bunche archives/Collection 2051/ Box 127/2, UCLA. See chapter 4:97.

9 Isaac Alteras, *Eisenhower and Israel: U.S.-Israeli Relations, 1953-1960* (Florida: University Press of Florida, 1993), 118.

10 The Eisenhower doctrine, which authorized economic and military assistance to any country that feared being taken over by communist forces, was not

formally approved by Congress as official foreign policy before 9 March 1957. For a discussion of the doctrine and its implications for US Middle East policy, see Peter L. Hahn, 'Securing the Middle East: The Eisenhower Doctrine of 1957', *Presidential Studies Quarterly* 36, no. 1 (1 March 2006): 38–47; Hahn, *Caught in the Middle East*, 224–7; Alteras, *Eisenhower and Israel*, 21, see also, 82–125.

11 Karp, *Missed Opportunities*, 140.

12 Interview with Roderic L. O'Connor, 2 April 1966, Dulles Oral History Collection, Public Policy Papers, Department of Rare Books and Special Collections, Dulles Collection Princeton University Library; Alteras, *Eisenhower and Israel*, 21.

13 Interview with Roderic L. O'Connor, 117–18.

14 Memorandum of Conversation, 27 January 1955, *FRUS*, 9 (part 1):31; See also Shuckburgh to Kirkpatrick, 2 February 1955, FO 371/115864, PRO.

15 Elath to Sharett, 12 November 1953, *DFPI*, 8:852–9.

16 Peretz, *Israel*, 27, 110–11.

17 For the reactions at the UN, see, for example, Eban to Sharett, 28 November 1953, RG 130/MFA/2310/4, ISA; for the British reactions see, for example, Note from Sir Francis Evans to Sharett, 16 October 1953; Elath to Sharett, 29 October 1953; Elath to Sharett, 12 November 1953, *DFPI*, 8:756–7, 818–19, 852–9; see also: Walid Khalidi and Neil Caplan, 'The 1953 Qibya Raid Revisited: Excerpts from Moshe Sharett's Diaries', *Journal of Palestine Studies* 31, no. 4 (1 July 2002): 77–98.

18 Pappé, 'Britain and the Palestinian Refugees', 19.

19 Raymond Hinnebusch, 'The Foreign Policy of Egypt', in *The Foreign Policy of Middle East States*, ed. Raymond Hinnebusch and Anoushiravan Ehteshami (Boulder, CO: Lynne Rienner Publishers, 2002), 97; Mark Tessler, *A History of the Israeli-Palestinian Conflict* (Bloomington: Indiana University Press, 1994), 337; Rogan, *The Arabs*, 282–7.

20 For a detailed discussion of the British presence in Egypt since 1882, see David Hurewitz, 'The Historical Context', in *Suez 1956: The Crisis and Its Consequences*, ed. Wm. Roger Louis and Roger Owen, 2nd edn (Oxford: Clarendon Press, 2003), 19–29.

21 The British contribution to UNRWA, for example, was cut at this time from 4 million to 2 million pounds sterling. 'Britain Reported Cutting Aid for Arab Refugees in Half', *Jewish Telegraphic Agency*, 9 April 1954, http://archive.jta.org/article/1954/04/09/3039370/britain-reported-cutting-aid-for-arab-refugees-in-half (Accessed 28 February 2019); Hurewitz, 'The Historical Context'.

22 For a detailed discussion of the Anglo-Egyptian settlement, see: Wm. Roger Louis, 'The Tragedy of the Anglo-Egyptian Settlement of 1954', in *Suez 1956: The Crisis and Its Consequences*, ed. Wm. Roger Louis and Roger Owen, 2nd edn (Oxford: Clarendon Press, 2003), 43–71; See also: Rogan, *The Arabs*, 287–8.

23 Evelyn Shuckburgh, *Descent to Suez: Diaries, 1951-56* (New York: W. W. Norton, 1987), 3, 245.

24 For the report itself, see Caplan, *Futile Diplomacy: Operation Alpha and the Failure of Anglo-American Coercive Diplomacy in the Arab-Israeli Conflict 1954-1956*, vol. 4 (New York: Routledge, 1997), 86–9.

25 Shimon Shamir, 'The Collapse of Project Alpha', in *Suez 1956: The Crisis and Its Consequences*, ed. Wm. Roger Louis and Roger Owen, 2nd edn (Oxford: Clarendon Press, 2003), 81.

26 Editorial note, *FRUS*, 9 (part 1), 1730.

27 Shamir, 'The Collapse', 74.

28 ''Ibid. In addition to Shamir's chapter on the Alpha Plan see also Caplan, *Futile Diplomacy*.

29 Dulles to Hoover, 17 December 1954, *FRUS*, 9 (part 1):1719–20. Eden and Dulles had loosely discussed the project in the previous autumn, before Shuckburgh was dispatched to the region. For the American thinking on the idea of an Arab–Israeli settlement initiative before the Paris meeting with the UK, see Jernegan to Dulles, 9 December 1954, *FRUS*, 9 (part 1):1707–10.

30 Shuckburgh, *Descent to Suez*, 242–3. Memorandum of Conversation, 22 January 1955, FO 371/115865, PRO; Summary of Meeting, 10.00 am, 22 January 1955, RG59/D518/28, NARA.

31 Keith Kyle, *Suez* (London: Weidenfeld and Nicolson, 1991), 56; See also: Shuckburgh, *Descent to Suez*, 266. Dulles repeated these same sentiments at a meeting with the British ambassador to the United States, Sir Roger Makins on 29 January 1955. See Memorandum of Conversation, 29 January 1955, FO 371/115865, PRO. And again a month later: UK Embassy Bangkok to FO, 23 February 1955, FO 371/115866, PRO.

32 Memorandum of Conversation, 27 January 1955, *FRUS*, 14:31; Shuckburgh, *Descent to Suez*, 247.

33 Memorandum of Conversation, 27 January 1955, *FRUS*, 14:31.

34 According to Israeli records, Stevenson met with Israeli UN diplomat Teddy Kollek on 30 September 1953 and with Eban on 2 October. Memorandum of Conversation, 8 October 1953, RG 130/MFA/2414/27, ISA; Eban to Bendor, 5 October 1953, RG 130/MFA/2310/4, ISA. Reports from 1956 suggest that Dulles made a similar effort before the 1956 presidential elections. See 'Dulles Seeks to

Prevent Congressional Debate on Arab-Israel Issue', *Jewish Telegraphic Agency*, 25 January 1956, Jewish News Archive, http://archive.jta.org/article/1956/01/25/304 6825/dulles-seeks-to-prevent-congressional-debate-on-arabisrael-issue (accessed 28 February 2019).

35 Memorandum of Conversation, 27 January 1955, *FRUS*, 14:31. Beeley to Shuckburgh, 16 February 1955, FO 371/115866, PRO; Editorial Note; Russell to Butterworth, 21 December 1955, *FRUS*, 9 (part 1):1730, 2.

36 This was the first round of meetings, after which the two partners developed their ideas in 'working groups' ahead of a second round of meetings, this time in London from 28 February 1955 to 10 March 1955. For this material, see especially, PRO/FO 371/115866.

37 Points of Agreement in London Discussion of Arab–Israeli Settlement, 10 March 1955, *FRUS*, 14:105.

38 Points of Agreement, 10 March 1955; Russell to Hoover, 2 February 1955, *FRUS*, 14:105, 41; Caplan, *Futile Diplomacy*, 1997, 4:94. Note that Caplan quotes the earlier memorandum, from 2 February, where this formulation is slightly different.

39 In NARA there are two different memoranda produced from this same meeting, and they vary somewhat in their level of detail. The following account is based on a combination of the two. Summary of Meeting, 2.30 pm, 24 January 1955, RG59/D518/28, NARA; Summary of Meeting, 3 pm, 24 January 1955, RG59/D518/28, NARA. For the British records of this first round of meetings, see PRO/FO 371/115865.

40 Shuckburgh in a letter to the British ambassador to the United States, Sir Ivone Kirkpatrick. Shuckburgh, *Descent to Suez*, 246.

41 Summary of Meeting, 2.30 pm, 24 January 1955, RG59/D518/28, NARA.

42 Ibid.

43 Summary of Meeting, 3.30 pm, 1 March 1955, RG59/D518/29, NARA.

44 Memorandum on UK–US Meeting on Arab–Israeli Settlement, 3 March 1955, RG59/D518/29, NARA.

45 Interview with George V. Allen, 29 July 1965, 28–9, Dulles Oral History Collection, Public Policy Papers, Department of Rare Books and Special Collections, Princeton University Library.

46 Summary of Meeting, 3 pm, 24 January 1955, RG59/D518/28, NARA.

47 Ogburn to Jernegan, 16 December 1954, RG59/D518/28, NARA. All quotes in this paragraph are from the same source.

48 Ibid.

49 Ibid.

50 Summary of Meeting, 3 pm, 24 January 1955, RG59/D518/28, NARA.

51 Summary of Meeting, 2.30 pm, 24 January 1955, RG59/D518/28, NARA.

52 Russell to Ludlow, 23 February 1955, RG59/D518/28, NARA.

53 *FRUS*, 14:102–5. The Arab secondary boycott blacklisted companies in or from non-Arab countries that did business with Israel. Famous examples included Pepsi and McDonald's, which because of this boycott, did not appear in Israel until the late 1980s. Under President Jimmy Carter, US Congress in 1977 passed two anti-boycott laws that sought to counteract the participation of US citizens in this boycott (or in any nation's economic boycott and/or embargoes): the Export Administration Act (EEA) and the Ribicoff Amendment to the 1976 Tax Reform Act (TRA). The laws are administered and enforced to this day by the Bureau of Industry and Security, under the US Department of Commerce.

54 Briefing Paper for Vice President Nixon, 16 September 1955, RG59/D518/30, NARA.

55 Zach Levey, 'Israel's Quest for a Security Guarantee from the United States, 1954-1956', *British Journal of Middle Eastern Studies* 22, no. 1/2 (1 January 1995), 44; Levey, *Israel and the Western Powers, 1952-1960* (Chapel Hill: University of North Carolina Press, 1997); Caplan, *Futile Diplomacy*, 4:112.

56 Sharett to Dulles, 12 April 1955, *FRUS*, 9 (part 1):149–50. Sharett was referring to the Anglo-Egyptian treaty, the Anglo-Jordanian treaty, the US–Iraq military aid agreement, the Turco-Iraqi pact and the Anglo-Iraqi agreement. See also: Sharett to Macmillan, 5 May 1955, FO 371/115868, PRO.

57 Dulles to Sharett, 18 April 1955, RG 130/MFA/2414/28, ISA.

58 Memorandum of Conversation, 27 January 1955, *FRUS*, 14:31.

59 Memorandum of Conversation, 12 May 1955, FO 371/115870, PRO; Dulles to Hoover, 12 May 1955, *FRUS*, 9 (part 1):185–6.

60 Ibid.

61 Shuckburgh, *Descent to Suez*, 255.

62 Russell to Secretary of State, 5 May 1955, RG59/D518/29, NARA.

63 Dulles to Byroade, 9 July 1955; Memorandum of Conversation, 14 July 1955, *FRUS*, 14:282–3; 295–9.

64 Macmillan to Washington, 12 July 1955, FO 371/115871, PRO; Shuckburgh to Beumont, 22 July 1955, FO 371/115872, PRO.

65 Shuckburgh to Beumont, 22 July 1955, FO 371/115872, PRO.

66 Russell to Dulles, 24 May 1955, *FRUS*, 9 (part 1): 206.

67 Shuckburgh, *Descent to Suez*, 266.

68 Memorandum of Conversation, 14 July 1955, *FRUS*, 14:297.

69 Shuckburgh, *Descent to Suez*, 266.

70   Ibid., 260, 288; Editorial note, *FRUS*, 14:301–2.

71   Macmillan to Washington, 12 July 1955, FO 371/115871, PRO; Baghdad to FO, 14 July 1955, FO 371/115871, PRO.

72   Elie Podeh, 'The Perils of Ambiguity: The US and the Baghdad Pact', in *The Middle East and the United States: A Historical and Political Reassessment*, ed. David W. Lesch, 4th edn (Boulder, CO: Westview Press, 2007), 90.

73   Macmillan to Washington, 12 July 1955, FO 371/115871, PRO; Shuckburgh to Beumont, 22 July 1955, FO 371/115872, PRO; Baghdad to FO, 14 July 1955, FO 371/115871, PRO; Podeh, 'The Perils', 86.

74   Macmillan to Washington, 12 July 1955, FO 371/115871, PRO; Shuckburgh to Beumont, 22 July 1955, FO 371/115872, PRO; Shuckburgh, *Descent to Suez*, 266.

75   Allen to Dulles, 9 August 1955, *FRUS*, 9 (part 1):341–2; Summary of Comments from the Field on Mr Russell's Letter of 22 July, 9 August 1955, RG59/D518/29, NARA.

76   Memorandum of Conversation, 3 August 1955, *FRUS*, 14:335–6.

77   For an overview of the election results see David Ben-Gurion, *Israel: A Personal History* (Tel Aviv: American Israel Publishing, 1971), 445.

78   The United Nations is *Ha-Oomot ha-Mookhadot* in Hebrew. Avi Shlaim, 'Conflicting Approaches to Israel's Relations with the Arabs: Ben Gurion and Sharett, 1953-1956', *Middle East Journal* 37, no. 2 (Spring 1983): 191. The Sharett cabinet officially resigned on 15 August 1955, and two days later Ben-Gurion was asked by Israeli president Yitzhak Ben-Zvi to form the new government. The Knesset then adjourned for the following two months, and the Sharett cabinet served in a caretaker capacity until November, when Ben-Gurion managed to assemble his new coalition. See: Lawson to State Department, 26 August 1955, *FRUS*, 14:399 (see footnote 2 in that memo).

79   Lawson (Tel Aviv) to Jernegan, 14 July 1955, RG59/D518/29, NARA.

80   Ibid.

81   Lawson (Tel Aviv) to Secretary of State, 21 February 1955, RG59/D518/32, NARA. The 'ingathering of Jews' was at the head of the program of Ben-Gurion's new government.

82   For the full text of Dulles' speech see: Caplan, *Futile Diplomacy*, 1997, 4:304–7 (appendix 6 in that book).

83   Alteras, *Eisenhower and Israel*.

84   Washington to FO, 31 August 1955, FO 371/115876, PRO. See also Harrison Salisbury, 'Political Overtone Noted in Dulles' Mid-East Plan', *New York Times*, 28 August 1955.

85   For a detailed account of the August 1955 raids and counter-raids, see Morris, *Israel's Border Wars, 1949-1956*, 361–5.

86 Though these numbers vary some in the literature, this account is based on the most thorough study of these events, in Morris, *Israel's Border Wars, 1949-1956*, 365–7; Alteras, *Eisenhower and Israel*, 158; Rogan, *The Arabs*, 290.

87 Washington to FO, 29 August 1955, FO 371/115876, PRO.

88 Memorandum from the Prime Minister's Office, 1 September 1955, FO 371/115876, PRO.

89 See Trevelyan to Shuckburgh, 20 September 1955, FO 371/115879, PRO; Memorandum of Conversation (3.30 pm Meeting), 21 September 1955, FO 371/115879, PRO; Baharain to FO, 3 March 1956, FO 371/121709, PRO.

90 Interview with Abba Eban, 28 May 1964, 22, Dulles Oral History Collection, Public Policy Papers, Department of Rare Books and Special Collections, Princeton University Library.

91 Memorandum of Conversation, 6 September 1955, RG59/D518/30, NARA.

92 Avner to Pinner, 21 October 1955, RG 130/MFA/328/12, ISA.

93 Both Blaustein of the American Jewish Committee and Abba Hillel Silver (a prominent Zionist) sent letters in which they 'warmly welcomed' Dulles's proposals. Morris to Rose, 12 September 1955, FO 371/115878, PRO.

94 Memorandum of Conversation, 16 September 1955, RG59/D518/30, NARA. The AZCPC was the forerunner to the American Israel Public Affairs Committee (AIPAC).

95 Ibid.

96 Memorandum of Conversation, 16 September 1955, RG59/D518/30, NARA.

97 Interview with Ambassador Francis H. Russell, 6.

98 Dulles to Eisenhower, 20 September 1955, MC108/Box 26/Folder 1, Princeton University Library Dulles Collection.

99 Shuckburgh, *Descent to Suez*, 275.

100 Motti Golani, 'The Historical Place of the Czech-Egyptian Arms Deal, Fall 1955', *Middle Eastern Studies* 31, no. 4 (1995): 803–27; Keith Kyle, 'Britain and the Crisis, 1955-1956', in *Suez 1956: The Crisis and Its Consequences*, edited by Roger Wm. Louis and Roger Owen, 2nd edn (Oxford: Clarendon Press, 2003)', 105; Alteras, *Eisenhower and Israel*, 139–41; Rogan, *The Arabs*, 297; Caplan, *Futile Diplomacy*, 1997, 4:154–5, 284.

101 Levey, *Israel and the Western Powers*, 25; Levey, 'Israel's Quest for a Security Guarantee from the United States, 1954-1956', 58; Alteras, *Eisenhower and Israel*, 173.

102 Dulles's statement to the committee as recounted in an Editorial Note in *Documents on the Foreign Policy of Israel, 1956, Companion Volume*, vol. 11 (Jerusalem: Israeli Government Printer, 2008), 106.

103   Russell to Secretary of State, 20 February 1956, RG59/D518/29, NARA. The
      Anderson mission is also referred to by its code name, 'Gamma'. For more
      detailed accounts of the Anderson mission, see Touval, *The Peace Brokers*, 106–
      33; Alteras, *Eisenhower and Israel*, 164–72; Caplan, *Futile Diplomacy*, 4:213–18.
104   Interview with Ambassador Francis H. Russell, 15–17; see also Caplan, *Futile
      Diplomacy*, 4:220–42.
105   Touval, *The Peace Brokers*, 131.
106   Morris, *Israel's Border Wars, 1949-1956*, 374–6.
107   Wm. Roger Louis and Roger Owen, eds, *Suez 1956: The Crisis and Its
      Consequences*, 2nd edn (Oxford: Clarendon Press, 2003); Kyle, *Suez*; Peter L.
      Hahn, *The United States, Great Britain, and Egypt, 1945-1956: Strategy and
      Diplomacy in the Early Cold War* (Chapel Hill: University of North Carolina
      Press, 1991); Avi Shlaim, 'The Protocol of Sevres, 1956: Anatomy of a War Plot',
      International Affairs 73, no. 3 (July 1997): 509–30; Rogan, *The Arabs*, 298–304;
      Tessler, *A History*, 336–43, 347–56.
108   Kyle, 'Britain and the Crisis, 1955-1956', 109.
109   Summary of Meeting, 2.30 pm, 24 January 1955, RG59/D518/28, NARA.
110   Morris, *Israel's Border Wars, 1949-1956*, 386–423.
111   Herter to Wilcox, 14 May 1957; Hanes to Dulles, 2 October 1957, *FRUS*, 17:618,
      745.

Chapter 4

1   Wilcox and Rountree to Dulles and Herter, 2 July 1957, *FRUS*, 17:662.
2   Wilcox to Herter, 10 May 1957, *FRUS*, 17:610–11.
3   Pub. L. 85-141, 14 August 1957, 71 Stat. 355 as quoted in Villard to Dulles, 30
     September 1957, *FRUS*, 17:743.
4   Villard to Dulles, 30 September 1957; Hanes to Dulles, 2 October 1957, *FRUS*,
     17:743, 745.
5   Herter to Wilcox, 14 May 1957; Dulles to Lodge, 13 June 1957, *FRUS*, 17:618,
     642.
6   Wilcox and Rountree to Dulles and Herter, 2 July 1957, *FRUS*, 17:661–77.
7   Ibid., 670. All of the quotes in the following three paragraphs are from the same
     memo.
8   Ibid., 672.
9   Wilcox and Rountree to Dulles and Herter, 2 July 1957, *FRUS*, 17:672.
10   Ibid.: 668.

11 Memorandum of Conversation, 24 June 1957, *FRUS*, 17:655.

12 Villard to Herter, 6 August 1957, *FRUS*, 17:699.

13 Howe to Herter, 8 August 1957, *FRUS*, 17:707.

14 Memorandum of Conversation, 8 August 1957, *FRUS*, 17:708, 707.

15 The Syrians accused the American embassy staff of plotting against the Syrian government. Editorial Note, *FRUS*, 17:708.

16 Villard to Dulles, 30 September 1957; Villard to Dulles, 21 November 1957, Attachment II (Palestine refugee problem), *FRUS*, 17:741–3, 808–9.

17 Villard to Dulles, 30 September 1957, *FRUS*, 17:742.

18 Memorandum of Conversation, 25 November 1957, *FRUS*, 17:823; Engen to MFA, 6 December 1957, UD 26.6/65, XVII.

19 Villard to Herter, 3 December 1957, *FRUS*, 17:835.

20 Villard to Herter, 3 December 1957 (see footnote 8); Memorandum of Conversation, 25 November 1957, *FRUS*, 17:836, 823–5.

21 Brian Urquhart, *Hammarskjold* (W. W. Norton and Company, Inc., 1994), 371.

22 Villard to Herter, 3 December 1957, *FRUS*, 17:835.

23 Wilcox to Dulles, 21 November 1957, *FRUS*, 17:816–19.

24 Ibid., 817. All of the following quotes in the subsequent paragraph are from the same memo.

25 Ibid., 837 (see footnote 9 of that memo).

26 Memorandum of Conversation, 24 June 1957, *FRUS*, 17:655.

27 Eban to US Division, 16 March 1956; Shiloah to US Division, 31 August 1956; Eban to US Division, 11 September 1956; Eban to Meir and Herzog, 28 September 1956; Eban to US Division, 9 October 1956; *DFPI Companion Vol*, 11:152–3, 384, 392, 418, 443.

28 This project, begun in 1953, had caused some uproar in the region and internationally because it was located in the demilitarized zone between Syria and Israel. Syria submitted a complaint to the UN Security Council and Israel that forced Israel to halt its activities. This was also the background for the appointment of Eric Johnston as Eisenhower's special envoy. *Documents on the Foreign Policy of Israel, 1958/59, Companion Volume*, vol. 13 (Jerusalem: Keter Press, 2001), xvii. See also chapter 5:90.

29 The Export–Import Bank had been prepared to dispatch a delegation on a fact-finding mission in October 1956, but because of the Suez Crisis, this never happened. See Eban to US Division, 9 October 1956 *DFPI Companion Vol*, 11:443 (see footnote 2 of this memorandum. See also Editorial note in same edition: 106); Memorandum of Conversation, 14 January 1958, *FRUS,* 8:10–15.

30 Eban to US Division, *DFPI Companion Vol*, 11:153; Memorandum of Conversation, 6 August 1957, *FRUS*, 17:701.

31 Editorial Note, *FRUS*, 17:825.

32 Heath to Dulles, 17 December 1957, *FRUS*, 17:859–60; Memorandum of Conversation, 1 January 1957, *FRUS*, 8:2.

33 Memorandum of Conversation, 20 June 1957; Memorandum of Conversation, 24 June 1957; Memorandum of Conversation, 12 October 1957; For the Anglo-American meetings where this was addressed, see Memorandum of Conversation, 22 October 1957; Memorandum of Conversation, 25 October 1957; *FRUS*, 17:649–51, 654–6, 759–62, 774–5.

34 US Division to Israeli Embassy in Washington, 14 January 1958, *DFPI Companion Vol*, 13:46.

35 Rountree to Dulles, October 28, 1957, RG59/CFD1955-1959/4931, NARA.

36 Using economic leverage was, for example discussed in this memo from Villard to Herter, 6 August 1957, *FRUS*, 17:199.

37 Rountree to Dulles, 6 December 1957, *FRUS*, 17:846.

38 Ibid.

39 Eban to MFA, 15 January 1958, Gilead, *DFPI Companion Vol*, 13:47; See also: Rountree to Dulles, 6 December 1957 *FRUS*, 17:846 (see footnote 7).

40 Eban to MFA, 15 January 1958, *DFPI Companion Vol*, 13:47; Rountree to Dulles, 6 December 1957, *FRUS*, 17:846; Memorandum of Conversation, 14 January 1958, *FRUS*, 8:10–15.

41 Eban to MFA, 15 January 1958, *DFPI Companion Vol*, 13:47; Memorandum of Conversation, 14 January 1958, *FRUS*, 8:10–15.

42 Memorandum of Conversation, 14 January 1958, *FRUS*, 8:10–15.

43 Memorandum of Conversation, 14 January 1958, *FRUS*, 8:13–14. See also Eban to MFA, 15 January 1958, *DFPI Companion Vol*, 13:47–8.

44 Ibid.

45 Specifically, this is a reference to a conversation among Golda Meir, Herzog and Eban on 12 October 1957, see Memorandum of Conversation, 12 October 1957, *FRUS*, 17:759–62.

46 Memorandum of Conversation, 14 January 1958, *FRUS*, 8:13–14. See also Eban to MFA, 15 January 1958, *DFPI Companion Vol*, 13:47–8. The quotes in the subsequent paragraph are from the same memo.

47 This had been discussed in several bilateral consultations: Memorandum of Conversation, 24 June 1957; Memorandum of Conversation, 12 October 1957; Memorandum of Conversation, 31 October 1957; *FRUS*, 17:656, 759–62, 779–85. It was addressed later, in the winter of 1958; see Eban to MFA, 15 January 1958, *DFPI Companion Vol*, 13:48.

48 Memorandum of Conversation, 14 January 1958, *FRUS*, 8:13–14.

49 Ibid. See also: Eban to MFA, 15 January 1958, *DFPI Companion Vol*, 13:47–8.

50 Memorandum of Conversation, 14 January 1958, *FRUS*, 8:13–14. See also: Eban to MFA, 15 January 1958, *DFPI Companion Vol*, 13:47–8.

51 Ibid.

52 Herter to Dulles, 30 January 1958, *FRUS*, 8:18.

53 Herter to McClintock, 13 February 1958, *FRUS*, 8:20.

54 Herter to Dulles, 30 January 1958, *FRUS*, 8:18.

55 Eban to Meir, 15 January 1958, *DFPI Companion Vol*, 13:49.

56 Golda Meir's view of the Arabs, as described by Abba Eban. The Israeli cabinet under Meir, Eban further notes, had a 'tendency to be apocalyptic about the Arab world'. Shlaim, 'Interview Eban'.

57 Meir to Eban, 19 January 1958, *DFPI Companion Vol*, 13:49 (see footnote 3 of that memo).

58 Eban to Meir, 15 January 1958, *DFPI Companion Vol*, 13:49.

59 Ibid.

60 Eban to Israeli Ministry of Foreign Affairs on 6 February 1958, as quoted in Herzog to the US Division, 4 March 1958, *DFPI Companion Vol*, 13:49–50 (see especially footnote 1).

61 Memorandum of Conversation, 9 January 1958, *FRUS*, 8:8–10.

62 Herter to Dulles, 30 January 1958, (attachment), *FRUS*, 8:16–18.

63 Ibid.

64 According to Israeli records, the exact amount was 24.2 million. See Herzog to US Division, 4 March 1958, *DFPI Companion Vol*, 13:50.

65 Herter to Dulles, 30 January 1958, *FRUS*, 8:17–18.

66 Ibid.

67 Ibid., 15.

68 Shlaim, *The Iron Wall*, 192–9; Trita Parsi, *Treacherous Alliance: The Secret Dealings of Israel, Iran, and the United States* (New Haven: Yale University Press, 2007).

69 Shlaim, *The Iron Wall*, 192; Parsi, *Treacherous Alliance*.

70 Shlaim, *The Iron Wall*, 192, 199; Rogan, *The Arabs*, 307–8; Tessler, *A History*, 357–8.

71 On 11 June 1958, in turn, the Security Council passed its resolution leading to the United Nations Observation Group in Lebanon (UNOGIL).

72 Rogan, *The Arabs*, 312–13.

73 Alteras, *Eisenhower and Israel*, 307–9; Rogan, *The Arabs*, 310–12, 314–15; Erika Alin, 'US Policy and Military Intervention in the 1958 Lebanon Crisis', in *The Middle East and the United States: A Historical and Political Reassessment*, ed. David W. Lesch, 4th edn (Boulder, CO: Westview Press, 2007), 122–40. By mid-October, all US troops had been withdrawn from Beirut.

74 Hanes to Dulles, 2 October 1957, *FRUS*, 8:745–7. Normally, this would be the president's job, but by executive order 10575 Eisenhower had delegated the authority to formulate US assistance to UNRWA to Dulles.

75 Herter to Hammarskjöld, 12 March 1959, *FRUS*, 8:154–6.

76 Ibid.

77 Ibid., 178–9.

78 Dag Hammarskjöld, Proposals for the Continuation of United Nations Assistance to Palestine Refugees, A/4121, 15 June 1959, UNISPAL; Aid to Palestine refugees, Yearbook of the United Nations, 1959, Questions Concerning the Middle East, 31 December 1959, UNISPAL.

79 Beirut to State Department, 27 August 1959, *FRUS*, 8:194–5.

80 For the text of the Casablanca resolution, see League of Arab States, Protocol for the Treatment of Palestinians in Arab States, 11 September 1959, UNHCR.

81 Comay to Israeli missions abroad, 28 June 1958, *DFPI Companion Vol*, 13:112. All subsequent quotes in the paragraph are from the same memo.

82 Memorandum Regarding Palestine Refugees, 2 November 1961, National security files/Palestine/148, JFK Library.

83 Ibid.; Robert David Johnson, *Congress and the Cold War* (New York: Cambridge University Press, 2006), 71–8.

84 Hare to State Department, 17 November 1959, *FRUS*, 8:224–26.

85 Memorandum of Conversation, 24 November 1959, *FRUS*, 8:231–3.

86 See: Tiller and Waage, 'Powerful State, Powerless Mediator'; Caplan, *The Lausanne Conference, 1949*; Neil Caplan, 'A Tale of Two Cities: The Rhodes and Lausanne Conferences, 1949', *Journal of Palestine Studies* 21, no. 3 (1 April 1992): 5–34; Caplan, *Futile Diplomacy*, vol. 3; Forsythe, *United Nations Peacemaking*, 1972.

87 A. Biran, Memorandum of Conversation, 30 August 1950, RG 130/MFA/2445/1, ISA.

88 Ibid.

89 Heian-Engdal, 'A Source of Considerable Annoyance': Michael R. Fischbach, *Records of Dispossession: Palestinian Refugee Property and the Arab-Israeli Conflict* (New York: Columbia University Press, 2003), 108–9.

Chapter 5

1 'A time for greatness: John F. Kennedy for president' was the main slogan employed in the Democratic Party's presidential campaign in 1960. Its ambitious policies in both domestic and international contexts became known as the 'New

Frontier'. Kennedy himself used this term first in his speech to the Democrats' national convention in 1960.

2 Warren Bass, *Support Any Friend: Kennedy's Middle East and the Making of the U.S.-Israel Alliance* (Oxford: Oxford University Press, 2003), 63, 65.

3 John F. Kennedy, as quoted in: Abraham Ben-Zvi, *John F. Kennedy and the Politics of Arms Sales to Israel* (London: Frank Cass Publishers, 2002), 67.

4 Interview with Myer Feldman (part 2), interview by John F. Stewart, 11 December 1966, para. 458, JFK Library, http://www.jfklibrary.org/Asset-Viewer/Archives/JFKOH-MF-10.aspx (Accessed 28 February 2019).

5 Speech by Senator John F. Kennedy, Zionists of America Convention, Statler Hilton Hotel, New York, NY, 26 August 1960, The American Presidency Project; see also Bass, *Support Any Friend*, 54–5.

6 Ball to Kennedy, 28 April 1961, National security files/Palestine/148, JFK Library. For the reference to the campaign speech, see above, note 1.

7 Ibid.

8 Memorandum of Conversation, 13 February 1961, *FRUS*, 1994, 17:20–5.

9 Ibid. Myer Feldman claims that he and Kennedy sat down 'a couple of weeks' after the inauguration and discussed the possibility of a refugee initiative, though this has been hard to verify while Feldman's documents remain classified at the US National Archives' John F. Kennedy Library in Boston, Massachusetts. It must be said, however, that considering the history of the problem (as well as the development of this initiative) it is more likely that the approach originated in the US State Department. For Feldman's version of the events see: Interview with Myer Feldman (part 1), interview by John F. Stewart, 20 August 1966, JFK Library, http://www.jfklibrary.org/Asset-Viewer/Archives/JFKOH-MF-09.aspx (Accessed 28 February 2019).

10 Ball to Kennedy, 28 April 1961, National security files/Palestine/148, JFK Library.

11 Bowles to McClintock, 5 May 1961, RG59/CDF/1960-1963/521, NARA.

12 Meyer to McClintock (Beirut), 30 May 1961, RG59/MF/C168/Roll 17, NARA.

13 All of the letters to the Arab leaders contained more or less the same message, with smaller passages tailored to the respective country and its leader. The drafts and the letters, as well as the reactions to them, can all be found in the JFK Library: National security files/Palestine/148.

14 Kennedy to King Hussein, 11 May 1961, National security files/Palestine/148, JFK Library.

15 Ibid.

16 Unknown Author, June 1961, RG59/A15632/24, NARA. Original emphasis.

17 That this worry was genuine is illustrated by the US initiative to invite all of the Arab ambassadors for a clarifying meeting just three days after the

Ben-Gurion–Kennedy meeting. See: Memorandum of Conversation, 2 June 1961, RG59/MF/C168/Roll 3, NARA.

18 Editorial Note, *FRUS*, 1994, 17:86.

19 Bass, *Support Any Friend*, 55.

20 Ibid., 57.

21 Etta Bick, 'Two-Level Negotiations and U.S. Foreign Policy: The Failure of the Johnson Plan for the Palestinian Refugees, 1961-1962', *Diplomacy and Statecraft* 17, no. 3 (2006): 456–7.

22 Editorial Note, *FRUS*, 1994, 17:86.

23 Israel: Security: Briefing Book, Ben-Gurion Visit, May 1961, National security files/JFK Library, http://www.jfklibrary.org/Asset-Viewer/Archives/JFKPOF-119-019.aspx. All references below can be accessed online from this same address; Feldman to Kennedy, 26 May 1961, Israel: Security, 1961–3, 30 January 1961, JFK Library.

24 Appendix: Arab Refugees (Discussion) in Israel: Security: Briefing Book, Ben-Gurion Visit, May 1961, National security files, JFK Library.

25 Appendix: Talking Outline for Subjects to be Raised by the President in Israel: Security: Briefing Book, Ben-Gurion Visit, May 1961, National security files, JFK Library, 2 (see point 2g. in appendix).

26 Appendix: Talking Outline for Subjects to be Raised by the President in Israel: Security: Briefing Book, Ben-Gurion Visit, May 1961, National security files, JFK Library, 1.

27 Ibid.

28 Feldman to Kennedy, 26 May 1961, Israel: Security, 1961–3, 30 January 1961, JFK Library.

29 Memorandum of Conversation, 30 May 1961, *FRUS*, 1994, 17:134–41.

30 'Ben Gurion Sees Gain on Refugees', *New York Times*, 2 June 1961.

31 Rusk to US Embassies, 16 June 1961, RG59/CDF/1960-1963/2809, NARA; McClintock to Rusk, 16 June 1961, National security files/Palestine/148, JFK Library; McClintock to Rusk, 19 June 1961, National security files/Palestine/148, JFK Library, 19 June 1961; McClintock to Rusk, 19 June 1961, National security files/Palestine/148, JFK Library, 19 June 1961.

32 Meyer to Feldman, 17 July 1961, RG59/CDF/1960-1963/521, NARA; Editorial note *FRUS*, 1994, 17:193–4. Meyer used the list as a set of talking points in a conversation with Israeli ambassador Avraham Harman on 22 August 1961. See Rusk to Tel Aviv, 22 August 1961, RG59/CDF/1960-1963/521, NARA.

33 Meyer to Feldman, 17 July 1961, RG59/CDF/1960-1963/521, NARA.

34 Memorandum of Conversation, 30 May 1961, *FRUS*, 1994, 17:134–41.

35 Stevenson to Secretary of State, 30 January 1962, RG59/CDF/1960-1963/522, NARA.

36 Ibid.

37 Meyer to McClintock, 27 April 1961, RG59/CDF/1960-1963/521, NARA.

38 The initial idea, a Turkish candidate derived from the fact that Turkey was already a member of the PCC. When it became clear that the Turks did not want the mission, the Americans decided on a Canadian, whose name I have been unable to find in the US records. Either way, once it became known that Ben-Gurion had scheduled a visit to Canada, the Canadian candidate had to be dropped. Finally, the Americans tried to get Swiss UN ambassador, Auguste Lindt, to take the job: he was a UN expert on refugee issues and was close to the UN secretary general Dag Hammarskjöld as well. As he was in 1957 (regarding the Villard study), Hammarskjöld was very sceptical about the whole refugee initiative, which might have been why Lindt rejected the American advances.

39 McClintok (Beirut) to Meyer, 22 May 1961, RG59/MF/C168/Roll 17, NARA. See also: Reminiscences of Joseph Esrey Johnson, 1968, 7–8, Carnegie Corporation project/NXCP88-A439, Colombia University Rare Book and Manuscript Library, United States.

40 Memorandum of Conversation, 17 August 1961, RG59/CDF/1960-1963/521, NARA; USSD to Various US Embassies, 31 August 1961, RG59/CDF/1960-1963/521, NARA.

41 USSD to Various US Embassies, 31 August 1961, RG59/CDF/1960-1963/521, NARA.

42 Two exceptions are: Bick, 'The Failure of the Johnson Plan'; Zaha Bustami, 'The Kennedy/Johnson Administrations and the Palestinians', *Arab Studies Quarterly* 12, no. 1–2 (1990): 101–20. Of these two, only Bick's is based on primary documents.

43 See: Forsythe, *United Nations Peacemaking*, 1972, 125–6; Bass, *Support Any Friend*, 147.

44 Davies to Talbot, 3 January 1963, RG59/CDF/1960-1963/525, NARA; see also Rusk to US Middle East Embassies, 17 August 1961, RG59/CDF/1960-1963/521, NARA.

45 Davies to Talbot, 3 January 1963, RG59/CDF/1960-1963/525. NARA; see also Rusk to US Middle East Embassies, 17 August 1961, RG59/CDF/1960-1963/521, NARA.

46 Stevenson to Secretary of State, 30 January 1962, RG59/CDF/1960-1963/522, NARA.

47 Memorandum of Conversation, 17 August 1961, RG59/CDF/1960-1963/521, NARA.

48 USUN Del to Rusk, 6 October 1961, RG59/CDF/1960-1963/522, NARA. Sherwood Moe was originally a UNRWA staff member. He was picked for the position by Johnson, who wanted a man who was not connected to the US government.

49 UNPCC, Summary Records of the 350th Meeting, A/AC.25/SR.350, 18 January 1962, 26 July 1962, (Accessed 28 February 2019).

50 Memorandum of Conversation, 29 September 1961, RG59/CDF/1960-1963/522, NARA.

51 Ibid.

52 Johnson's analysis of the situation was communicated back to Washington via the US Embassy in Amman. Macomber to Secretary of State, 26 September 1961, RG59/CDF/1960-1963/522, NARA.

53 Ibid.

54 Memorandum of Conversation, 17 January 1962, RG59/CDF/1960-1963/522, NARA.

55 Memorandum of Conversation, 29 September 29 RG59/CDF/1960-1963/522, NARA.

56 Memorandum of Conversation, 6 February 1962, RG59/CDF/1960-1963/523, NARA.

57 Meyer to Rusk, 23 March 1962, National security files/Palestine/148, JFK Library.

58 Barbour to Secretary of State, 12 October 1961, RG59/CDF/1960-1963/522, NARA.

59 Ibid. The Americans also thought the statement was made to enhance Israel's tactical position before the upcoming UNGA debate. See also US Embassy Tel Aviv to USSD, Weekly Report, 2–8 November 1961, 9 November 1961, RG59/MF/C168/Roll 3, NARA.

60 US Embassy Tel Aviv to USSD, Weekly Report, 2–8 November 1961, 9 November 1961, RG59/MF/C168/Roll 3, NARA.

61 In Robert Putnam's metaphor of international bargaining as a two-level game, 'tying hands' is described as one of the tactics parties can employ to manipulate their domestic constraints (level 2), in order to enhance their own negotiation position at the international level (level 1). See: Robert D. Putnam, 'Diplomacy and Domestic Politics: The Logic of Two-Level Games', *International Organization* 42, no. 3 (1988): 427–60; Andrews Moravcsik, 'Introduction: Integrating International and Domestic Theories of International Bargaining', in *Double-Edged Diplomacy: International Bargaining and Domestic Politics*, ed. Peter B. Evans, Harold K. Jacobson and Robert D. Putnam (Berkeley: University of California Press, 1993), 28.

62 Tel Aviv to USSD, 8 February 1962, RG59/CDF/1960-1963/523, NARA.

63 Ibid.

64 Ibid.

65 Johnson to Secretary of State, 18 September 1961, RG59/CDF/1960-1963/522, NARA.

66 The Brazzaville block's original member states were Dahomey (now Benin), Cameroon, Congo (Brazzaville), the Central African Republic, Chad, Gabon, Ivory Coast, Madagascar, Mauritania, Niger, Upper Volta (now Burkina Faso) and Senegal. The alliance was formed in 1961 and was one of three main African blocs, the others being the Casablanca and Monrovia group, the former of which was Brazzaville's arch-rival. The Casablanca group sided with the Eastern block at the UN and included Nasser's Egypt. Isaac N. Endeley, *Bloc Politics at the United Nations: The African Group* (Lanham: University Press of America, 2009).

67 Stevenson to Secretary of State, 3 November 1961, RG59/CDF/1960-1963/522, NARA.

68 UN General Assembly Resolution, A/Res/1725 (XVI), 20 December 1961, UNISPAL. The resolution merely referred to Resolution 194 and paragraph 11, without including the specific language in it that referred to repatriation. This was the result of an Arab–Israeli thug of war over the draft resolution in the days prior to its introduction. See Stevenson to Secretary of State, 13 December 1961, RG59/CDF/1960-1963/522, NARA.

69 Memorandum of Conversation, 17 January 1962, RG59/CDF/1960-1963/522, NARA.

70 A month before Johnson's arrival, the border conflict between Syria and Israel had flared up and dramatically heightened the levels of tension in the region. On the night of 16 March Syria and Israel had clashed in the demilitarized zone of Lake Tiberias, where Israel claimed absolute sovereignty over the lake and the southern part of the zone, despite a lack of international support for this claim. The Syrians had fired earlier as well, on 8 March a week before the Israeli attack. The Security Council passed a near unanimous resolution addressing the situation (with French abstention) on 9 April 1962, UN SC Res. 171 (1962)/S 5111, 9 April 1962, UNISPAL.

71 Working paper five was simply the fifth draft produced by the Johnson mission before his departure for the Middle East. All of the working papers had been discussed in detail with the State Department throughout the spring. Extracts from Summary of Records of Dr Johnson's Talks in Israel, May 1962, RG/130/MFA/4315/10, ISA.

72 Extracts from Summary of Records of Dr Johnson's Talks in Israel, May 1962, RG/130/MFA/4315/10, ISA; Johnson to Talbot and Cleveland, 19 April 1962, RG59/CDF/1960-1963/523, NARA.

73 Johnson to Talbot and Cleveland, 19 April 1962, RG59/CDF/1960-1963/523,
    NARA; The same was reported by a source in the Israeli UN delegation, see
    Plimpton to Rusk, 24 April 1962, RG59/CDF/1960-1963/523, NARA.

74 Johnson to Talbot and Cleveland, 19 April 1962, RG59/CDF/1960-1963/523,
    NARA; Plimpton to Rusk, 24 April 1962, RG59/CDF/1960-1963/523, NARA.

75 Ibid.

76 Johnson to Talbot and Cleveland, 19 April 1962, RG59/CDF/1960-1963/523,
    NARA; Extracts from Summary of Records of Dr Johnson's Talks in Israel, May
    1962, RG/130/MFA/4315/10, ISA.

77 Plimpton to Rusk, 24 April 1962, RG59/CDF/1960-1963/523, NARA; Rusk to
    USUN Del, 24 April 1962, RG59/CDF/1960-1963/523, NARA.

78 Stevenson to Rusk, 4 May 1962, RG59/CDF/1960-1963/523, NARA.

79 Strong to Talbot and Cleveland, 7 June 1962, RG59/CDF/1960-1963/523, NARA.

80 Stevenson to Rusk, 4 May 1962, RG59/CDF/1960-1963/523, NARA.

81 Johnson visited Beirut on 19–23 April, Damascus 24–26 April, Cairo
    28 April–3 May, Amman 3–7 May and Beirut again on 10–12 May. Strong to
    Talbot and Cleveland, 7 June 1962, RG59/CDF/1960-1963/523, NARA.

82 Meyer (Beirut) to Secretary of State, 21 April 1962, RG59/CDF/1960-1963/523,
    NARA; Strong to Talbot and Cleveland, 7 June 1962, RG59/CDF/1960-1963/523,
    NARA.

83 Johnson to Talbot and Cleveland, 10 May 1962, RG59/CDF/1960-1963/523,
    NARA; see also Meyer to Rusk, 9 May 1962, RG59/CDF/1960-1963/523, NARA.

84 Meyer (Beirut) to Secretary of State, 21 April 1962, RG59/CDF/1960-1963/523,
    NARA.

85 Rogan, *The Arabs*, 309–10; Alin, 'US Policy and Military Intervention in the 1958
    Lebanon Crisis', 124.

86 Macomber to USSD, 9 May 1962, RG59/CDF/1960-1963/523, NARA.

87 Ibid.

88 Ibid.; see also Strong to Talbot and Cleveland, 7 June 1962, RG59/CDF/1960-
    1963/523, NARA.

89 Macomber to USSD, 9 May 1962, RG59/CDF/1960-1963/523, NARA.

90 Ibid.

91 Meyer to Secretary of State, 24 April 1962, RG59/CDF/1960-1963/523, NARA.

92 Ibid.

93 Memorandum of Conversation, 7 June 1962, RG59/CDF/1960-1963/523, NARA.

94 Johnson to Davis (UNWRA), 6 July 1962, Johnson Papers: UN Conciliation
    Commission, Herbert Hoover Presidential Library.

95 Johnson to Cleveland and Talbot, 15 May 1962, *FRUS*, 1994, 17:670–1.

Chapter 6

1 For the questionnaire-draft see: Talbot to Secretary of State, 27 July 1962, RG59/ CDF/1960-1963/523, NARA.

2 Johnson to USSD, 27 July 1962, RG59/MF/C168/Roll 6, NARA.

3 Ibid.

4 Memorandum of Conversation, 14 March 1962, *FRUS*, 1994, 17:531 (see note 4 in that memo).

5 Russell to Ludlow, 23 February 1955, RG59/D518/28, NARA. See chapter 5:153.

6 Johnson to USSD, 27 July 1962, RG59/MF/C168/Roll 6, NARA.

7 Ibid.

8 Ibid.

9 Ibid.

10 Talbot to Secretary of State, 27 July 1962, RG59/CDF/1960-1963/523, NARA.

11 Talbot to Secretary of State, 27 July 1962, RG59/CDF/1960-1963/523, NARA; Talbot and Cleveland to Secretary of State, 4 August 1962, RG59/CDF/1960-1963/2809, NARA.

12 'I do not share the Department's views on this point [i.e. compensation] and am not convinced by the arguments in its memorandum', Johnson stated at the conclusion of his letter. Johnson to USSD, 7 August 1962, RG59/CDF/1960-1963/523, NARA. See also: Talbot and Cleveland to Secretary of State, 4 August 1962, RG59/CDF/1960-1963/2809, NARA.

13 Rusk to Kennedy, 7 August 1962, National security files/Palestine/148, JFK Library.

14 See for example: Meyer to Bundy, 2 July 1962, RG59/MF/C168/Roll 14, NARA; Meyer to Talbot, 6 July 1962, RG59/CDF/1960-1963/523, NARA; Talbot to Secretary of State, 28 July 1962, RG59/CDF/1960-1963/523, NARA.

15 Talbot to Rusk, 9 July 1962, RG59/MF/C168/Roll 14, NARA.

16 Formally, the nuclear plant in Dimona is called the Negev Nuclear Research Center. See, for example, Avner Cohen, *Israel and the Bomb* (New York: Columbia University Press, 1999); Avner Cohen, *The Worst-Kept Secret: Israel's Bargain with the Bomb* (New York: Columbia University Press, 2010). At the Woodrow Wilson Institute's online website, one can access Avner Cohen's newest material. For a detailed account of the Kennedy administration's handling of the issue of Israel's nuclear program and the reactor in Dimona, see also: Bass, *Support Any Friend*, 186–238.

17 Arthur M. Schlesinger Jr., *A Thousand Days: John F. Kennedy in the White House* (New York: First Mariner Books/Houghton Mifflin Company, 2002); David

Schoenbaum, *The United States and the State of Israel* (Oxford: Oxford University Press, 1993), 131, 134; Bass, *Support Any Friend.*

18 Ibid.
19 Ibid.
20 Bass, *Support Any Friend*, 57; Ben-Zvi and Bick both refer to Feldman as the president's 'political liaison' to the American-Jewish Community. See Ben-Zvi, *John F. Kennedy and the Politics of Arms Sales to Israel*, 41; Bick, 'The Failure of the Johnson Plan', 456.
21 Interview with Myer Feldman (part 2), para. 475.
22 Ibid.
23 Ibid.
24 Bass, *Support Any Friend*, 212.
25 Ibid., 58–59.
26 Schlesinger Jr., *A Thousand Days*, 412–13, 417–20; Interview with Robert W. Komer, 22 December 1969, JFK Library; Ben-Zvi, *John F. Kennedy and the Politics of Arms Sales to Israel*, 77.
27 Ben-Zvi, *John F. Kennedy and the Politics of Arms Sales to Israel*, 77.
28 Talbot to Feldman, 9 August 1962, *FRUS*, 1995, 18:51–2.
29 Ibid.
30 Bass, *Support Any Friend*, 167.
31 Ibid., 145.
32 Ben-Zvi, *John F. Kennedy and the Politics of Arms Sales to Israel*, 2; See also: Bass, *Support Any Friend*, 144–85.
33 Ben-Zvi, *John F. Kennedy and the Politics of Arms Sales to Israel*, 65–101.
34 Talbot to Feldman, 9 August, 1962, *FRUS*, 1995, 18:51–2. All quotes in the two subsequent paragraphs are from the same memo.
35 Rusk to Feldman, 20 August, 1962, *FRUS*, 1995, 18:66–7; Bass, *Support Any Friend*, 170.
36 Bick, 'The Failure of the Johnson Plan', 468; Thomas Preston, *The President and His Inner Circle: Leadership Style and the Advisory Process in Foreign Affairs* (New York: Columbia University Press, 2001), 99–112.
37 Feldman to Kennedy, 10 August 1962, *FRUS*, 1995, 18:53–4.
38 Bass, *Support Any Friend*, 166.
39 Feldman to Kennedy, 10 August 1962, *FRUS*, 1995, 18:53–4. See also Interview with Myer Feldman (part 3), interview by John F. Stewart, 29 July 1967, para. 532, JFK Library (accessible online).
40 Interview with Myer Feldman (part 3), para. 535–6; Ben-Zvi, *John F. Kennedy and the Politics of Arms Sales to Israel*, 75; See also: Interview with Myer Feldman (part 1), para. 431–3.

41 Ben-Zvi, *John F. Kennedy and the Politics of Arms Sales to Israel*, 75.

42 Bick, 'The Failure of the Johnson Plan', 458. Talbot to Rusk, 12 September 1962, National security files/Papers of Robert W. Komer/436, JFK Library.

43 Interview with Myer Feldman (part 2), para. 471.

44 Memorandum of Conversation, 14 August 1962, *FRUS*, 1995, 18:54–8. See also: Interview with Myer Feldman (part 2), para. 470.

45 Interview with Myer Feldman (part 3), para. 535–6.

46 Memorandum of Conversation, 19 August 1962, RG93/MFA/1619/11, ISA.

47 After having returned to the United States, Feldman later reiterated to Meir that the 'matter of the 10%' was a matter strictly between the United States and Israel. Gazit to Meir, 28 August 1962, RG93/MFA/1619/11, ISA.

48 Memorandum of Conversation, August 1962, RG93/MFA/1619/11, ISA; Bick, 'The Failure of the Johnson Plan', 457.

49 Ibid.

50 Ibid.

51 Memorandum of Conversation, 19 August 1962, RG93/MFA/1619/11, ISA, 8. All of the quotes in the subsequent paragraph are from the same memo.

52 Badeau to Kennedy, Rusk and Grant, 24 August 1962, National security files/Palestine/148, JFK Library; Badeau to Secretary of State, 24 August 1962, RG59/MF/C168/Roll 17, NARA; Badeau to Secretary of State, 24 August 1962, RG59/MF/C168/Roll 17, NARA.

53 White House, *Meeting on Arab Israeli Questions*, Sound recording, vol. 1, tape 17, 17 vols., The Presidential Recordings: John F. Kennedy, The Great Crises: Meeting Recordings, July–August 1962 (New York: W.W. Norton, 1962), Kennedy Presidential Recordings, JFK Library.

54 Davis to Grant, 25 August 1962, National security files/Palestine/148, JFK Library.

55 Stevenson to Rusk, 22 August 1962, RG59/CDF/1960-1963/523, NARA. The Israelis had their own legal advisor, Shabtai Rosenne, write a detailed eight-page memorandum on his legal analysis of the Johnson plan and in particular on the UN machinery that was envisioned to help decide matters of disagreement. Rosenne concluded that Israel was under no obligation to 'avail itself of any such machinery'. See Shabtai Rosenne, Notes on Dr Johnson's Proposal by the Legal Advisor, 24 September 1962, RG130/MFA/4315/11, ISA.

56 White House, *Meeting on Arab Israeli Questions*.

57 Gazit to Meir, 28 August 1962, RG93/MFA/1619/11, ISA.

58 Ibid.

59 Memorandum, 30 August 1962, RG93/MFA/1619/11, ISA.

60 Komer to Kaysen, 28 September 1962, National security files/Palestine/148, JFK
    Library; Memorandum of Conversation, 26 September 1962, RG59/CDF/1960-
    1963/524, NARA; Memorandum of Conversation, 26 September 1962, RG130/
    MFA/4312/2, ISA; Memorandum of Conversation, 28 September 1962, RG130/
    MFA/4312/2, ISA.
61 The NSC advises the US president in matters pertaining to foreign policy and
    national security. It is part of the executive office of the president. Richard A.
    Best, *National Security Council: An Organizational Assessment* (Washington D.C.:
    Diane Publishing, 2010).
62 Shepard to Kennedy, 21 September 1962, National security files/Palestine/148,
    JFK Library; Memorandum of Conversation, 20 September 1962, RG59/
    CDF/1960-1963/524, NARA; Bundy to Komer, 20 September 1962, National
    security files/Palestine/148, JFK Library; Bick, 'The Failure of the Johnson Plan',
    461. Shepard's memorandum is dated 21 September, but from a handwritten note
    on the memo it appears as though Feldman talked directly with the president
    after the dinner, that is, on 20 September.
63 Talbot to Rusk, 20 September 1962, RG59/CDF/1960-1963/524, NARA; Bundy
    to Komer, 20 September 1962, National security files/Palestine/148, JFK Library;
    Bick, 'The Failure of the Johnson Plan', 460.
64 Bundy to Komer, 20 September 1962, National security files/Palestine/148, JFK
    Library.
65 Komer to Kaysen, 25 September 1962, National security files/Palestine/148,
    JFK Library; Komer to Kaysen, 22 September 1962, National security files/
    Palestine/148, JFK Library.
66 Komer to Kennedy, 25 September 1962, National security files/Palestine/148,
    JFK Library; Komer to Kaysen, 22 September 1962, National security files/
    Palestine/148, JFK Library; Talbot to Rusk, 30 September 1962, RG59/
    CDF/1960-1963/524, NARA; Bick, 'The Failure of the Johnson Plan', 462.
67 Bick, 'The Failure of the Johnson Plan', 458; Talbot to Rusk, 12 September 1962,
    National security files/Papers of Robert W. Komer/436, JFK Library.
68 Komer to Kaysen, 25 September 1962, National security files/Palestine/148, JFK
    Library, 25 September 1962.
69 Talbot to Rusk, 20 September 1962, RG59/CDF/1960-1963/524, NARA;
    Komer to Feldman, 20 September 1962, National security files/Palestine/148,
    JFK Library; Komer to Kaysen, 22 September 1962, National security files/
    Palestine/148, JFK Library; Kaysen to Kennedy, 23 September 1962, National
    security files/Palestine/148, JFK Library.

70 Komer to Kaysen, 22 September 1962, National security files/Palestine/148, JFK Library.

71 Kaysen to Kennedy, 23 September 1962, National security files/Palestine/148, JFK Library; Bick, 'The Failure of the Johnson Plan', 462.

72 Talbot to Rusk, 20 September 1962, RG59/CDF/1960-1963/524, NARA; Brubeck to Bundy, 19 September 1962, National security files/Palestine/148, JFK Library; Talbot and Cleveland to Rusk, 28 September 1962, RG59/CDF/1960-1963/524, NARA.

73 Ibid.

74 Ibid. This concept, the 'Algerianization' of the conflict, referred to recent developments in Algeria, where the Algerian nationalist National Liberation Front consolidated its power over the thousands of Algerians who would eventually join the fight for independence and also succeed in bringing its cause to the international stage. With the help of other countries in the Non-Aligned Movement, they brought the question in front of the General Assembly in 1957. The next year, they established a provisional government in exile (in Cairo). Eventually an Algerian plebiscite for independence was held, and when the Algerians voted overwhelmingly for independence, it was granted them on 3 July 1962. Rogan, *The Arabs*, 322–30.

75 Kimmerling and Migdal, *The Palestinian People*, 246.

76 Brubeck to Bundy, 9 August 1962, RG59/CDF/1960-1963/2809, NARA.

77 Komer to Kaysen, 22 September 1962, National security files/Palestine/148, JFK Library.

78 Memorandum of Conversation, 26 September 1962, RG59/CDF/1960-1963/524, NARA; The same message was repeated in a later conversation on 28 September. See Rusk to USSD, 29 September 1962, RG59/CDF/1960-1963/524, NARA; Komer to Kaysen, 29 September 1962, National security files/Palestine/148, JFK Library.

79 Talbot to Rusk, 30 September 1962, RG59/CDF/1960-1963/524, NARA.

Chapter 7

1 Talbot to Rusk, 30 September 1962, RG59/CDF/1960-1963/524, NARA.

2 Rusk to USSD, 29 September 1962, RG59/CDF/1960-1963/524, NARA.

3 Rusk to Kennedy, 7 August 1962, National security files/Palestine/148, JFK Library; Secretary of State to President Kennedy, 12 November 1962, RG59/CDF/1960-1963/524, NARA.

4   Rusk to Kennedy, 7 August 1962, National security files/Palestine/148, JFK
    Library.

5   One of the first news articles revealing the existence of the plan was Milton
    Freudenheim, 'Plan Is Proposed to Settle Palestine Refugee Problem', *Chicago
    Daily News*, 1 October 1962, AG20/S0161/0004/1, UN ARMS. Freudenheim's
    article was, according to Joseph Johnson, one of few factually accurate reports
    about the plan. Joseph E. Johnson, 'Arab Vs. Israeli: A Persistent Challenge to
    Americans', *Middle East Journal* 18, no. 1 (Winter 1966): 8 (see footnote 4 of
    that article). It has been difficult to locate the origin of the leak to the press. In
    theory, anybody opposed to the plan could have been behind it, as publicity was
    sure to complicate matters. Both Israel and the United States adamantly denied
    involvement, though. See Stevenson to Rusk, 2 October 1962, RG59/CDF/1960-
    1963/524, NARA.

6   Rusk to Kennedy, 4 October 1962, RG59/CDF/1960-1963/524, NARA.

7   Moynihan to Cleveland, undated 1962, National security files/Papers of Harland
    Cleveland/94, JFK Library; Talbot to Rusk, 30 September 1962, RG59/CDF/1960-
    1963/524, NARA.

8   Talbot to Rusk, 30 September 1962, RG59/CDF/1960-1963/524, NARA.

9   Rusk to Kennedy, 4 October 1962, RG59/CDF/1960-1963/524, NARA.

10 Rusk to USSD, 29 September 1962, RG59/CDF/1960-1963/524, NARA.

11 For the *note verbale* itself, see Stevenson to Rusk, 15 October 1962, RG59/
    CDF/1960-1963/524, NARA. For more on the Arab reactions, see, Meyer to
    Rusk, 25 September 1962, RG59/CDF/1960-1963/524, NARA; Stevenson to
    Rusk, 28 September 1962, RG59/CDF/1960-1963/524, NARA; Macomber to
    USSD, 12 September 1962, RG59/MF/C168/Roll 6, NARA; Meyer to USSD,
    18 September 1962, NARA; Macomber to Rusk, 20 September 1962, RG59/
    CDF/1960-1963/524, NARA; Knight to Secretary of State, 23 September 1962,
    RG59/CDF/1960-1963/524, NARA; Stevenson to Rusk, 9 October 1962, RG59/
    CDF/1960-1963/524, NARA; Brubeck to Bundy, 2 October 1962, RG59/
    CDF/1960-1963/524, NARA.

12 Talbot to Rusk, 30 September 1962, RG59/CDF/1960-1963/524, NARA.

13 Rusk to US UN Del, 16 October 1962, RG59/CDF/1960-1963/524, NARA.

14 Stevenson to Rusk, 17 October 1962, RG59/CDF/1960-1963/524, NARA.

15 Michael Comay, The Johnson Proposals and the Refugee Debate, 7 November
    1962, RG130/MFA/4331/1, ISA.

16 The meetings were all located in Washington, D.C., and took place on 12 and
    22 October and 1, 9, and 14. See: Memorandum of Conversation, 12 October
    1962, RG59/CDF/1960-1963/524, NARA; Memorandum of Conversation,

15 October 1962, RG130/MFA/4312/2, ISA; Memorandum of Conversation, 22 October 1962, RG59/MF/C168/Roll 6, NARA; Summary of Conversations, 22 October 1962, RG93/MFA/1619/12, ISA; Memorandum of Conversation, 23 October 1962, RG130/MFA/4312/2, ISA; Memorandum of Conversation, 23 October 1962, RG59/MF/C168/Roll 6, NARA; Memorandum of Conversation, 1 November 1962, RG130/MFA/4312/2, ISA; Memorandum of Conversation, 1 November 1962, RG59/CDF/1960-1963/524, NARA; Memorandum of Conversation, 14 November 1962, RG130/MFA/4312/3, ISA; Memorandum of Conversation, 14 November 1962, RG130/MFA/4312/3, ISA; Memorandum of Conversation, 14 November 1962, RG59/CDF/1960-1963/524, NARA.

17 Memorandum of Conversation, 12 October 1962, RG59/CDF/1960-1963/524, NARA.

18 Memorandum of Conversation, 21 November 1962, RG59/CDF/1960-1963/524, NARA.

19 Ibid.

20 Secretary of State to President Kennedy, 12 November 1962, RG59/CDF/1960-1963/524, NARA.

21 Memorandum of Conversation, 21 November 1962, RG59/CDF/1960-1963/524, NARA.

22 Memorandum of Conversation, 29 November 1962, RG59/CDF/1960-1963/524, NARA; Memorandum of Conversation, 29 November 1962, RG130/MFA/4312/3, ISA.

23 Ibid.

24 Ibid.

25 Ibid.

26 Talbot to Rusk, 4 December 1962, *FRUS*, 18:251–3 (see footnote 1 of that memo).

27 This comment is from an attachment to Komer's memo to the president, addressed to Bundy. Komer to Bundy, 16 November 1962, White House Classified Staff Files/Papers of Schlesinger/WH39, JFK Library.

28 Schlesinger Jr, *A Thousand Days*, 412–17.

29 Ibid., 407.

30 Ibid; Ben-Zvi, *John F. Kennedy and the Politics of Arms Sales to Israel*, 77; Interview with Robert W. Komer, para. 18.

31 Schlesinger Jr, *A Thousand Days*, 406–17.

32 Ibid., 413; See also: Best, *National Security Council*, 10–11.

33 Schlesinger Jr, *A Thousand Days*, 421; Best, *National Security Council*, 10.

34 The expression 'the best and the brightest' comes from the title of a book by journalist David Halberstam about the Vietnam War and specifically the way in

which Kennedy and his men tended to arrogantly insist on 'brilliant policies that defied common sense'. The term has since stuck as a popular reference to the Kennedy administration. David Halberstam, *The Best and Brightest* (New York: Random Housing Publishing, 1992).

35 Komer to Bundy, 16 November 1962, White House Classified Staff Files/Papers of Schlesinger/WH39, JFK Library.

36 Interview with Myer Feldman (part 3), 511.

37 Kaysen to Bundy, 5 December 1962, National security files/Palestine/148, JFK Library.

38 Ibid.

39 Komer to Bundy, 5 December 1962, National security files/Palestine/148, JFK Library.

40 Kaysen to Bundy, 5 December 1962, National security files/Palestine/148, JFK Library.

41 Ibid; Komer to Bundy, 5 December 1962, National security files/Palestine/148, JFK Library.

42 Komer to Bundy, 5 December 1962, National security files/Palestine/148, JFK Library.

43 Komer to Kennedy, 5 December 1962, National security files/Palestine/148, JFK Library.

44 Points Regarding Understanding between US and Israel Delegations Regarding Refugee Item at 17th Assembly, 9 December 1962, RG130/MFA/4312/3, ISA.

45 Ibid.

46 Points Regarding Understanding between US and Israel Delegations Regarding Refugee Item at 17th Assembly, 9 December 1962, RG130/MFA/4312/3, ISA; Memorandum of Conversation, 4 December 1962, RG130/MFA/4312/3, ISA.

47 Points Regarding Understanding between US and Israel Delegations Regarding Refugee Item at 17th Assembly, 9 December 1962, RG130/MFA/4312/3, ISA.

48 Ibid.

49 Ibid.

50 Komer to Kennedy, 5 December 1962, National security files/Palestine/148, JFK Library.

51 Feldman had even managed to secure the Israelis a deal on the Hawks that until then had been reserved only for Australia. Ordinarily, the Americans demanded payment for the missiles in cash or instalments over a three-year period at a 6 per cent interest rate per year. Secretary of Defense Robert McNamara was prepared to sell the Hawks under these auspices, until Feldman apparently intervened and got Kennedy to call McNamara and direct him to give Israel the

same deal as the Australians: a ten-year loan at 3.5 per cent. The deal established a powerful precedent for future military deals between Israel and the United States. Interview with Myer Feldman (part 3), para. 542–6.

52 Interview with Myer Feldman (part 4), interview by John F. Stewart, 26 August 1967, para. 576–80, JFK Library, http://www.jfklibrary.org/Asset-Viewer/Archiv es/JFKOH-MF-12.aspx (Accessed 28 February 2019).

53 Komer to Kennedy, 5 December 1962, National security files/Palestine/148, JFK Library.

54 Davies to Talbot and Cleveland, 28 September 1962, National security files/ Papers of Harland Cleveland/94, JFK Library.

55 Cohen, *Israel and the Bomb*; Cohen, *The Worst-Kept Secret*.

56 For the NTBT discussions in Vienna, see, for example, Schlesinger Jr, *A Thousand Days*, 368–70.

57 Schlesinger Jr, *A Thousand Days*, 897.

58 Walworth Barbour, Oral History Interview, interview by Sheldon M. Stern, 22 May 1981, para. 2, JFK Library, http://www.jfklibrary.org/Asset-Viewer/Archiv es/JFKOH-WB-01.aspx (Accessed 28 February 2019).

59 Avner Cohen and Marvin Miller, Bringing Israel's Bomb Out of the Basement, *Foreign Affairs*, 1 September 2010.

60 Israel crossed the nuclear threshold before the 1967 War. It has never admitted to or denied having a nuclear weapons program. This posture is known as nuclear opacity (or ambiguity) – *amimut* in Hebrew. Israel is the only nation in the world that has adopted this particular code of conduct and has not signed the nuclear non-proliferation treaty (NPT). Cohen and Miller, 'Bringing Israel's Bomb Out of the Basement'.

61 Press Release PAL/925, 1 February 1963, UNISPAL; Stevenson to Rusk, 31 January 1963, NARA RG59/CDF/1960-1963/525, NARA. Johnson returned to serving as the president of the Carnegie Institute until 1971. In the early 1970s, however, he was once again engaged in Middle East issues, this time as a part of a US 'Commission on the Middle East', a private and unofficial body that produced two reports on the Palestinian refugee issue and the economic development of the areas in which they lived. See Johnson to Urquhart, 13 December 1972, AG20/S0668/0001/06, UN ARMS.

62 Brief for President Kennedy, 5 February 1963, Israel: Security, 1961–3, 30 January 1961, JFK Library; Memorandum of Conversation, 6 February 1963, *FRUS*, 1995, 18:336–8.

63 Press Release PAL/925, 1 February 1963, UNISPAL.

64 Yost to Rusk, 28 January 1963, RG59/CDF/1960-1963/525, NARA.

65 Talbot and Cleveland to Rusk, 21 November 1962, RG59/CDF/1960-1963/524, NARA.

66 Talbot and Cleveland to Rusk, 18 January 1963, RG59/CDF/1960-1963/524, NARA.

67 Memorandum of Conversation, 3 January 1963, RG59/CDF/1960-1963/525, NARA.

68 Johnson, 'Arab Vs. Israeli', 8–9. In the collection of his private papers at the Herbert Hoover Presidential Library in Iowa, there are original paper clippings of some of the examples of inaccurate reporting – for example, the newspaper article: 'Were Refugees Proposals a Trap?', *The Jewish Observer and Middle East Review*, 12 October 1962, Herbert Hoover Presidential Library. On the margin of the clipping is the handwritten comment, most likely Johnson's: 'A fine collection of misapprehensions and outright lies'. See also Johnson to Talbot, 22 June 1964, RG59/A15632/24. NARA; Talbot and Cleveland to Rusk, 21 November 1962, RG59/CDF/1960-1963/524, NARA.

69 Memorandum of Conversation, 27 December 1962, RG93/MFA/1619/12, ISA. According to Meir's account this meeting, Kennedy leaned over to her, took her hand and told her: 'Don't worry. *Nothing* will happen to Israel.'

70 Meir as quoted in: Martin Gilbert, *Israel: A History*, 2nd edn (New York: Harper Perennial, 2008), 348.

71 Memorandum of Conversation, 27 December 1962, RG93/MFA/1619/12, ISA.

72 Ibid.

73 Ben-Gurion to Barbour, 22 January 1963, RG59/CDF/1960-1963/525, NARA.

74 Rusk to Bundy, 29 January 1963, RG59/CDF/1960-1963/525, NARA.

75 Talbot and Cleveland to Rusk, 18 January 1963, RG59/CDF/1960-1963/524, NARA.

76 Kennedy to Ben-Gurion, 30 January 1963, RG 130/MFA/4331/2, ISA.

77 Interview with Myer Feldman (part 1), para. 436.

Chapter 8

1 As quoted in Bustami, 'The Kennedy/Johnson Administrations and the Palestinians', 115, 114.

2 Ibid.

3 Shuqayri was a Palestinian lawyer who for years had served as the Saudi Arabian representative to the UN. He was known for his long and bombastic anti-Israeli speeches at the UN. Yezid Sayigh, *Armed Struggle and the Search for State the*

Palestinian National Movement, 1949-1993 (Oxford: Oxford University Press, 1999), 96–7; Yezid Sayigh, 'Armed Struggle and State Formation', *Journal of Palestine Studies* 26, no. 4 (1997): 17–32; Tessler, *A History*, 373–4; Rogan, *The Arabs*, 344; Baruch Kimmerling and Joel S. Migdal, *The Palestinian People: The Palestinian People: A History* (Cambridge, MA: Harvard University Press, 2003), 248–9; Rashid Hamid, 'What Is the PLO?', *Journal of Palestine Studies* 4, no. 4 (1975): 93–4; Shlaim, *The Iron Wall*, 230.

4 Tessler, *A History*, 373–4.

5 The first Fatah operation in Israel came in January 1965. Sayigh, 'Armed Struggle'; Sayigh, *Armed Struggle and the Search for State the Palestinian National Movement, 1949-1993*, 114–15; Rashid Khalidi, 'The 1967 War and the Demise of Arab Nationalism', in *The 1967 Arab-Israeli War: Origins and Consequences*, ed. Roger Wm. Louis and Avi Shlaim (Cambridge: Cambridge University Press, 2012), 283.

6 In his book, Khalidi discusses both this 'reemergence' of Palestinian nationalism and what he refers to as the 'lost years' of Palestinian national identity (1948–64). Khalidi, *Palestinian Identity*, 192. Similarly, Sayigh notes that there was a 'Palestinianness' rather than a 'Palestinianism' that marked the first period of the Palestinian diaspora's identity. Sayigh, 'Armed Struggle', 18; see also Sayigh, *Armed Struggle and the Search for State the Palestinian National Movement, 1949-1993*, chap. 1.

7 This was a struggle that was played out rhetorically as well: Fatah's own magazine, *Filastinuna*, was dedicated to promoting the strategy of provoking war between the Arab states and Israel. Kimmerling and Migdal, *The Palestinian People*, 245.

8 Louis and Shlaim, *The 1967 Arab-Israeli War: Origins and Consequences*; Michael B. Oren, *Six Days of War: June 1967 and the Making of the Modern Middle East* (New York: Ballantine Books, 2003), 33–126; Tessler, *A History*, 378–97; Rogan, *The Arabs*, 333–6; William B. Quandt, *Peace Process: American Diplomacy and the Arab-Israeli Conflict since 1967*. 3rd edn (Washington, D.C.: Brookings Institution Press and the University of California Press, 2005), 23–41; Ray Hinnebusch, *The International Politics of the Middle East* (Manchester: Manchester University Press, 2003), 163–71; Shlaim, *The Iron Wall*, 236–41.

9 Louis and Shlaim, *The 1967 Arab-Israeli War: Origins and Consequences*.

10 Ibid.; Shlaim, *The Iron Wall*, 236–41.

11 Louis and Shlaim, *The 1967 Arab-Israeli War: Origins and Consequences*, 8.

12 Quandt, *Peace Process*, 34, 41; Louis and Shlaim, *The 1967 Arab-Israeli War: Origins and Consequences*, 8–9.

13   Air Force Commander Motti Hod as quoted in Oren, *Six Days of War*, 170.

14   Shlaim, *The Iron Wall*, 241; Rogan, *The Arabs*, 337; Oren, *Six Days of War*, 170–82.

15   Tessler, *A History*, 399–405, 401–5; Rogan, *The Arabs*, 339.

16   Tessler, *A History*, 403–4; Shlaim, *The Iron Wall*, 251; Shlomo Gazit, *Trapped Fools: Thirty Years of Israeli Policy in the Territories* (New York: Routledge, 2003), 327–9.

17   Raz, *The Bride and the Dowry*.

18   Ibid., 39.

19   *From the 1948 Nakba to the 1967 Naksa*, Bulletin (Badil, 2004).

20   Masalha, *The Politics of Denial*, 178.

21   'Begin with the Refugees', *Richmond Times-Dispatch*, 11 June 1967, Johnson Papers: UN Conciliation Commission, 1964–70, Herbert Hoover Presidential Library.

22   Kochavi, 'The US, Britain and the Palestinian Refugee Question after the Six Day War', *Middle Eastern Studies* 48, no. 4 (2012): 537–52.

23   For standard accounts of the passing of resolution see: Shlaim, *The Iron Wall*, 260; Tessler, *A History*, 418–22; Quandt, *Peace Process*, 46–7; Kochavi, 'The US, Britain and the Palestinian Refugee Question after the Six Day War'; Fawaz A. Gerges, 'The 1967 Arab-Israeli War: US Actions and Arab Perceptions', in *The Middle East and the United States: A Historical and Political Reassessment*, ed. David W. Lesch, 4th edn (Boulder, CO: Westview Press, 2007), 174; Hulda Kjeang Mørk, 'The Jarring Mission: A Study of the UN Peace Effort in the Middle East, 1967–1971' (MA Thesis, University of Oslo, 2008), 39.

24   Shlaim, *The Iron Wall*, 260; Tessler, *A History*, 418; Mørk, 'The Jarring Mission', 39–40. For a detailed discussion of the role played by the British in the resolution, see Roger Wm. Louis, 'The Ghost of Suez and Resolution 242', in *The 1967 Arab-Israeli War: Origins and Consequences*, ed. Roger Wm. Louis and Avi Shlaim (Cambridge: Cambridge University Press, 2012).

25   After an interlude of sixteen months, the Jarring mission started its second phase in August 1970 and lasted until March 1971. The second phase was equally unsuccessful. Hilde Henriksen Waage and Hulda Kjeang Mørk, 'Mission Impossible: UN Special Representative Gunnar Jarring and His Quest for Peace in the Middle East', *The International History Review* 38, no. 4 (2015): 830–53.

26   Kochavi, 'The US, Britain and the Palestinian Refugee Question after the Six Day War', 537.

27   The Palestinian Refugee Problem: Options in an Arab-Israeli Settlement, 6 November 1970, NARA RG59/A15632/17, NARA.

28 Michael R. Fischbach, *The Peace Process and the Palestinian Refugee Claims: Addressing Claims for Property Compensation and Restitution* (Washington, D.C.: United States Institute for Peace Press, 2006), 82.

29 Tessler, *A History*, 422.

30 Ibid., 422–3; Khalidi, 'The 1967 War'; Kimmerling and Migdal, *The Palestinian People*, 240–73.

31 Sayigh, 'Armed Struggle', 18; Khalidi, *Palestinian Identity*, 182.

32 Fischbach, *The Peace Process and the Palestinian Refugee Claims: Addressing Claims for Property Compensation and Restitution*, 82–3; Sayigh, 'Armed Struggle'; Rosemary Sayigh, *The Palestinians: From Peasants to Revolutionaries*, 2nd edn (London: Zed Books, 2008); Kimmerling and Migdal, *The Palestinian People*; Rogan, *The Arabs*; Khalidi, *The Iron Cage: The Story of the Palestinian Struggle for Statehood*; Khalidi, *Palestinian Identity*, 192.

33 Rogan, *The Arabs*, 343; Khalidi, *Palestinian Identity*, 192.

34 Sayigh, 'Armed Struggle', 19.

35 Ibid., 19; Sayigh, *Armed Struggle and the Search for State the Palestinian National Movement, 1949-1993*, 114–16, 121; Shlaim, *The Iron Wall*, 230; Tessler, *A History*, 372–3; Rogan, *The Arabs*, 344–5; Kimmerling and Migdal, *The Palestinian People*, 248–9; Hamid, 'What Is the PLO?'

36 Sayigh, 'Armed Struggle', 19–20; Sayigh, *Armed Struggle and the Search for State the Palestinian National Movement, 1949-1993*, 174–5. See also: Tessler, *A History*, 425–6; Sayigh, *Armed Struggle and the Search for State the Palestinian National Movement, 1949-1993*, 174–9; Rogan, *The Arabs*, 346; Kimmerling and Migdal, *The Palestinian People*, 354; Mark Heller, 'Politics and Social Change in the West Bank Since 1967', in *Palestinian Society and Politics*, ed. Joel S. Migdal (Princeton, NJ: Princeton University Press, 1980), 202; William B. Quandt, Fouad Jabber and Ann M. Lesch, *The Politics of Palestinian Nationalism* (Berkeley: University of California Press, 1973), 55–8.

37 Bustami, 'The Kennedy/Johnson Administrations and the Palestinians', 115.

38 The Palestinian Refugee Problem: Options in an Arab-Israeli Settlement, 6 November 1970, NARA RG59/A15632/17, NARA.

39 90 Days Transition Paper: US Position on Arab Israel Confrontation and Efforts at Settlement, 21 November 1968, NARA RG59/A15632/2, NARA; Saunders to Atherton, 27 November 1968, NARA RG59/A15632/2, NARA; Saunders Comment on Further Studies on Middle East Policy-Report, 13 February 1969, NARA RG59/A15632/16, NARA.

40 Shadid, *US Policy*, 82–92. According to Shadid, Senator William Fulbright was possibly the first American official to express in public his recognition of some

form of Palestinian self-determination, including the possibility of a Palestinian state in the West Bank and the Gaza Strip.

41 The Palestinian Refugee Problem: Options in an Arab-Israeli Settlement, 6 November 1970, NARA RG59/A15632/17, NARA.

42 Ibid.

43 Ibid.

44 Ibid.

45 Ibid.

46 For a recent study of the policy discussion regarding the so-called 'Palestine option', that is, active US support for the establishment of an independent Palestinian state, see S. Zernichow and H. H. Waage, 'The Palestine Option: Nixon, the National Security Council, and the Search for a New Policy, 1970', *Diplomatic History* 38, no. 1 (2013): 182–209; see also Avi Raz, *The Bride and the Dowry: Israel, Jordan, and the Palestinians in the Aftermath of the June 1967 War* (New Haven: Yale University Press, 2012); In Arieh Kochavi's study of the refugee question after the 1967 War, the same idea surfaces, only this time as the possibility of a 'Palestine Republic', a quasi-independent state in the West Bank and Gaza Strip. See Kochavi, 'The US, Britain and the Palestinian Refugee Question after the Six Day War', 541.

47 Shadid, *US Policy*, 97.

48 The Palestinian Refugee Problem: Options in an Arab-Israeli Settlement, 6 November 1970, NARA RG59/A15632/17, NARA.

49 Ibid.

50 Zernichow and Waage, 'The Palestine Option'.

51 US diplomat Stephen Campbell attributed the coining of the phrase to Moshe Dayan. Campbell to Atherton, 18 July 1969, NARA RG59/A15632/3, NARA.

52 Gershom Gorenberg, *Accidental Empire: Israel and the Birth of the Settlements, 1967–1971* (New York: Times Books, 2006), 346. See also: Nadia Abu El-Haj, *Facts on the Ground: Archaeological Practice and Territorial Self-Fashioning in Israeli Society* (Chicago: University of Chicago Press, 2002).

53 Ibid.

54 Avi Raz has solidly rebuked the myth of Israel offering land for peace in the summer of 1967. See Avi Raz, 'The Generous Peace Offer That Was Never Offered: The Israeli Cabinet Resolution of June 19, 1967', *Diplomatic History* 37, no. 1 (2013): 85–108.

55 Gazit, *Trapped Fools*, 281, 268–83. Initially, after the 1967 War, the settlement project was driven by the religious block *Gush Emunim* (Bloc of the Faithful). With Ariel Sharon as minister of agriculture in 1977, however, the settlement

project became a venture for and driven by the Israeli state. The main point was to move swiftly so that future withdrawal from the territories could not be feasible. For an analysis of the religious component of the settlement project, see, for example, Gadi Taub, *The Settlers* (New Haven: Yale University Press, 2010).

Chapter 9

1 See Mitchell Geoffrey Bard, *The Water's Edge and Beyond: Defining the Limits to Domestic Influence on U.S. Middle East Policy* (New Brunswick, NJ: Transaction Publishers, 1991); John Mearsheimer et al., 'The Israeli Lobby', *Journal of Palestine Studies* 35, no. 3 (1 April 2006): 83–114; John J. Mearsheimer and Stephen M. Walt, *The Israel Lobby and U.S. Foreign Policy* (New York: Farrar, Straus and Giroux, 2007).

2 Edward W. Said and Christopher Hitchens, eds, *Blaming the Victims: Spurious Scholarship and the Palestinian Question*, 4th edn (London: Verso, 2001), 10.

3 Interview with Joseph Esrey Johnson.

4 Ibid.

5 Interview with Myer Feldman (part 2), para. 482.

6 Etta Bick, 'Transnational Actors in a Time Crisis: The Involvement of American Jews in Israel-United States Relations, 1956-57', *Middle Eastern Studies* 39, no. 3 (July 2003): 144–68.

7 Interview with Joseph Esrey Johnson.

8 Ibid.

9 See Etta Bick's contributions: Bick, 'Transnational Actors'; Bick, 'The Failure of the Johnson Plan'. Otherwise, this remains a topic that has mostly attracted attention in non-academic literature.

10 'No-agreement' as an analytical concept is borrowed here from Robert Putnam and his 'Diplomacy and Domestic Politics', 442.

11 Ben-Gurion as quoted Morris, *The Birth*, 577. See also Shlaim, *The Iron Wall*.

12 Khalidi, *Palestinian Identity*, 1998, 191–2.

Bibliography

Archives visited

Archives of the United Nations (UNARMS) in New York City.

Colombia University Rare Book and Manuscript Library, Colombia University, New York City.

Herbert Hoover Presidential Library, West Branch, Iowa (NARA).

Israeli State Archives (ISA), Jerusalem.

John F. Kennedy Library in Boston, Massachusetts (NARA).

National Archives in College Park, Maryland (NARA).

Seeley G. Mudd Manuscript Library, Princeton University, Princeton, New Jersey.

United Kingdom Foreign Office Files at the Public Record Office (PRO), Kew Gardens, London.

Edited Archival records

Documents on the Foreign Policy of Israel, October 1948–April 1949. Vol. 2, Jerusalem: Israel State Archives Keter Press, 1984.

Documents on the Foreign Policy of Israel, December 1948–July 1949. Vol. 3. Jerusalem: Israel State Archives Hamakor Press, 1983.

Documents on the Foreign Policy of Israel, May-December 1949. Vol. 4. Jerusalem: Israeli Government Printer, 1986.

Documents on the Foreign Policy of Israel, 1949, Companion Volume. Vol. 4. Jerusalem: Israeli Government Printer, 1986.

Documents on the Foreign Policy of Israel, 1950. Vol. 5. Jerusalem: Israel State Archives Keter Press, 1988.

Documents on the Foreign Policy of Israel, 1950, Companion Volume. Vol. 5. Jerusalem: Israel State Archives Keter Press, 1988.

Documents on the Foreign Policy of Israel, 1951, Companion Volume. Vol. 6. Jerusalem: Israeli Government Printer Keter Press, 1991.

Documents on the Foreign Policy of Israel, 1952. Vol. 7. Jerusalem: Israeli Government Printer Keter Press, 1991.

Documents on the Foreign Policy of Israel, 1952, Companion Volume. Vol. 7. Jerusalem: Israeli Government Printer Keter Press, 1991.

Documents on the Foreign Policy of Israel, 1953. Vol. 8. Jerusalem: Israeli Government Printer, 1995.

Documents on the Foreign Policy of Israel, 1953, Companion Volume. Vol. 8. Jerusalem: Israeli Government Printer, 1995.

Documents on the Foreign Policy of Israel, 1954. Vol. 9. Jerusalem: Israeli Government Printer, 2004.

Documents on the Foreign Policy of Israel, 1954, Companion Volume. Vol. 9. Jerusalem: Israeli Government Printer, 2004.

Documents on the Foreign Policy of Israel, 1956, Companion Volume. Vol. 11. Jerusalem: Israeli Government Printer, 2008.

Documents on the Foreign Policy of Israel, 1958/59, Companion Volume. Vol. 13. Jerusalem: Keter Press, 2001.

Foreign Relations of the United States, 1949, The Near East, South Asia and Africa. Vol. 6. US Government Printing Office, 1977.

Foreign Relations of the United States, 1950, The Near East, South Asia and Africa. Vol. 5. Washington, D.C.: United States Government Printing Office, 1978.

Foreign Relations of the United States, 1952-1954, The Near and Middle East. Vol. 9 (part 1). Washington, D.C.: United States Government Printing Office, 1986.

Foreign Relations of the United States, 1955-1957, Arab-Israeli Dispute 1955. Vol. 14. Washington, D.C., 1989.

Foreign Relations of the United States, 1955-1957, Near East. Vol. 17. Washington, D.C.: United States Government Printing Office, 1990.

Foreign Relations of the United States, 1958-1960, Arab-Israeli Dispute. Vol. 8. Washington, D.C.: United States Government Printing Office, 1992.

Foreign Relations of the United States, 1961-1962, Near East. Vol. 17. U.S. Government Printing Office, 1994.

Foreign Relations of the United States, 1962-1963, Near East. Vol. 18. United States Government Printing, 1995.

Political Documents of The Jewish Agency. Vol. 2. Jerusalem: Publishing House of the World Zionist Organization, 1998.

Yearbook of the United Nations, 1958.

Yearbook of the United Nations, 1959.

Interviews/oral sources

Interview with Mark F. Etheridge. Interview by Richard D. McKinzie, 4 June 1974. Truman Library (accessible online).

From Dulles Oral History Collection, Public Policy Papers, Department of Rare Books and Special Collections. Princeton University Library:

Interview with Abba Eban, 28 May 1964.

Interview with Ambassador Francis H. Russell, 6 April 1966.

Interview with George V. Allen, 29 July 1965.

Interview with Roderic L. O'Connor, 2 April 1966.

Interview with Senator Jacob Javits, 2 March 1966.

From JFK Library (accessible online):

Interview with Myer Feldman (part 1). Interview by John F. Stewart, 20 August 1966.

Interview with Myer Feldman (part 2). Interview by John F. Stewart, 11 December 1966.

Interview with Myer Feldman (part 3). Interview by John F. Stewart, 29 July 1967.

Interview with Myer Feldman (part 4). Interview by John F. Stewart, 26 August 1967.

Interview with Robert W. Komer, 22 December 1969.

White House. *Meeting on Arab Israeli Questions*. Sound recording. Vol. 1, tape 17. 17 vols. The Presidential Recordings: John F. Kennedy, *The Great Crises: Meeting Recordings*, July–August 1962. New York: W.W. Norton, 1962. Kennedy Presidential Recordings.

Interview with Joseph Esrey Johnson. Interview by William Quandt, 6 December 1968. In author's possession.

Official documents/reports

'Annual Report of the Director of UNRWA, 1 July 1954–30 June 1955'. Official Records, Tenth Session, Supplement No. 15 (A/2978). *United Nations*, 30 June 1955.

'Annual Report of the Director of UNRWA, 1 July 1956–30 June 1957/ A 3686'. *United Nations*, 30 June 1957.

'Bringing Back the Palestinian Refugee Question'. *Middle East Report*, International Crisis Group, October 2014.

'From the 1948 Nakba to the 1967 Naksa'. *Bulletin*. Badil, 2004.

Grandi, Filippo. 'Crossroads of Crisis: Yarmouk, Syria and the Palestine Refugee Predicament'. Lecture, *American University of Beirut*, 25 February 2014.

'Interim Report of the Director of UNRWA, General Assembly Official Records: 5th Session Supplement, No. 19 (A/1451/Rev.1)'. *United Nations*, 6 October 1950.

'Middle East Endgame I: Getting to a Comprehensive Arab-Israeli Settlement'. *Middle East Report*, International Crisis Group, July 2002.

'Progress Report of the United Nations Mediator on Palestine'. *United Nations*, 16
    September 1948. (Folke Bernadotte report)
'Proposals for the Continuation of United Nations Assistance to Palestine Refugees,
    A/4121'. *United Nations*, 15 June 1959. (Dag Hammarskjöld report)
'Refugee Repatriation, Resettlement and Compensation - UNCCP Special Rep.
    (Joseph E. Johnson report) - Proposal/Non-UN Document'. *United Nations*, 31
    August 1962.

Newspaper articles

'Arab Refugees on U.N. Payroll Resist Solution of Refugee Problem'. *Jewish Telegraphic
    Agency*, 15 November 1957.
'Arab Threatens Refugee Uprising'. *New York Times*, 7 May 1949.
'Begin with the Refugees'. *Richmond Times-Dispatch*, 11 June 1967.
'Ben Gurion Sees Gain on Refugees'. *New York Times*, 2 June 1961.
'Britain Reported Cutting Aid for Arab Refugees in Half'. *Jewish Telegraphic Agency*,
    9 April 1954.
Currivan, Gene. '100,000 Figure given'. *New York Times*, 2 August 1949.
Currivan, Gene. 'Egyptians Moving Refugees to Gaza'. *New York Times*, 21 August
    1949.
'Dulles Seeks to Prevent Congressional Debate on Arab-Israel Issue'. *Jewish
    Telegraphic Agency*, 25 January 1956.
Freedland, Jonathan. 'Maybe Israel Just Needs to Acknowledge Palestinian Pain'.
    Haaretz, 18 September 2009.
Freudenheim, Milton. 'Plan Is Proposed to Settle Palestine Refugee Problem'. *Chicago
    Daily News*, 1 October 1962.
Hamilton, Thomas J. 'Arab Refugee Case Placed before UN'. *New York Times*, 6
    August 1948.
Hamilton, Thomas. 'Israel Assails U.S. on Arab Re-Entry'. *New York Times*, 10 June
    1949.
Hazkani, Shay. 'Catastrophic Thinking: Did Ben-Gurion Try to Rewrite History?'
    Haaretz, 16 May 2013.
Hoffman, Michael L. 'US Gives U.N. Unit New Palestine Aim'. *New York Times*, 24
    August 1949.
'Israel Agrees to Release All Assets of Palestine Arab Refugees'. *Jewish Telegraphic
    Agency*, 30 September 1954.
'Israel's Reply to U.S. on Dulles' Statement Revealed at Bond Conference'. *Jewish
    Telegraphic Agency*, 12 September 1955.

Kashti, Or. 'Israeli Textbook under Review for Giving Palestinian Version of "Nakba"'. *Haaretz*, 22 September 2009.

'Lieberman's Party Proposes Ban on Arab Nakba'. *Haaretz*, 14 May 2009.

McCormick, Anne O'Hare. 'Israel Speeds Resettlement of Areas Left by the Arabs'. *New York Times*, 18 January 1949.

Morris, Benny. 'In '48, Israel Did What It Had to Do'. *Los Angeles Times*, 26 January 2004.

'Over 85 Percent Palestinians Fled Syria's Yarmouk Camp: UNRWA'. *Alarabia*, 12 March 2013.

Pipes, Daniel. 'Israel's Domestic Enemy'. *New York Sun*, 19 December 2006.

Ross, Albion. 'Boycott Move Reported'. *New York Times*, 8 September 1949.

Ross, Albion. 'Jordan and Israel in Refugee Plans'. *New York Times*, n.d., 14 September 1949 edition.

Ross, Albion. 'U.N. Mid-East Unit Facing Hostility'. *New York Times*, 3 September.

Salisbury, Harrison. 'Political Overtone Noted In Dulles' Mid-East Plan'. *New York Times*, 28 August 1955.

Schechter, Asher. 'Requiem for the Shekel'. *Haaretz*, 24 February 2012, sec. Week's End.

Shavit, Ari. 'Survival of the Fittest'. *Haaretz*, 7 January 2004.

'Stop Rewriting History'. *Haaretz.com*.

'Were Refugees Proposals a Trap?' *The Jewish Observer and Middle East Review*, 12 October 1962.

Yashar, Avi. 'Liberman Calls Arab Protesters A "Fifth Column"'. *Israel National News*, 7 May 2014.

Books and journal articles

Abdel Jawad, Saleh. 'The Arab and Palestinians Narratives of the 1948 War'. In *Israeli and Palestinian Narratives of Conflict: History's Double Helix*, edited by Robert I. Rothberg, 72–114. Bloomington: Indiana University Press, 2006.

Adwan, Sami, Dan Bar-On and Eyal Naveh, eds. *Side by Side: Parallel Histories of Israel-Palestine*. New York: The New Press, 2012.

Alin, Erika. 'US Policy and Military Intervention in the 1958 Lebanon Crisis'. In *The Middle East and the United States: A Historical and Political Reassessment*, edited by David W. Lesch, 4th edn, 122–40. Boulder: Westview Press, 2007.

Alteras, Isaac. *Eisenhower and Israel: U.S.-Israeli Relations, 1953-1960*. Florida: University Press of Florida, 1993.

Alund, Atle. 'Hans Engen: En utenrikspolitisk biografi'. MA Thesis, University of Oslo, 2014.

Artz, Donna E. 'Negotiating The Last Taboo: Palestinian Refugees', January 1996. http://prrn.mcgill.ca/prrn/papers/arzt1.html.

Aruri, Naseer, ed. *Palestinian Refugees: The Right of Return*. London: Pluto Press, 2001.

Ashton, Nigel. *King Hussein of Jordan: A Political Life*. New Haven: Yale University Press, 2008.

Azcárate, Pablo De. *Mission in Palestine 1948-1952*. Washington, D.C.: The Middle East Institute, 1966.

Ball, George W. and Douglas B. Ball. *The Passionate Attachment: America's Involvement with Israel, 1947 to the Present*. New York: Norton, 1992.

Bard, Mitchell Geoffrey. *The Water's Edge and Beyond: Defining the Limits to Domestic Influence on U.S. Middle East Policy*. New Brunswick: Transaction Publishers, 1991.

Bar-On, Dan and Sami Adwan. 'The Psychology of Better Dialogue between Two Separate but Interdependent Narratives'. In *Israeli and Palestinian Narratives of Conflict: History's Double Helix*, edited by Robert I. Rothberg. Bloomington: Indiana University Press, 2006.

Bar-On, Mordechai. 'Cleansing History of Its Content: Some Critical Comments on Ilan Pappe's The Ethnic Cleansing of Palestine'. *The Journal of Israeli History* 27, no. 2 (2008): 269–75.

Bar-On, Mordechai. 'Conflicting Narratives or Narratives of Conflict: Can the Zionist and Palestinian Narratives of the 1948 War Be Bridged?' In *Israeli and Palestinian Narratives of Conflict: History's Double Helix*, edited by Robert I. Rothberg. Bloomington: Indiana University Press, 2006.

Bar-Siman-Tov, Yaacov. 'The United States and Israel since 1948: A "Special Relationship"?'. *Diplomatic History* 22, no. 2 (1998): 231–62.

Bar-Tal, Daniel and Dikla Antebi. 'Siege Mentality in Israel'. *International Journal of Intercultural Relations* 16 (1992): 251–75.

Bar-Tal, Daniel and Gavriel Salomon. 'Israeli-Jewish Narratives of the Israeli-Palestinian Conflict: Evolution, Contents, Functions and Consequences'. In *Israeli and Palestinian Narratives of Conflict: History's Double Helix*, edited by Robert I. Rothberg, 19–46. Indiana Series in Middle East Studies. Bloomington: Indiana University Press, 2006.

Bass, Warren. *Support Any Friend: Kennedy's Middle East and the Making of the U.S.-Israel Alliance*. Oxford: Oxford University Press, 2003.

Beinin, Joel. 'No More Tears: Benny Morris and the Road Back from Liberal Zionism'. *Middle East Report*, 2004. http://www.merip.org/mer/mer230/no-more-tears.

Ben-Gurion, David. *Israel: A Personal History*. Tel Aviv: American Israel Publishing, 1971.

Benson, Michael T. *Harry S. Truman and the Founding of Israel*. Westport, CT: Praeger Publishers, 1997.

Benvenisti, Eyal, Chaim Gans and Sari Hanafi, eds. *Israel and the Palestinian Refugees*. Berlin: Springer, 2007.

Ben-Zvi, Abraham. *John F. Kennedy and the Politics of Arms Sales to Israel*. London: Frank Cass Publishers, 2002.

Ben-Zvi, Abraham. *Lyndon B. Johnson and the Politics of Arms Sales to Israel: In the Shadow of the Hawk*. New York: Routledge, 2012.

Berg, Kjersti G. 'The Unending Temporary: United Nations Relief and Works Agency (UNRWA) and the Politics of Palestinian Refugee Camps, 1950-2012'. PhD thesis, University of Bergen, 2014.

Bernadotte, Folke. *To Jerusalem*. Translated by Joan Bulman. London: Hodder and Stoughton, 1951.

Best, Richard A. *National Security Council: An Organizational Assessment*. Washington, D.C.: DIANE Publishing, 2010.

Bick, Etta. *Reasoning Together: Three Decades of Discussions between American and Israeli Jews*. New York: The American Jewish Committee, 1985.

Bick, Etta. 'Transnational Actors in a Time Crisis: The Involvement of American Jews in Israel-United States Relations, 1956-57'. *Middle Eastern Studies* 39, no. 3 (July 2003): 144–68.

Bick, Etta. 'Two-Level Negotiations and U.S. Foreign Policy: The Failure of the Johnson Plan for the Palestinian Refugees, 1961-1962'. *Diplomacy and Statecraft* 17, no. 3 (2006): 447–74.

Brown, Nathan. 'Contesting National Identity in Palestinian Education'. In *Israel and Palestinian Narratives of Conflict: History's Double Helix*, edited by Robert I. Rothberg, 225–43. Bloomington: Indiana University Press, 2006.

Brynen, Rex. 'Much Ado About Nothing: The Refugee Working Group and the Perils of Multilateral Quasi-negotiation'. *International Negotiation* 2 (1997): 279–302.

Brynen, Rex and Roula El-Rifai, eds. *Palestinian Refugees: Challenges of Repatriation and Development*. London: I.B. Tauris, 2007.

Brynen, Rex and Roula El-Rifai, eds. *The Palestinian Refugee Problem: The Search for a Resolution*. London: Pluto Press, 2014.

Buheiry, Marwan R. 'The Saunders Document'. *Journal of Palestine Studies* 8, no. 1 (October 1978): 28–40.

Bustami, Zaha. 'The Kennedy/Johnson Administrations and the Palestinians'. *Arab Studies Quarterly* 12, no. 1–2 (1990): 101–20.

Caplan, Neil. 'A Tale of Two Cities: The Rhodes and Lausanne Conferences, 1949'. *Journal of Palestine Studies* 21, no. 3 (1 April 1992): 5–34.

Caplan, Neil. *Futile Diplomacy: Early Arab-Zionist Negotiation Attempts, 1913-1931*. Vol. 2. New York: Routledge, 1983.

Caplan, Neil. *Futile Diplomacy: Operation Alpha and the Failure of Anglo-American Coercive Diplomacy in the Arab-Israeli Conflict 1954-1956*. Vol. 4. New York: Routledge, 1997.

Caplan, Neil. *Futile Diplomacy: Palestine Jewry and the Arab Question, 1917-1925*. Vol. 1. New York: Routledge, 1978.

Caplan, Neil. *Futile Diplomacy: The United Nations, the Great Powers and Middle East Peacemaking 1948-1954*. Vol. 3. New York: Routledge, 1997.

Caplan, Neil. *The Israel-Palestine Conflict: Contested Histories*. West Sussex: Wiley-Blackwell, 2010.

Caplan, Neil. *The Lausanne Conference, 1949: A Case Study in Middle East Peacemaking*. Tel Aviv: Tel Aviv University, Moshe Dayan Center for Middle Eastern and African Studies, 1993.

Carr, E. H. *What Is History?*. 2nd edn. London: Penguin Press, 1990.

Charlton, Thomas Lee, Lois E. Myers and Rebecca Sharpless, eds. *Handbook of Oral History*. Oxford: AltaMira Press, 2006.

Charlton, Thomas Lee, Lois E. Myers and Rebecca Sharpless, eds. *History of Oral History: Foundations and Methodology*. Oxford: AltaMira Press, 2007.

Christison, Kathleen. *Perceptions of Palestine: Their Influence on U.S. Middle East Policy*. Berkeley: University of California Press, 2001.

Christison, Kathleen. 'U.S. Policy and the Palestinians: Bound by a Frame of Reference'. *Journal of Palestine Studies* 26, no. 4 (1997): 46–59.

Clapp, Gordon R. 'First Interim Report of the United Nations Economic Survey Mission for the Middle East', 16 November 1949. UNISPAL. http://unispal.un.org/UNISPAL.NSF/0/648C3D9CF58AF0888525753C00746F31.

Cohen, Avner. *Israel and the Bomb*. New York: Columbia University Press, 1999.

Cohen, Avner. *The Worst-Kept Secret: Israel's Bargain with the Bomb*. New York: Columbia University Press, 2010.

Cohen, Avner and Marvin Miller. 'Bringing Israel's Bomb Out of the Basement'. *Foreign Affairs*, 1 September 2010. http://www.foreignaffairs.com/print/66682.

Cohen, Michael Joseph. *Truman and Israel*. Berkeley: University of California Press, 1990.

Davidson, L. 'Truman the Politician and the Establishment of Israel'. *Journal of Palestine Studies* 39, no. 4 (2010): 28–42.

Davis, Rochelle A. *Palestinian Village Histories: Geographies of the Displaced*. Stanford: Stanford University Press, 2011.

Devine, Michael J. *Harry S. Truman, the State of Israel and the Quest for Peace in the Middle East*. Kirksville: Truman State University Press, 2010.

Devine, Michael J., Robert P. Watson and Robert J. Wolz. *Israel and the Legacy of Harry S. Truman*. Kirksville: Truman State University Press, 2008.

Dumper, Michael. *The Future for Palestinian Refugees: Toward Equity and Peace*. Boulder: Lynne Rienner Publishers, 2007.

Eban, Abba Solomon. *Abba Eban: An Autobiography*. New York: Random House, 1977.

El-Haj, Nadia Abu. *Facts on the Ground: Archaeological Practice and Territorial Self-Fashioning in Israeli Society*. Chicago: University of Chicago Press, 2002.

Elmusa, Sharif. 'Toward a Unified Management Regime in the Jordan Basin: The Johnston Plan Revisited'. *Yale Forestry and Environmental Studies Bulletin*, no. 103 (n.d.): 297–313.

Endeley, Isaac N. *Bloc Politics at the United Nations: The African Group*. Lanham: University Press of America, 2009.

Enstad, Johannes Due. 'De Arabiske Jødenes Eksodus: Bakgrunn Og Årsaker [The Exodus of the Arab Jews: Context and Causes]'. *Babylon* 8, no. 2 (2010): 120–31.

Enstad, Johannes Due. 'Ilan Pappe: The Ethnic Cleansing of Palestine (Review)'. *Historisk Tidsskrift* 86, no. 3 (2007): 529–33.

Eshel, Amir, Hannan Hever and Vered Karti Shemtov. 'History and Responsibility: Hebrew Literature and 1948'. *Jewish Social Studies*, Special Issue, 18, no. 3 (2012): 1–9.

Evans, Peter B., Harold K. Jacobson and Robert D. Putnam, eds. *Double-Edged Diplomacy: International Bargaining and Domestic Politics*. Berkeley: University of California Press, 1993.

Evensen, Bruce J. 'Truman, Palestine and the Cold War'. *Middle Eastern Studies* 28, no. 1 (1 January 1992): 120–56.

Fischbach, Michael R. *Jewish Property Claims Against Arab Countries*. New York: Columbia University Press, 2008.

Fischbach, Michael R. 'Palestinian Refugee Compensation and Israeli Counterclaims for Jewish Property in Arab Countries'. *Journal of Palestine Studies* 38, no. 1 (2008): 6–24.

Fischbach, Michael R. *The Peace Process and the Palestinian Refugee Claims: Addressing Claims for Property Compensation and Restitution*. Washington, D.C.: United States Institute for Peace Press, 2006.

Fischbach, Michael R. *Records of Dispossession: Palestinian Refugee Property and the Arab-Israeli Conflict*. New York: Columbia University Press, 2003.

Fleischmann, Ellen L. *The Nation and Its 'New' Women: The Palestinian Women's Movement, 1920-1948*. Berkeley: University of California Press, 2003.

Forsythe, David P. 'The Palestine Question: Dealing with a Long-Term Refugee Situation'. *Annals of the American Academy of Political and Social Science* 467 (1 May 1983): 89–101.

Forsythe, David P. *United Nations Peacemaking: The Conciliation Commission for Palestine*. Baltimore: Johns Hopkins University Press, 1972.

Forsythe, David P. 'UNRWA, the Palestine Refugees, and World Politics: 1949-1969'. *International Organization* 25, no. 01 (1971): 26–45.

Fried, Shelly. 'The Refugee Problem at the Peace Conferences, 1949-2000'. *Palestine-Israel Journal* 9, no. 2 (2002). Available online https://pij.org/articles/144/the-re fugee-problem-at-the-peace-conferences-19492000.

Fried, Shelly. '"They Are Not Coming Back" - The Crystallization of Israeli Foreign Policy toward Possible Solutions of the Palestinian Refugee Problem, 1947-1956'. [Hebrew] PhD thesis, Tel Aviv University, 2003.

Gabbay, Rony E. *A Political Study of the Arab-Jewish Conflict: The Arab Refugee Problem (A Case Study)*. Genève: Librarie E. Droz, 1959.

Ganin, Zvi. *Truman, American Jewry and Israel, 1945-1948*. Teaneck: Holmes & Meier Publishers, 1978.

Gazit, Shlomo. *Trapped Fools: Thirty Years of Israeli Policy in the Territories*. New York: Routledge, 2003.

Gerges, Fawaz A. 'The 1967 Arab-Israeli War: US Actions and Arab Perceptions'. In *The Middle East and the United States: A Historical and Political Reassessment*, edited by David W. Lesch, 4th edn, 163–81. Boulder: Westview Press, 2007.

Gerges, Fawaz A. 'The Kennedy Administration and the Egyptian-Saudi Conflict in Yemen: Co-Opting Arab Nationalism'. *Middle East Journal* 49, no. 2 (1 April 1995): 292–311.

Gilbert, Martin. *Israel: A History*. 2nd edn. New York: Harper Perennial, 2008.

Ginat, Joseph and Edward J. Perkins, eds. *The Palestinian Refugees: Old Problems – New Solutions*. Norman: University of Oklahoma Press, 2001.

Golani, Motti. 'The Historical Place of the Czech-Egyptian Arms Deal, Fall 1955'. *Middle Eastern Studies* 31, no. 4 (1995): 803–27.

Gorenberg, Gershom. *Accidental Empire: Israel and the Birth of the Settlements, 1967-1971*. New York: Times Books, 2006.

Grose, Peter. *Israel in the Mind of America*. New York: Schocken, 1984.

Grossman, Grace Cohen, Stanley Chyet and Michael T. Benson. *On Moral Grounds: President Harry S. Truman and the Birth of the State of Israel*. Skirball Cultural Center, 1998.

Haddad, Mohanna. 'Palestinian Refugees in Jordan and Palestinian Identity'. In *Palestinian Refugees: Old Problems-New Solutions*, edited by Joseph Ginat and Edward J. Perkins. Norman: University of Oklahoma Press, 2001.

Hahn, Peter L. 'Alignment by Coincidence: Israel, the United States, and the Partition of Jerusalem, 1949-1953'. *The International History Review* 21, no. 3 (1999): 665.

Hahn, Peter L. *Caught in the Middle East: U.S. Policy toward the Arab-Israeli Conflict, 1945-1961*. Chapel Hill: University of North Carolina Press, 2006.

Hahn, Peter L. *Crisis and Crossfire: The United States and the Middle East since 1945.* Issues in the History of American Foreign Relations. Washington, D.C.: Potomac Books, 2005.

Hahn, Peter L. 'Glasnost in America: Foreign Relations of the United States and the Middle East, 1955–1960'. *Diplomatic History* 16, no. 4 (1992): 631–42.

Hahn, Peter L. 'Securing the Middle East: The Eisenhower Doctrine of 1957'. *Presidential Studies Quarterly* 36, no. 1 (1 March 2006): 38–47.

Hahn, Peter L. *The United States, Great Britain, and Egypt, 1945-1956: Strategy and Diplomacy in the Early Cold War.* Chapel Hill: University of North Carolina Press, 1991.

Halberstam, David. *The Best and Brightest.* New York: Random Housing Publishing, 1992.

Halperin, Eran, Daniel Bar-Tal, Rafi Nets-Zehngut and Erga Drori. 'Emotions in Conflict: Correlates of Fear and Hope in the Israeli-Jewish Society'. *Peace and Conflict: Journal of Peace Psychology* 14, no. 3 (2008): 233–58.

Hamid, Rashid. 'What Is the PLO?' *Journal of Palestine Studies* 4, no. 4 (1975): 90–109.

Heian-Engdal, Marte. '"A Source of Considerable Annoyance": An Israeli–Palestinian Backchannel in the Efforts to Release the Blocked Palestinian Bank Accounts'. *British Journal of Middle Eastern Studies* 43, no. 4 (2016): 644–60.

Heian-Engdal, Marte, Jørgen Jensehaugen and Hilde Henriksen Waage. '"Finishing the Enterprise": Israel's Admission to the UN'. *International History Review* 35, no. 3 (2013): 465–85.

Heller, Joseph. 'Failure of a Mission: Bernadotte and Palestine, 1948'. *Journal of Contemporary History* 14, no. 3 (July 1979): 515–34.

Heller, Mark. 'Politics and Social Change in the West Bank Since 1967'. In *Palestinian Society and Politics*, edited by Joel S. Migdal, 185–211. Princeton: Princeton University Press, 1980.

Hinnebusch, Ray. *The International Politics of the Middle East.* Manchester: Manchester University Press, 2003.

Hinnebusch, Raymond. 'The Foreign Policy of Egypt'. In *The Foreign Policy of Middle East States*, edited by Raymond Hinnebusch and Anoushiravan Ehteshami, 91–114. Boulder: Lynne Rienner Publishers, 2002.

Hinnebusch, Raymond and Anoushiravan Ehteshami, eds. *The Foreign Policy of Middle Eastern States.* Boulder: Lynne Rienner Publishers, 2002.

Hovdenak, A. 'Trading Refugees for Land and Symbols: The Palestinian Negotiation Strategy in the Oslo Process'. *Journal of Refugee Studies* 22, no. 1 (2008): 30–50.

Hurewitz, David. 'The Historical Context'. In *Suez 1956: The Crisis and Its Consequences*, edited by Wm. Roger Louis and Roger Owen, 2nd edn, 19–29. Oxford: Clarendon Press, 2003.

Hussein, Agha and Robert Malley. 'The Last Negotiation: How to End the Middle East Peace Process'. *Foreign Affairs*, June 2002.

Jacobs, Matthew F. *Imagining the Middle East: The Building of an American Foreign Policy, 1918-1967*. Chapel Hill: University of North Carolina Press, 2011.

Jensehaugen, Jørgen. 'Friendship Reanimated: The Israeli-Transjordanian Armistice Negotiations 1948-1949'. MA Thesis, University of Oslo, 2008.

Jensehaugen, Jørgen and Hilde Henriksen Waage. 'Coercive Diplomacy: Israel, Transjordan and the UN—a Triangular Drama Revisited'. *British Journal of Middle Eastern Studies* 39, no. 1 (2012): 79–100.

Jensehaugen, Jørgen, Marte Heian-Engdal and Hilde Henriksen Waage. 'Securing the State: From Zionist Ideology to Israeli Statehood'. *Diplomacy and Statecraft* 23, no. 2 (June 2012): 280–303.

Jiryis, Sabri. 'The Legal Structure for the Expropriation and Absorption of Arab Lands in Israel'. *Journal of Palestine Studies* 2, no. 4 (July 1973): 82–104.

Johnson, Joseph E. 'Arab Vs. Israel: A Persistent Challenge to Americans'. *Middle East Journal* 18, no. 1 (Winter 1966): 1–13.

Johnson, Robert David. *Congress and the Cold War*. New York: Cambridge University Press, 2006.

Jordanova, Ludmilla. *History in Practice*. 2nd edn. London: Hodder Headline Group, 2006.

Kafkafi, Eyal. 'Ben-Gurion, Sharett and the Johnston Plan'. *Studies in Zionism* 13, no. 2 (1992): 165–86.

Kagan, Michael. 'The (Relative) Decline of Palestinian Exceptionalism and Its Consequences for Refugee Studies in the Middle East'. *Journal of Refugee Studies* 22, no. 4 (2009): 417–38.

Karmi, Ghada. *Married to Another Man Israel's Dilemma in Palestine*. London: Pluto Press, 2007.

Karp, Candace. *Missed Opportunities: US Diplomatic Failures And The Arab-Israeli Conflict 1947-1967*. Claremont: Regina Books, 2005.

Karsh, Efraim. 'Benny Morris and the Reign of Error'. *Middle East Quarterly*, 1 March 1999.

Karsh, Efraim. 'Benny Morris's Reign of Error, Revisited'. *Middle East Quarterly*, 1 March 2005.

Karsh, Efraim. 'The Unbearable Lightness of My Critics'. *Middle East Quarterly*, 1 June 2002.

Khalidi, Muhammad Ali, ed. *Manifestations of Identity: The Lived Reality of Palestinian Refugees in Lebanon*. Beirut: Institute for Palestine Studies, 2010.

Khalidi, Rashid. 'The 1967 War and the Demise of Arab Nationalism'. In *The 1967 Arab-Israeli War: Origins and Consequences*, edited by Roger Wm. Louis and Avi Shlaim, 264–84. Cambridge: Cambridge University Press, 2012.

Khalidi, Rashid. *The Iron Cage: The Story of the Palestinian Struggle for Statehood*. Boston: Beacon Press, 2006.

Khalidi, Rashid. *Palestinian Identity: The Construction of Modern National Consciousness*. New York: Columbia University Press, 1998.

Khalidi, Rashid. *Palestinian Identity: The Construction of Modern National Consciousness*. New York: Columbia University Press, 2009.

Khalidi, Rashid. 'The Palestinians and 1948: The Underlying Causes of Failure'. In *The War for Palestine: Rewriting the History of 1948*, edited by Eugene L. Rogan and Avi Shlaim, 12–36. Cambridge: Cambridge University Press, 2007.

Khalidi, Walid. *All That Remains: The Palestinian Villages Occupied and Depopulated by Israel in 1948*. Washington, D.C.: Institute for Palestine Studies, 2006.

Khalidi, Walid. *Before Their Diaspora: A Photographic History of the Palestinians 1876-1948*. Washington, D.C.: Institute for Palestine Studies, 2010.

Khalidi, Walid. 'Plan Dalet: Master Plan for the Conquest of Palestine'. *Middle East Forum*, 1961.

Khalidi, Walid. 'Plan Dalet Revisited'. *Journal of Palestine Studies*, n.d.

Khalidi, Walid. 'Why Did the Palestinians Leave?' *Middle East Forum*, 1959.

Khalidi, Walid. 'Why Did the Palestinians Leave, Revisited'. *Journal of Palestine Studies* 34, no. 2 (2005): 42–54.

Khalidi, Walid and Neil Caplan. 'The 1953 Qibya Raid Revisited: Excerpts from Moshe Sharett's Diaries'. *Journal of Palestine Studies* 31, no. 4 (1 July 2002): 77–98.

Khouri, Fred J. *The Arab-Israeli Dilemma*. Syracuse: Syracuse University Press, 1968.

Khouri, Fred J. 'United Nations Peace Efforts'. In *The Elusive Peace in the Middle East*, edited by Malcolm H. Kerr, 19–101. Albany: State University of New York Press, 1975.

Kimmerling, Baruch and Joel S. Migdal. *The Palestinian People: A History*. Cambridge: Harvard University Press, 2003.

Kochavi, Arieh J. 'The US, Britain and the Palestinian Refugee Question after the Six Day War'. *Middle Eastern Studies* 48, no. 4 (2012): 537–52.

Kolinsky, M. 'The Efforts of the Truman Administration to Resolve the Arab-Israeli Conflict'. *Middle Eastern Studies* 20, no. 1 (1 January 1984): 81–94.

Kyle, Keith. 'Britain and the Crisis, 1955-1956'. In *Suez 1956: The Crisis and Its Consequences*, edited by Roger Wm. Louis and Roger Owen, 2nd edn, 103–30. Oxford: Clarendon Press, 2003.

Kyle, Keith. *Suez*. London: Weidenfeld and Nicolson, 1991.

Landis, Joshua. 'Early US Policy toward Palestinian Refugees: The Syrian Option'. In *The Palestinian Refugees: Old Problems - New Solutions*, edited by Joseph Ginat and Edward J. Perkins, 77–87. Norman: University of Oklahoma Press, 2001.

Laqueur, Walter. *The History of Zionism*. 3rd edn. London: I.B. Tauris, 2003.

Leffler, Melvyn P. and Odd Arne Westad. *The Cambridge History of the Cold War.* Vol. 1. Cambridge: Cambridge University Press, 2011.

Leffler, Melvyn P. and Odd Arne Westad. *The Cambridge History of the Cold War.* Vol. 2. Cambridge: Cambridge University Press, 2011.

Leibovich, Ariel. 'The Palestinian Refugee Issue in Israeli Foreign Policy, 1948-1967'. PhD thesis, University of Haifa, 2012.

LeoGrande, W. M. 'From Havana to Miami: U.S. Cuba Policy as a Two-Level Game'. *Journal of Interamerican Studies and World Affairs* 40, no. 1 (1997): 67–86.

Levey, Zach. 'Anglo-Israeli Strategic Relations, 1952-56'. *Middle Eastern Studies* 31, no. 4 (October 1995): 772–802.

Levey, Zach. 'Israel's Quest for a Security Guarantee from the United States, 1954-1956'. *British Journal of Middle Eastern Studies* 22, no. 1/2 (1 January 1995): 43–63.

Levey, Zach. *Israel and the Western Powers, 1952-1960*. Chapel Hill: University of North Carolina Press, 1997.

Lewis, Samuel W. 'The United States and Israel: Evolution of an Unwritten Alliance'. *Middle East Journal* 53, no. 3 (1 July 1999): 364–78.

Lieberfeld, Daniel. 'Secrecy and & "Two-Level Games" in the Oslo Accord: What the Primary Sources Tell Us'. *International Negotiation* 13, no. 1 (2008): 133–46.

Lisowski, M. 'Playing the Two-Level Game: US President Bush's Decision to Repudiate the Kyoto Protocol'. *Environmental Politics* 11, no. 4 (2002): 101–19.

Little, Douglas. 'The Making of a Special Relationship: The United States and Israel, 1957-68'. *International Journal of Middle East Studies* 25, no. 04 (1993): 563–85.

Louis, Wm. Roger. *The British Empire in the Middle East, 1945-1951: Arab Nationalism, the United States, and Postwar Imperialism*. Oxford: Oxford University Press, 2006.

Louis, Wm. Roger. 'The Ghost of Suez and Resolution 242'. In *The 1967 Arab-Israeli War: Origins and Consequences*, edited by Wm. Roger Louis and Avi Shlaim. Cambridge: Cambridge University Press, 2012.

Louis, Wm. Roger. 'The Tragedy of the Anglo-Egyptian Settlement of 1954'. In *Suez 1956: The Crisis and Its Consequences*, edited by Wm. Roger Louis and Roger Owen, 2nd edn, 43–71. Oxford: Clarendon Press, 2003.

Louis, Wm. Roger and Roger Owen, eds. *Suez 1956: The Crisis and Its Consequences*. 2nd edn. Oxford: Clarendon Press, 2003.

Louis, Wm. Roger and Avi Shlaim, eds. *The 1967 Arab-Israeli War: Origins and Consequences*. Cambridge: Cambridge University Press, 2012.

Masalha, Nur. *Catastrophe Remembered: Palestine, Israel and the Internal Refugees*. London: Zed Books, 2005.

Masalha, Nur. 'A Critique of Benny Morris'. *Journal of Palestine Studies* 21, no. 1 (October 1991): 90–7.

Masalha, Nur. *Expulsion of the Palestinians: The Concept of 'Transfer' in Zionist Political Thought, 1882-1948*. 5th edn. Washington, D.C.: Institute for Palestine Studies, 2009.

Masalha, Nur. 'The Historical Roots of the Palestinian Refugee Question'. In *The Palestinian Refugees and the Right of Return*, edited by Naseer Aruri. London: Pluto Press, 2001.

Masalha, Nur. *The Palestine Nakba: Decolonizing History, Narrating the Subaltern, Reclaiming Memory*. London: Zed Books, 2012.

Masalha, Nur. *The Politics of Denial: Israel and the Palestinian Refugee Problem*. London: Pluto Press, 2003.

McCann, Paul. 'The Role of UNRWA and the Palestine Refugees'. *Palestine-Israel Journal* 15, no. 4 (2008).

McGhee, George. *Envoy to the Middle World: Adventures in Diplomacy*. New York: Harper and Row, 1983.

Mearsheimer, John J. and Stephen M. Walt. *The Israel Lobby and U.S. Foreign Policy*. New York: Farrar, Straus and Giroux, 2007.

Mearsheimer, John, Stephen Walt, Geoffrey Wheatcroft, William Pfaff, Daniel Levy, Joseph Massad, Noam Chomsky and Mark Mazower. 'The Israeli Lobby'. *Journal of Palestine Studies* 35, no. 3 (1 April 2006): 83–114.

Migdal, Joel, ed. *Palestinian Society and Politics*. Princeton: Princeton University Press, 1980.

Moravcsik, Andrews. 'Introduction: Integrating International and Domestic Theories of International Bargaining'. In *Double-Edged Diplomacy: International Bargaining and Domestic Politics*, edited by Peter B. Evans, Harold K. Jacobson and Robert D. Putnam. Berkeley: University of California Press, 1993.

Mørk, Hulda Kjeang. 'The Jarring Mission: A Study of the UN Peace Effort in the Middle East, 1967-1971'. MA Thesis, University of Oslo, 2008.

Morris, Benny. *1948: A History of the First Arab-Israeli War*. New Haven: Yale University Press, 2008.

Morris, Benny. *The Birth of the Palestinian Refugee Problem Revisited*. 2nd edn. Cambridge: Cambridge University Press, 2004.

Morris, Benny. *Israel's Border Wars, 1949-1956: Arab Infiltration, Israeli Retaliation, and the Countdown to the Suez War*. 2nd edn. Oxford: Oxford University Press, 1997.

Morris, Benny. 'The Liar as Hero'. *New Republic*, 17 March 2011.

Morris, Benny. 'Response to Finkelstein and Masalha'. *Journal of Palestine Studies* 21, no. 1 (1991): 98–114.

Morris, Benny. 'Revisiting the Palestinian Exodus'. In *The War for Palestine: Rewriting the History of 1948*, edited by Eugene L. Rogan and Avi Shlaim. Cambridge: Cambridge University Press, 2007.

Morris, Benny. *Righteous Victims: A History of the Zionist-Arab Conflict, 1881-2001*. New York: Vintage, 2001.

Morris, Benny. 'Yosef Weitz and the Transfer Committees, 1948-49'. *Middle Eastern Studies* 22, no. 4 (1986): 522–61.

Naveh, Eyal. 'Identity Construction in Israel through Education in History'. In *Israel and Palestinian Narratives of Conflict: History's Double Helix*, edited by Robert I. Rothberg, 244–70. Bloomington: Indiana University Press, 2006.

Neff, Donald. 'US Policy and the Palestinian Refugees'. *Journal of Palestine Studies* 18, no. 1 (1988): 96–111.

Nets-Zehngut, Rafi. 'Origins of the Palestinian Refugee Problem: Changes in the Historical Memory of Israelis/Jews 1949–2004'. *Journal of Peace Research* 48, no. 2 (2011): 235–48.

Nets-Zehngut, Rafi. 'Palestinian Autobiographical Memory Regarding the 1948 Palestinian Exodus'. *Political Psychology* 32, no. 2 (2011): 271–95.

Nichols, David A. *Eisenhower 1956: The President's Year of Crisis--Suez and the Brink of War*. New York: Simon and Schuster, 2011.

Njølstad, Olav. 'Norge Og USA'. In *Norges Utenrikspolitikk*, edited by Thorbjørn L. Knutsen, Gunnar M. Sørbø and Svein Gjerdåker, 295–315. Oslo: Cappelen Akademisk Forlag, 1997.

Nye Jr, Joseph S. *Soft Power*. New York: Public Affairs, 2004.

Oren, Michael B. *Six Days of War: June 1967 and the Making of the Modern Middle East*. New York: Ballantine Books, 2003.

Palestinian Refugees and the Politics of Peacemaking. Middle East Report. International Crisis Group, February 2004.

Pappé, Ilan. 'The 1948 Ethnic Cleansing of Palestine'. *Journal of Palestine Studies* 36, no. 1 (2006): 6–20.

Pappé, Ilan. *Britain and the Arab-Israeli Conflict, 1948-51*. London: Macmillan Press, 1988.

Pappé, Ilan. 'Britain and the Palestinian Refugees, 1948-1950'. *Middle East Focus*, Fall 1986.

Pappé, Ilan. *The Ethnic Cleansing of Palestine*. Oxford: Oneworld Publications, 2007.

Pappé, Ilan. 'The History, Historiography and Relevance of the Palestinian Refugee Problem'. *Journal of Philosophy of International Law and Global Politics* 1, no. 1 (2005): 1–13.

Pappé, Ilan. *The Idea of Israel: A History of Power and Knowledge*. London: Verso/New Left Books, 2014.

Pappé, Ilan. 'Israeli Perceptions of the Refugee Question'. In *The Palestinian Refugees and the Right of Return*, edited by Naseer Aruri, 71–7. London: Pluto Press, 2001.

Pappé, Ilan. *The Making of the Arab-Israeli Conflict, 1947-1951*. 4th edn. London: I.B. Tauris, 2006.

Pappé, Ilan. 'Visible and Invisible in the Israeli-Palestinian Conflict'. In *Exile and Return: Predicaments of Palestinians and Jews*, edited by Ann M. Lesch and Ian S. Lustick. Philadelphia: University of Pennsylvania Press, 2005: 279–96.

Parsi, Trita. *Treacherous Alliance: The Secret Dealings of Israel, Iran, and the United States*. New Haven: Yale University Press, 2007.

Parsons, Laila. 'The Ethnic Cleansing of Palestine (review)'. *Comparative Studies of South Asia, Africa and the Middle East* 29, no. 3 (2009): 585–6.

Pelcovits, Nathan A. *The Long Armistice: UN Peacekeeping and the Arab-Israeli Conflict, 1948-1960*. Boulder: Westview Press, 1993.

Peled, Kobi. 'Oral Testimonies, Archival Sources, and the 1948 Arab-Israeli War: A Close Look at the Occupation of a Galilean Village'. *Journal of Israeli History* 33, no. 1 (2 January 2014): 41–61.

Peretz, Don. *Israel and the Palestine Arabs*. Washington, D.C.: Middle East Institute, 1958.

Perla, Shlomo. 'Israel and the Palestine Conciliation Commission'. *Middle Eastern Studies* 26, no. 1 (January 1990): 113–18.

Plascov, Avi. *The Palestinian Refugees in Jordan 1948-1957*. London: Psychology Press, 1981.

Podeh, Elie. 'The Perils of Ambiguity: The US and the Baghdad Pact'. In *The Middle East and the United States: A Historical and Political Reassessment*, edited by David W. Lesch, 4th edn, 86–105. Boulder: Westview Press, 2007.

Preston, Thomas. *The President and His Inner Circle: Leadership Style and the Advisory Process in Foreign Affairs*. New York: Columbia University Press, 2001.

Putnam, Robert D. 'Diplomacy and Domestic Politics: The Logic of Two-Level Games'. *International Organization* 42, no. 3 (1988): 427–60.

Quandt, William B. 'America and the Middle East: A Fifty-Year Overview'. In *Diplomacy in the Middle East: The International Relations of Regional and Outside Powers*, edited by L. Carl Brown, 2nd edn, 59–73. London: I.B. Tauris, 2004.

Quandt, William B. 'Domestic Influences on the United States Foreign Policy in the Middle East: The View from Washington'. In *The Middle East: Quest for an American Policy*, edited by Willard Beling, 264–85. Albany: State University of New York Press, 1973.

Quandt, William B. *Peace Process: American Diplomacy and the Arab-Israeli Conflict since 1967*. 3rd edn. Washington, D.C.: Brookings Institution Press and the University of California Press, 2005.

Quandt, William B., Fouad Jabber and Ann M. Lesch. *The Politics of Palestinian Nationalism*. Berkeley: University of California Press, 1973.

Radosh, Ronald and Allis Radosh. *A Safe Haven: Harry S. Truman and the Founding of Israel*. 1st edn. New York: Harper Perennial, 2010.

Raz, Avi. *The Bride and the Dowry: Israel, Jordan, and the Palestinians in the Aftermath of the June 1967 War*. New Haven: Yale University Press, 2012.

Raz, Avi. 'The Generous Peace Offer That Was Never Offered: The Israeli Cabinet Resolution of June 19, 1967'. *Diplomatic History* 37, no. 1 (2013): 85–108.

Reich, Bernard. 'The United States and Israel: The Nature of a Special Relationship'. In *The Middle East and the United States: A Historical and Political Reassessment*, edited by David W. Lesch, 4th edn. Boulder: Westview Press, 2007.

Rogan, Eugene L. *The Arabs: A History*. 2nd edn. New York: Basic Books, 2011.

Rogan, Eugene L. and Avi Shlaim. *The War for Palestine: Rewriting the History of 1948*. 2nd edn. Cambridge: Cambridge University Press, 2007.

Rothberg, Robert I., ed. *Israeli and Palestinian Narratives of Conflict: History's Double Helix*. Bloomington: Indiana University Press, 2006.

Roy, Sara. 'Humanism, Scholarship, and Politics: Writing on the Palestinian-Israeli Conflict'. *Journal of Palestine Studies* 36, no. 2 (2007): 54–65.

Rubenberg, Cheryl, ed. *Encyclopedia of the Israeli-Palestinian Conflict*. Vol. 1. 3 vols. Boulder: Lynne Rienner Publishers, 2010.

Rubenberg, Cheryl, ed. *Encyclopedia of the Israeli-Palestinian Conflict*. Vol. 2. Boulder: Lynne Rienner Publishers, 2010.

Sa'di, Ahmad H. 'Catastrophe, Memory and Identity: Al-Nakbah as a Component of Palestinian Identity'. *Israel Studies* 7, no. 2 (2002): 175–98.

Said, Edward. 'Introduction: The Right of Return At Last'. In *Palestinian Refugees: The Right of Return*, edited by Naseer Aruri. London: Pluto Press, 2001.

Said, Edward W. *The Question of Palestine*. 2nd edn. New York: Vintage Books, 1992.

Said, Edward W. and Christopher Hitchens, eds. *Blaming the Victims: Spurious Scholarship and the Palestinian Question*. 4th edn. London: Verso, 2001.

Sayigh, Rosemary. *The Palestinians: From Peasants to Revolutionaries*. 2nd edn. London: Zed Books, 2008.

Sayigh, Rosemary. *Too Many Enemies: The Palestinian Experience in Lebanon*. London: Zed Books, 1994.

Sayigh, Yezid. *Armed Struggle and the Search for State the Palestinian National Movement, 1949-1993*. Oxford: Oxford University Press, 1999.

Sayigh, Yezid. 'Armed Struggle and State Formation'. *Journal of Palestine Studies* 26, no. 4 (1997): 17–32.

Sayigh, Yezid and Avi Shlaim. *The Cold War and the Middle East*. Oxford: Oxford University Press, 1997.

Schiff, Benjamin N. *Refugees unto a Third Generation: UN Aid to Palestinians*. New York: Syracuse University Press, 1995.

Schiffer, Varda. 'The 1949 Israeli Offer to Repatriate 100.000 Palestinian Refugees'. *Middle East Focus*, no. Fall (1986).

Schlesinger Jr, Arthur M. *A Thousand Days: John F. Kennedy in the White House*. New York: First Mariner Books/Houghton Mifflin Company, 2002.

Schoenbaum, David. *The United States and the State of Israel*. Oxford: Oxford University Press, 1993.

Schvindlerman, Julián. 'Israel's Parliamentary Intifada'. *Middle East Quarterly* 9, no. 2 (Spring 2002): 22–31.

Segev, Tom. *1967: Israel, the War, and the Year That Transformed the Middle East*. New York: Metropolitan Books, 2008.

Segev, Tom. 'The June 1967 War and the Palestinian Refugee Problem'. *Journal of Palestine Studies* 36, no. 3 (2007): 6–22.

Shadid, Mohammed K. *United States Policy Towards Palestinian Refugees*. New York: St. Martin's Press, 1981.

Shamir, Jacob and Khalil Shikaki. 'Public Opinion in the Israeli-Palestinian Two-Level Game'. *Journal of Peace Research* 42, no. 3 (2005): 311–28.

Shamir, Shimon. 'The Collapse of Project Alpha'. In *Suez 1956: The Crisis and Its Consequences*, edited by Wm. Roger Louis and Roger Owen, 2nd edn. Oxford: Clarendon Press, 2003.

Sharqieh, Ibrahim. 'What About the Palestinian Double Refugees?' *Harvard Journal of Middle Eastern Politics and Policy*, 25 February 2014.

Shiblak, Abbas. *The Palestinian Refugee Issue: A Palestinian Perspective*. Briefing Paper. Chatham House, February 2009.

Shiffer, Varda. 'The 1949 Israeli Offer to Repatriate 100.000 Palestinian Refugees'. *Middle East Focus*, 1986.

Shlaim, Avi. 'Conflicting Approaches to Israel's Relations with the Arabs: Ben Gurion and Sharett, 1953-1956'. *Middle East Journal* 37, no. 2 (Spring 1983): 180–201.

Shlaim, Avi. 'The Debate about 1948'. *International Journal of Middle East Studies* 27, no. 03 (1995): 287–304.

Shlaim, Avi. 'Husni Za'im and the Plan to Resettle Palestinian Refugees in Syria'. *Journal of Palestine Studies* 15, no. 4 (1 July 1986): 68–80.

Shlaim, Avi. 'Huzni Zaim and the Plan to Resettle Palestinian Refugees in Syria'. *Middle East Focus*, 9/2 (1986): 27–31.

Shlaim, Avi. 'Interview with Abba Eban, 11 March 1976'. *Israel Studies* 8, no. 1 (2003): 153–177.

Shlaim, Avi. *The Iron Wall: Israel and the Arab World*. New York: W.W. Norton, 2001.

Shlaim, Avi. 'Israel between East and West, 1948-56'. *International Journal of Middle East Studies* 36, no. 4 (1 November 2004): 657–73.

Shlaim, Avi. *Israel and Palestine: Reappraisals, Revisions, Refutations*. London: Verso, 2009.

Shlaim, Avi. *Lion of Jordan: The Life of King Hussein in War and Peace*. London: Penguin Books, 2009.

Shlaim, Avi. *The Politics of Partition: King Abdullah, the Zionists, and Palestine 1921-1951*. Abridged. Oxford: Oxford University Press, 1999.

Shlaim, Avi. 'The Protocol of Sevres, 1956: Anatomy of a War Plot'. *International Affairs* 73, no. 3 (July 1997): 509–30.

Shlaim, Avi. 'The War of Israeli Historians'. *Annales* 59, no. 1 (2004): 161–7.

Shlaim, Avi and Avner Yaniv. 'Domestic Politics and Foreign Policy in Israel'. *International Affairs* (Royal Institute of International Affairs 1944-) 56, no. 2 (1 April 1980): 242–62.

Shuckburgh, Evelyn. *Descent to Suez: Diaries, 1951-56*. New York: W.W. Norton, 1987.

Sluglett, Peter. 'The Cold War in the Middle East'. In *International Relations of the Middle East*, edited by Louise Fawcett, 41–54. Oxford: Oxford University Press, 2005.

Spiegel, Steven L. *The Other Arab-Israeli Conflict: Making America's Middle East Policy, from Truman to Reagan*. Chicago: University Of Chicago Press, 1986.

Stein, Kenneth W. 'A Historiographic Review of Literature on the Origins of the Arab-Israeli Conflict'. *American Historical Review* 96, no. 5 (1991): 1450–65.

Suleiman, Jaber. 'The Palestinian Liberation Organization: From the Right of Return to Bantustan'. In *The Palestinian Refugees and the Right of Return*, edited by Naseer Aruri. London: Pluto Press, 2001.

Suleiman, Michael W., ed. *U.S. Policy on Palestine: From Wilson to Clinton*. Normal: AAUG Press, 1995.

Talhami, Ghada Hashem. *Palestinian Refugees: Pawns to Political Actors*. New York: Nova Science Publishers, 2003.

Taub, Gadi. *The Settlers*. New Haven: Yale University Press, 2010.

Tessler, Mark. *A History of the Israeli-Palestinian Conflict*. Bloomington: Indiana University Press, 1994.

Tiller, Stian Johansen. 'Defending the UN Agenda: The Peace Efforts of the Palestine Conciliation Commission 1949-1951'. MA thesis, University of Oslo, 2009.

Tiller, Stian Johansen and Hilde Henriksen Waage. 'Powerful State, Powerless Mediator: The United States and the Peace Efforts of the Palestine Conciliation Commission, 1949-51'. *International History Review* 33 (2011): 501–24.

Touval, Saadia. *The Peace Brokers: Mediators in the Arab-Israeli Conflict, 1948-1979*. Princeton: Princeton University Press, 1982.

Tovy, Jacob. 'All Quiet on the Eastern Front; Israel and the Issue of Reparations from East-Germany, 1951-1956'. *Israel Studies* 18, no. 1 (2013): 77–100.

Tovy, Jacob. *Israel and the Palestinian Refugee Issue: The Formulation of Policy, 1948-1956*. New York: Routledge, 2014.

Tovy, Jacob. 'Negotiating the Palestinian Refugees'. *Middle East Quarterly*, Spring 2003.

Tschirgi, Dan. *The Politics of Indecision: Origins and Implications of American Involvement with the Palestine Problem*. Praeger Publishers, 1983.

'UNRWA and the Palestinian Refugees 60 Years Later'. *Refugee Studies Quarterly*, Special Issue, 28, no. 2–3 (2010): 227–661.

Urquhart, Brian. *Hammarskjold*. W.W. Norton and Company, Inc., 1994.

Urquhart, Brian. *Ralph Bunche: An American Odyssey*. W.W. Norton, 1998.

Waage, Hilde Henriksen. *Da staten Israel ble til: Et stridsspørsmål i norsk politikk 1945-49*. Oslo: Gyldendal Norsk Forlag, 1989.

Waage, Hilde Henriksen. *Norge, Israels Beste Venn: Norsk Midtøsten-Politikk 1949-1956*. Oslo: Universitetsforlaget, 1996.

Waage, Hilde Henriksen. 'The Winner Takes All: The 1949 Island of Rhodes Armistice Negotiations Revisited'. *The Middle East Journal* 65 (Spring 2011): 279–304.

Waage, Hilde Henriksen and Hulda Kjeang Mørk 'Mission Impossible: UN Special Representative Gunnar Jarring and His Quest for Peace in the Middle East'. *The International History Review* 38, no. 4 (2015): 830–53.

Waage, Hilde Henriksen and Petter Stenberg. 'Cementing a State of Belligerency: The 1949 Armistice Negotiations between Israel and Syria'. *Middle East Journal* 71, no. 1 (Winter 2016): 69–89.

Wishart, David M. 'The Breakdown of the Johnston Negotiations over the Jordan Waters'. *Middle Eastern Studies* 26, no. 4 (1990): 536–46.

Zernichow, S. and H. H. Waage. 'The Palestine Option: Nixon, the National Security Council, and the Search for a New Policy, 1970'. *Diplomatic History* 38, no. 1 (2013): 182–209.

Index

www.ingramcontent.com/pod-product-compliance
Lightning Source LLC
Chambersburg PA
CBHW050436280326
41932CB00013BA/2134